T0305331

# Institutional Change for Sustainable Development

## THE AUTHORS

Robin Connor has worked in fisheries management policy in New Zealand, and in community-based integrated conservation and development in Melanesia. He is currently providing contract services to the New Zealand Ministry of Fisheries, and engaged in research into fisheries quota management through the Centre for Resource and Environmental Studies (CRES), The Australian National University.

Stephen Dovers is a Senior Fellow at CRES, with interests in policy and institutional aspects of sustainability, integration in the science and policy of resource management, and environmental history. Among his recent works are the co-edited volumes *South Africa's Environmental History* (Ohio University Press 2002), *Uncertainty, Ecology and Policy* (Prentice-Hall 2001), *Strategic Environmental Assessment in Australasia* (Federation Press 2002), *Managing Australia's Environment* (Federation Press 2003) and *New Dimensions in Ecological Economics* (Edward Elgar 2003).

# Institutional Change for Sustainable Development

Robin Connor and Stephen Dovers

*Centre for Resource and Environmental Studies,*
*The Australian National University, Canberra, Australia*

**Edward Elgar Publishing**

Cheltenham, UK • Northampton, MA, USA

Published by
Edward Elgar Publishing Limited
Glensanda House
Montpellier Parade
Cheltenham
Glos GL50 1UA
UK

Edward Elgar Publishing, Inc.
136 West Street
Suite 202
Northampton
Massachusetts 01060
USA

A catalogue record for this book
is available from the British Library

**Library of Congress Cataloging in Publication Data**
Connor, Robin, 1954–
   Institutional change for sustainable development / Robin Connor, Stephen Dovers.
     p. cm.
   Includes bibliographical references and index.
   1. Industrial management—Environmental aspects. 2. Organizational change. 3. Sustainable development. 4. Environmental policy. I. Dovers, Stephen. II. Title.

HD30.255.C654 2004
338.9'27—dc21                                         2003049267

ISBN 1 84376 569 1

Printed and bound in Great Britain by MPG Books Ltd, Bodmin, Cornwall

# Contents

# Figures and tables

# Acknowledgements

This book originated in research supported by Land & Water Australia, a research and development agency of the Australian Commonwealth Government. Although specifically initiated to inform – indeed to engender – Australian debates on institutional reform for sustainability, the themes and topics surveyed are, by definition, of universal interest, and were approached in that vein. The authors thank the steering committee for the project for their comments and guidance: Catherine Mobbs and Ken Moore (Land & Water Australia), Lorraine Elliott (Australian National University), John Handmer (Centre for Risk and Community Safety, RMIT University), and Alison Reid (Murray Darling Basin Commission). Catherine was also central to the early design of the research. Rob Dyball assisted in the foundational stages. A number of people provided leads into the grey and policy literature. We also thank the staff of Edward Elgar for their interest, professionalism and efficiency.

# Acronyms

| | |
|---|---|
| AAE | assessment of environmental effects |
| CA | cumulative assessment |
| CEC | Commission of the European Communities |
| COM | Council of Ministers |
| CORINE | Coordination of Information on the Environment |
| CP | common pool |
| CPR | common pool resource |
| DG | Directorate General |
| EA | environmental assessment |
| EAP | Environmental Action Programme |
| EC | European Community |
| ECJ | European Court of Justice |
| ECOFIN | Council of the Economic and Finance Ministers |
| EEA | European Environment Agency |
| EEB | European Environment Bureau |
| EEC | European Economic Community |
| EFR | ecological fiscal reform |
| EIA | environmental impact assessment |
| EIONET | European Environment Information and Observation Networks |
| EP | European Parliament |
| EPBC | Environment Protection and Biodiversity Conservation Act |
| EPIP | Environment Protection (Impact of Proposals) Act |
| ESD | ecologically sustainable development |
| Espoo Convention | Convention on Environmental Impact Assessment in a Transboundary Context |
| EU | European Union |
| FRDO-CFDD | Belgian Federal Council for Sustainable Development |
| GEC | global environment conventions |
| GIS | geographical information system |
| IA | integrated assessment |
| IEM | integrated environmental management |
| IMPEL | Network for Implementation and Enforcement of Community Law |

| | |
|---|---|
| ITQ | individual transferable quota |
| MBI | market based instruments |
| MfE | Ministry for the Environment |
| NCP | National Competition Policy |
| NCSA | National Conservation Strategy for Australia |
| NCSD | National Council for Sustainable Development |
| NEPMs | National Environmental Protection Measures |
| NES | National Environmental Standards |
| NGO | non-governmental organization |
| NPS | National Policy Statement |
| NRM | natural resource management |
| NRTEC | National Round Table on the Environment and the Economy |
| NSESD | National Strategy for Ecologically Sustainable Development (Australia) |
| OECD | Organization for Economic Cooperation and Development |
| PP | precautionary principle |
| PPPs | policies, plans and programmes |
| PRI | property rights instrument |
| PUCM | planning under a corporate mandate |
| QMV | qualified majority voting |
| RFA | Regional Forest Agreement |
| RPS | Regional Policy Statement |
| RMA | Resource Management Act |
| RMLR | Resource Management Law Reform |
| SA | sustainability assessment |
| SD | sustainable development |
| SDS | Strategy for Sustainable Development |
| SEA | Single European Act |
| SEA | strategic environmental assessment |
| SMF | Sustainable Management Fund |
| SoE | state of environment |
| TLA | territorial local authority |
| UNCED | United Nations Conference on Environment and Development |
| WCED | World Commission on Environment and Development |
| WSSD | World Summit on Sustainable Development |

# Introduction

This book explores international experiences of institutional reform for sustainable development through a series of case studies, seeking to identify positive principles from existing practice to inform further institutional change. Underlying this investigation is the proposition that countries should be making purposeful efforts to reform environmental and resource management policies and practice, and those in other sectors, consistent with the notion of sustainable development and with commitments made under international agreements at, and subsequent to, the 1992 United Nations Conference on Environment and Development (UNCED).

The institutionalization of the sustainability idea, and its eventual integration as a fundamental and mainstream principle of governance, is a long-term project only recently begun. Arguably sustainability has an inexorable logic, on a plane with other deep social logics such as democracy, justice and human rights. Inevitably, it seems, these central animating ideas of modern societies are all intertwining and inseparable; the identification of these strands may be viewed as part of the definition of a moral rationality for global civilization. However, sustainability has yet to attain the recognition and status of its natural partners at national or global levels. This will require both broad normative change and purposive institutional change, and these are key themes of this book.

Now is certainly an important historical point for humanity with respect to institutional development, and one that demands that we attend closely to the task of better understanding the substance and the ways of our institutions. Sustainability, as a newly recognized strand of the moral fibre by which we propose to survive and prosper in a full world, requires urgent practical development within our institutional systems. How can we purposively develop social rules and organizational structures and relationships to support and promote sustainable behaviour? This is certainly a learning project, and one that must attempt to extract lessons as efficiently as possible both from general institutional experience and from the initial attempts at purposive change. This book is an effort to share the experience of one study that has approached this problem.

The study originated from the perspective of informing institutional and policy change in Australia, utilizing international experiences. As we proceeded, however, it became obvious that the themes and principles underlying the issue of institutional change for sustainability are more often universal, even though their translation into a specific context must be closely considered. So, while the Australian setting is used from time to time as a reference point, the analysis, content and conclusions of the book are more global than local. This is to be expected, as sustainability is nothing if not an intrinsically global idea.

## THE PLAN OF THE BOOK

The book is organized into three parts. The first part attempts to provide some mental furniture – a landscape of concepts and language to assist later empirical analysis. This is followed, in Part II, by a set of five case studies (Chapters 3 to 7), and Part III works to distil general lessons from the project.

Chapter 1 attempts first to define some reference points within institutional language and link these conceptually to everyday experience of complex organized society. It explores the notion of institutions and the environment of institutional systems. Second, this chapter investigates notions of policy-relevant learning in an institutional context and how they might relate to the task of institutional learning and development for sustainability policy. Chapter 2 develops a framework for the choice of case studies in institutional change through exploring the practical issues of what it is we might wish to learn about and from where the lessons might come. It explores the meaning of 'sustainable development' and how policy and institutional systems might, and do, respond to its imperatives, using Australian institutional responses as examples. The chapter then develops a set of criteria for the selection of case studies and develops a matrix of analytical targets for the study. Finally the chapter briefly describes the case study topics chosen, along with some that might have been but were not, and how the criteria were applied in the choices made.

The first case study in Part II examines the development of the environmental policies of the European Union (EU) into a major institutional commitment to sustainability principles. The EU represents the most advanced, complex and sustained example of integrated policy and institutional development in the history of modern government. The evolution of EU environmental policy from the time of the Stockholm Conference in 1972 to the Maastricht Treaty of 1992 reflects an official concern for accumulating evidence of environmental damage and normative change – particularly in Northern Europe. This same constituency is the source of the 'sustainable development' conceptual synthesis, and since 1992 the EU policy discourse has focused increasingly on sustainable development. The case study traces this developmental path through its core modality, the periodic Environmental Action Plan. Complexity of political relationships and governmental structures has led to a variety of modes and paths being explored for the integration of sustainability principles into sectoral policies, and a great richness of experience is only partially uncovered here.

The second case study (Chapter 4) looks at the New Zealand legislative reforms resulting in the Resource Management Act 1991. The Resource Management Act (RMA) began as an attempt to consolidate a large fragmented body of legislation and other institutional arrangements for natural resource management. This reform was carried out concurrently with a structural reform of local government. Twenty major statutes and 50 other laws affecting the environment were replaced by the RMA, and more than six hundred units of local government were reduced to about eighty-six. Resource management and the maintenance of environmental quality were placed at the centre of concerns for local government. Planning and regulation of all land use is subject to the singular purpose of the RMA – the sustainable management of natural and physical resources. The focus of planning and decision making was switched from the activities carried out on land to the effects of land and resource use on the environment. This dual reform – structure and policy mandate – held much promise, but this has only been partially realized. Close attention reveals a lapse in policy scrutiny at the centre following the decentralizing reform, and the critical need for ongoing political commitment to the values behind sustainability policy.

The third case study surveys the widespread use of a sustainability-specific institutional innovation. From WCED to UNCED and since, great emphasis has been placed on national scale coordination and integration of policy for sustainable development, and the cooperation of government and civil society in communication and policy development. In response over seventy nations – developed, developing and transitional alike – have established a National Council for Sustainable Development (NCSD) or equivalent body. Coordination is provided through a network serviced by the Earth Council, an NGO. In the ideal form, NCSDs have the following features:

- membership representing different levels of government, research, the private sector and community organizations, and through that membership a network of formal and informal linkages
- a focus on a long term, integrated sustainability agenda, with the ability to maintain a purposeful dialogue and environment of policy learning over time
- sufficient status within the institutional system, including through mandated roles viewed as necessary by others, to have an impact on policy and institutional change.

Together these functions are necessary and logical expressions of the policy task of sustainability. The core rationale of the NCSD is maintenance of an inclusive policy discourse around the broader field of sustainable development, complementing but not replacing inclusive approaches to subsidiary issues. This study examines the roles adopted by, variability among, and comparative success of examples of NCSDs around the world, assessing strengths and weakness and contribution to advancing the sustainability policy agenda in different national settings.

The fourth case study examines the under-recognised policy integration tool termed Strategic Environmental Assessment (SEA). For three decades environmental impact assessment (EIA) of individual development projects has been central to environmental policy. While important, project-EIA does not attend impacts that are cumulative in space or time or the policy settings that establish the directions and parameters of development. Over the same three decades, and well before the emergence of the sustainable development policy agenda, the need for assessment of policies, plans and programmes (PPPs) above the discrete project level has been recognized and advocated. In its various guises, such Strategic Environmental Assessment proposes to insert environmental considerations into policy development in other sectors.

Project-EIA addresses the more obvious, direct causes of environmental degradation. SEA targets less obvious but crucial indirect causes of unsustainable patterns of production and consumption across all policy sectors, focusing on government policy and legislative proposals (for example, in areas such as tax, trade, transport, regional development). SEA thus represents a prime option for implementing policy integration for sustainability. SEA is recommended in major international agreements, and statutory or policy provisions exist in a number of countries. Experience with sustainable development in the 1990s has strengthened interest in SEA, but there is a clear gap between recommending SEA and actual implementation.

This case study examines SEA as a mechanism for policy integration for sustainability, in theory and in (limited) practice in parts of the world. It offers a summary history of SEA, describes the basic elements of SEA, reviews its status in selected countries and regions, and identifies apparent barriers to implementation. The level of detail is kept to the minimum required for the purpose: more detailed sources are available and cited.

The last of the case studies explores the issue of property rights based policy reform in the sustainability arena. Over the past two decades, coincident with the rise of the sustainability discourse, the application of property rights instruments (PRIs) to natural resource management has been advocated as a means to efficiently allocate scarce resources. PRIs have been implemented in a range of applications including the control of sulphur emissions from fossil fuel burning power stations, in controlling discharges into rivers affecting water quality, for the allocation of water abstraction, and most notably in marine fisheries management. They have also been proposed in other areas, including carbon emissions and sequestration, and biodiversity conservation. Although often characterized as 'just another tool in the policy toolbox' the case study argues that PRIs involve a fundamental change in social parameters.

Property rights are primary aspects of institutional systems around which resource use regimes are built. Resulting incentives and behaviour patterns structure social relations and cultural values over the long term. The distributional consequences of access and allocation rights and rules contribute a particular logic to social constructions of fairness and equity. Therefore changes to existing property rights regimes need to be considered carefully in light of the specific social and cultural context.

This case study first presents a framework for understanding the nature of common pool resources and the various property regime types that can apply to their management and use, including private property. PRIs are located within this framework, not as a means of privatizing the commons but as an option for regulation of access and withdrawal rights as operational-level sticks in a bundle of rights associated with common pools. The study next elucidates the origin of PRIs in applied economics and the development of the ideas for application in actual policy making using the 'environmental bottom line' approach.

The chapter then turns to the notion of equity in resource use and its linkages with prevailing property regimes. As party to the sustainability troika of concerns, equity is perhaps the least understood and least considered in policy proposals. We explore the implications of the required integration of equity into policy for change in management regimes brought on by over-exploitation of resources. The remainder of the chapter sets out to explore differences in the culture of resource use from frontier to commons and aspects of process and path dependence relevant to the application of PRIs, and considerations of the inherent adaptability of different cultures. These elements serve to construct a broad understanding of the nature of, and potential for, the use of PRIs in sustainability policy.

Part III of the book provides a synthesis from the analysis of the cases. On the basis of the conceptual framework established in Part I, and utilizing lessons from the case studies presented in Part II, this final section derives some principles and distils some positive themes of institutional and policy change for sustainable development from the experiences surveyed. These emergent principles and elements are grouped under the two classes of 'objects of learning' identified in Chapter 1 as targets of this investigation: problem reframing and organizing government. These empirically derived themes are key to understanding both the potential of institutional change consistent with the sustainability idea and the nature of reforms reviewed in this research. They are not forms or models of institutional change in themselves but rather conceptual and practical principles crucial to progress in institutional change for sustainability.

Grouped under problem reframing are four elements operating on the formation of an explicit conception of the sustainability problem: the institutional accommodation of a sustainability discourse; normative change; legal change; and international law and policy as drivers. Under organizing government, three characteristics emerged as critical to the organizational logic of sustainability: integration of policy and practice; subsidiarity; and reiteration. The central discussion of this concluding chapter is based around this framework of emergent themes and principles, drawing on the case study material to illustrate and develop the lessons. Following that a brief translation of some of these generic principles into a specific jurisdictional context (Australia) is undertaken to illustrate the practical potential for their application to institutional change and policy learning for sustainable development.

PART I

Approaching institutional change and
policy learning

# 1. Conceptions of institutions and policy learning

## INTRODUCTION

The broad questions prompting this study are about what and how we might learn from early experiences with institutional development in response to the sustainability imperative. The application of any lessons drawn from a case study approach was to be to inform further policy making and institutional reform in a modern democracy. In approaching the study it seemed prudent to reflect first on the nature of institutions in this context and second upon the notion of policy learning.

Here we first explore the issue of defining the focus of our attention – institutions. It is important analytically that a shared and well-understood meaning for the term 'institution' and associated language is established at the outset, and that consistent usage is maintained as much as possible throughout the book. We argue that clear and consistent terminology will promote a deeper understanding of the dynamics of institutional systems and of the later analysis of case studies. This section looks at various meanings of the term 'institution', exploring linkages in the use of language and concepts. It adopts a specific approach to institutional language from the literature that we believe offers an analytical escape route from what can become something of an interdisciplinary quagmire of ambiguity. At the close of this preliminary discussion we set ourselves some rules for language in the rest of the study.

Second, as this investigation is an exercise in policy and institutional learning, some exploration of what might comprise learning in this context is worthwhile. The second part of the chapter briefly explores concepts of policy learning from the literature, yielding a working typology for the study and building blocks for an analytical framework. This framework is put to work in Chapter 2 to derive analytical targets for the research and to select case studies.

## INSTITUTIONS: FORM, FUNCTION AND RELATIONS

This section sets out a framework for the consideration of institutions in the context of the objectives of the study. It develops a general conception of institutional systems based on the analytical definition and explanation of institutions developed in the New Institutional literature and particularly in the work of Douglass North.[1] The account given seeks to reconcile this analytical definition of institutions with meanings underlying common usage, reducing apparent conflict through the view that the need for analysis forces refinement and precision in defining the objects of study. This theoretical work in turn facilitates clearer understanding of the commonalities of meaning behind seemingly disparate common usages. It also allows us to develop a systems view of institutional form and function that will facilitate a deeper appreciation of how and why particular institutional arrangements may be more or less effective in addressing the problems of sustainability policy.

**Defining Institutions**

The term institution has been used in many ways to refer to a range of different things. It is used in everyday language to refer to entities as seemingly disparate as banks and insurance companies, a nation's constitution, or an older member of the community reliably seated at the bar of the local hotel. This broad scope in common usage of the term has been reflected in the language of institutionally related theorising dating back a century. Most definitions of institutions are descriptive and encompass a diversity of social entities. Following a period of neglect, institutional theory has recently undergone a revival throughout the social sciences.[2] However, references to institutions and the use of institutional language often remain vague and, despite a greater emphasis on analysis, somewhat conflictual. Some of this is a deliberate attempt to accommodate a range of disciplinary theoretical perspectives with disparate traditions, or merely traditions of similar imprecision, with an associated view that a restrictive definition would not be helpful to scholarship. In recent Australian literature Henningham,[3] for example, relies on a dictionary definition originating in the sixteenth century, describing an institution as 'an established law, custom, usage, practice, organization, or other element in the political or social life of a people'. Dovers builds on this to produce a more detailed meaning but one that retains the ambiguity of the original, and summarizes this as '[a]n institution is an underlying, durable pattern of rules and behaviour'.[4]

   Theoretical work in other areas has led to attempts to provide a more precise definition to assist analysis. However, as foreshadowed above, such definitions have contributed to confusion over how to utilize the term in a discourse that refers to several of the differing entities that in various contexts are called institutions. A particular difficulty arises in the distinction of institutions and organizations. Where the term institution is used to refer to an organization, those that use it so would not agree that all organizations could be described as institutions. So a key question must concern what it is that distinguishes one type of organization from another in this way. Dovers, for example, argues that persistence and widespread recognition are features of institutions, and therefore an organization that persists over time and is widely recognized might be termed an institution.[5] However, here we explore a different approach.

One of the most widely used theoretical definitions of institutions is that of Douglass North.

> Institutions are the rules of the game in a society or, more formally, are the humanly devised constraints that shape human interaction.[6]

> They are made up of formal constraints (e.g., rules, laws, constitutions), informal constraints (e.g., norms of behaviour, conventions, self-imposed codes of conduct), and their enforcement characteristics. Together they define the incentive structure of societies and specifically economies.[7]

This definition can be interpreted as referring to an institution as being a single rule (such as that proscribing the forward pass in rugby football or that prescribing which side of the road to drive on) but it is also possible and of considerable utility to allow a hierarchy of aggregation of individual rules. Thus the set of official formal rules of a sport can be considered an institution. North also proposes the primary purpose of institutions.

> Institutions reduce uncertainty by providing structure to everyday life. They are a guide to human interaction ...

Thus the way others will respond in a given interaction is made more predictable by institutions, whether by formal rules of the road or sport, or through informal social and cultural norms of behaviour. This allows us to move through many interactions with others every day without having to renegotiate ground rules every time.

The scope of this view of institutions is important to appreciate. It includes all socially devised rules of governance such as articles of constitutions, statute and common law, regulations and by-laws, policies, legal rulings, contracts, codes of conduct and honour, and the myriad of social and cultural traditions and norms that constrain the way individuals and groups act in social contexts. This vast array of constraints and guides to appropriate behaviour forms an institutional matrix within which all social actors interact.

North specifically enjoins us to separate institutions from organizations conceptually, warning against confusing the rules of the game with the players. 'The purpose of the rules', he explains, 'is to define the way the game is played. But the objective of the team within that set of rules is to win the game – by a combination of skills, strategy, and coordination; by fair means and sometimes by foul means.'[8] Thus teams (the organizations) and their strategies are responses to the rule set, and are different in kind to the rules themselves (the institutions).

North's conception and definition of institutions derives from his underlying purpose in theorizing: to explain an economic history in which firms (economic organizations) are primary actors. This makes the separation of institutions from organizations crucial to his analysis, and it is a distinction we hold to be well made and valid. However, it does present a challenge to consistency in the institutional language of a broad and cross-disciplinary public discussion, where that distinction is much less often made.

One approach to this problem is to view North's definition as an analytical refinement of common usage of the term 'institution', rather than a departure. In North's model, institutions are environmental variables set by society that condition behaviour generally, and therefore the emergence, form and actions of organizations. They do this in combination with other variables, particularly the purpose and objectives of actors and organizations, cost structures and potential benefits, risks involved in breaking rules, and so on, although these other factors themselves are all conditioned by, or are direct products of, the broader institutional environment. General agreement may be had on the proposition that at least a minimum set of such rules is essential for orderly and predictable social life.

Now, some organizations are also essential for orderly social life as we know it, because they provide the essential service infrastructure required for the degree of social coordination and assurance necessary to support the level of governance and economic activity that is the norm in a particular society. These services provide the regularities upon which we build our social lives. To this extent they, and the organizations that deliver them, form part of the institutional system. If we attempt to identify such essential services and their associated organizational structures we find that many of these tend to be referred to as institutions. Schools, universities, hospitals, banks, the key arms of government, are all referred to in this way, arguably because they serve to facilitate the fundamental workings of our society, just as the basic rules do. These are expectable regularities, or norms, in a given social context. They provide us with a 'normalized' social environment and are entirely integral to our way of life.

From this perspective it may also be appreciated that particular organizational entities might, for convenience, be substituted in common parlance and perception for the system of infrastructure of which they are merely a delivery point. Thus residents of a small community are shaken by the closure of a bank branch or postal agency not only because this may require changes in the way they go about their daily business and the possible extra costs involved but also because they regard the branch, and sometimes even the building, as an institution in its own right. Whether the closure of a particular bank branch represents real erosion of essential institutional infrastructure is in part an empirical question, and is certainly a matter of social discourse. However, this is not itself relevant to the task of separating out the underlying meaning of the use of the term institution in the current context.

In the context of the advanced Western economies, it is the underlying service delivered by the infrastructure of institutional systems that is critical, and we have become increasingly acculturated to changes in their organizational configuration. Regulatory reform, including privatization of government-owned assets and government-controlled services, has brought altered modes of delivery that continue changing with technological and economic change. These regulatory changes are the real institutional changes in the Northian sense of the rules of the game rather than the organizational changes consequent to them.

However, we cannot so easily discard common usage for an analytical convenience. Remember that old fellow at the bar? Both he and the bank building on Main Street are regularities in the socio-physical environment that are directly analogous to those produced by rules. It is this socio-physical reality that people experience most directly on a daily basis and that represents in the sensorial world the kind of order and predictability that institutions as rules bring to behaviour.

It is now becoming clear how the seemingly conflicting notions of institutions as rules, organizations, or other long-standing socio-physical phenomena, are related as social regularities. The analytical cleavage emerges when we ask what is cause and what is effect. In complex dynamic systems like human societies there are few truly independent variables. Each social entity, whether individual, group, organization, process or institution, is interlinked with many others and bound into the whole, and these linkages are not arranged in a strict linear hierarchy. Hence the relationships between a rule and the entities (for example, organizations) acted upon by it are often two-way, with feedback from the results of the rule being applied used to modify it so as to improve future outcomes.

The New Institutional literature makes a convincing analytical case for institutions-as-rules providing the fundamental infrastructure of coordinated social action and thereby setting the stage for the emergence of other regularities such as organizations. Some authors have suggested that the regularities themselves should be treated as the institutional analytical unit but this seems less helpful than using the cause of the regularity. However, the answer to the question of what is an institution depends to some extent on why the question is being asked. In any case it is still a work in progress, in that interest in the issue has undergone a recent resurgence and it will take time for the analytical utility of particular definitions to be demonstrated and accepted. The range of disciplinary traditions in the use of institutional language is likely to remain quite broad,[9] and hence analytical definitions such as North's will not be appropriate in all discussions.

For those engaged in discussions of public policy for sustainability, however, it seems that North's framework provides a significant clarification in language as a crucial building block for an improved analytic theory. Although founded on a micro-behavioural model of the boundedly rational actor, the framework views individual action as fundamentally constrained by social choice as expressed in the institutional system. This allows more scope for addressing sustainability concerns through purposive institutional development and reform, and for learning about how to approach this, than do other views of institutions more concerned with exploring multiple theoretical perspectives. However, the bounded rationality caveat is important in its implications for institutional change. Herbert Simon comments:

> If … we accept the proposition that the knowledge and computational power of the decision-maker are severely limited, then we must distinguish between the real world and the actor's perception of it and reasoning about it. That is to say we must construct a theory (and test it empirically) of the process of decision. Our theory must include not only the reasoning processes but also the processes that generated the actor's subjective representation of the decision problem, his or her frame.[10]

The implication is that perceptions are built on cultural norms as well as experience. Because humans have limited cognitive capacity and incomplete information our judgements of the world are based on perceptions guided by beliefs – our mental models. Cultural beliefs about resources and environment are difficult to change, and to an important extent determine both the demand for institutional change to support sustainability and the effectiveness of new rules for a given level of enforcement.

## Structural Logic in Institutions

In the context of this discussion, establishing the distinction between institutions and organizations, and the consideration of cause and effect relations between these classes of entity, promotes a systems view of institutions and of the contribution that they make to the functioning of society. Institutions are fundamental building blocks of social systems, providing the generalized regulatory framework for socially acceptable behaviour. Without institutions-as-rules, social and economic coordination would not be possible and social life would be reduced to face-to-face negotiations of terms for every interaction. Even language is an institution, or institutional system, in this view.

The complexity of the general institutional environment can be appreciated from the consideration of many everyday activities that require coordination of individuals. From the running of the formal mechanisms of governance such as parliamentary or court processes to driving a private car through the city, successful negotiation of daily tasks is mediated by a plethora of socially defined rules, norms and expectations. The very purpose of these rules – reducing uncertainty in interaction – means that they remain unchanged for long enough to often become suppressed from conscious consideration. We do not think constantly about which side of the road we should be driving on or whether to stop for a red light. However, should the traffic lights go out or start operating in a random fashion, chaos soon results.

In the wider institutional environment there is often a considerable degree of redundancy in the system, particularly at higher levels of group decision making where results, and therefore mistakes, have far-reaching impacts. The separation of powers and the notion of checks and balances in government are an institutional expression of the principle of redundancy supporting several subsystems that must agree to, or at least agree not to veto, policy proposals for them to succeed. Having such multiple parallel institutional channels has the effect of broadening the range of views included in policy debates and tends to increase both their sophistication and acceptance. This redundancy built into governance mechanisms again emphasizes the systems nature of the institutional matrix. A hierarchy is evident, but democratic government is not a rigid single-headed beast. It is, rather, a system of actors and resources whose, sometimes almost unfathomably, complex relations and interactions are defined and constrained by a large set of institutions-as-rules.

The concept of policy systems is familiar enough,[11] and we can directly observe many of the processes and actors involved in the formation of policy. In a broader institutional system model these can be viewed as subsystems, often acting as feedback loops as well as producing new or altered institutions as policy edicts or legislative change. Existing institutional settings prescribe, encourage or allow certain organizations and processes to emerge and develop that consider issues of importance for government policy. Through resulting interactions the facilitating framework may itself be modified and developed, changing conditions for further policy work. In addition, policy processes result in outputs that address substantive issues, setting the rules and parameters for action in the real world, thus adding new substance and often complexity to the institutional system.

Organizational form in state-run resource and environmental management has traditionally adopted standard departmental bureaucratic modes as a means of dealing with distinct and separable sectors of government responsibility. This form is based on an assumption of discrete issue areas and a hierarchical model of administration and decision making, and is reproduced by convention (another institutional form). Such models have been argued to be particularly inadequate for environmental policy problems due to important characteristics such as complexity, uncertainty, and cross-sectoral impacts,[12] and proposed alternative models embody different fundamental principles.

The notion of organizational form and culture having an embedded rationality is worth developing briefly. Popular arguments over what comprises rational action have become dominated in recent decades by a single view or form of rationality based on economic theory. Here, efficiency is the key principle upon which rationality is judged, and its purpose is the maximization of a plurality of goals (social welfare) through the mechanism of individual utility maximization. However, many still recognise that other rationalities exist based on different principles of order and their own sets of values and goals. Easily distinguishable ones include legal rationality, political rationality, technical rationality and social rationalities.

Each form of rationality is supported by what has been termed a discourse: 'a shared way of apprehending the world. Embedded in language, it enables those who subscribe to it to interpret bits of information and put them together into coherent stories or accounts. Each discourse rests on assumptions, judgements, and contentions that provide the basic terms for analysis, debates, agreements, and disagreements'.[13] John Dryzek sees the discourse as 'institutional software,' interacting with the hardware of rules, rights, operating procedures, customs and principles.[14] The system will not work without the software, and this has arguably been demonstrated in attempts to introduce a free market economy to the former Soviet bloc countries. Formal changes were wheeled in, but the informal systems of understanding that support the kind of response expected by the reformers were not widespread and policy failure and even chaos have been the predominant results. The discourse concept is perhaps a more socially developed version of the Simon–North view of cultural norms and subjective mental models of reality.

Standard bureaucratic administration of environmental and natural resource policy, as seen in many state agencies, has been built on a pre-existing administrative rationality that privileges scientific and managerial expertise and is strictly hierarchical (the Weberian model). The underlying purpose is to be able to deal with large and complex problems facing society by reduction – breaking them down into sub-problems, solving each separately, with the process controlled, and the value of outputs judged, from the top. This rationality is built into the structures and processes of administration, but it is also (to some extent) built into the mindset, thought processes and language (the discourse) of the occupants of the hierarchy. Thus both structure and culture are integral to the maintenance of administrative rationality. This approach has worked to deal with many policy issues arising in complex developed economies over the past century. However, it seems particularly inappropriate to sustainability issues due to several important characterizing features, including the key factors of complexity and uncertainty.[15]

Over the last four decades a range of changes to the basic model have been made through the modification of organizational structures such as the flattening of management hierarchies, and the adoption of new practices such as stakeholder consultation. Such changes can have transformative effects on attitudes, organizational culture and policy discourse. However, they can contribute confusion and conflict, particularly where the changes are adopted as a means of neutralizing political pressure rather than in an attempt to change system dynamics. This is because institutional structure has an embedded logic, and a 'mix and match' system may, unthinkingly, embody conflicting rationalities.

One example of this type of conflict has been created where an NRM agency, in responding to stakeholder demand and policy fashion, has adopted a formalized consultative structure to advise policy decision making. The implicit structural logic in this arrangement is at least three-fold. It acknowledges that those with a stake in the outcome:

- have a right to a voice in decision making because they bear the consequences of decisions made under considerable uncertainty
- hold local environmental, social and economic knowledge not available to agency staff in other ways
- will be more likely to accept management decisions and comply with subsequent rules because they have been part of the process (that is, ownership).

However, in this case, in compliance with the Weberian expertise-based hierarchical model of bureaucratic problem solving, the members of the consultative groups are selected from stakeholders (by the hierarchy) on the basis of 'expertise', and specifically not as representative of stakeholders. This potentially allows relevant expertise to be defined in a manner convenient to the agency in determining which stakeholders will be part of the process. Control is maintained. The systemic conflict resulting from this clash of rationalities may well not be recognized for what it is, at least until there is recognition that such a thing is possible. However, solving actual problems may be made considerably more difficult, and stakeholders may become frustrated and factionalized. This points to an important issue in policy learning that will be explored later – that learning must involve improved understanding, not just mimicry.

A systems view of institutions makes it clear that the specification of new types of organization, on its own, is an ad hoc approach and likely to prove inadequate to the task of institutionalizing sustainability. It is the rationality, the principles and goals that organizational form must embody and implement, that is required to be elaborated within the institutional system first, along with a credible commitment from government to support it. This implies sincere and believable high-level avowals of principle and the establishment of pragmatic policies and ongoing initiatives with adequate resources to back them up. Of course we cannot start with a blank canvas, and changing the cultures of existing organizations to employ a new logic is a difficult task precisely because the formal rules are only part of the institutional system. The critical role of informal institutions such as cultural norms and social and policy discourses must not be disregarded. Normative change is required at all levels along with formal institutional change. In the case of sustainability, this suggests directed effort to re-educate policy making and implementation agency staff and stakeholders.

It also suggests that the level at which sustainability is embedded in the general institutional system of governance needs to be raised, perhaps to constitutional level, to provide some insulation from the rapid fluctuations of partisan political economy. For many, it seems a self-evident truth that governance of human societies should subscribe to the principles of sustainability at the same level as justice, human rights and democratic self-determination. Like these other foundation social values, sustainability is an ideal and not something likely to be fully achieved any time soon. It is a matter for ongoing social consideration at the most serious level and requires mechanisms to accumulate experience and knowledge of decision making so that learning may proceed into the far future.

**Rules for Institutional Language**

The core questions this book seeks to answer are: in what ways and to what degree have nations succeeded in establishing credible and working institutional instantiations for sustainable development, and how can we learn from them? In seeking answers it is proposed that the arguments put here be adopted for the consistent use of institutional language. In particular, 'institution' should not be used as a synonym for 'organization'.[16] Such usage is of little analytical utility and can be perceived as a merely rhetorical device aimed at imbuing the said organization with socially critical relevance. Some organizations, as argued above, provide services that are critical to social functioning. Where these are prescribed directly through a policy or set of rules, and particularly where they are part of the machinery of government for policy development and delivery, they can accurately be referred to as part of the 'institutional arrangements' with respect to that policy. 'Institutional arrangements' encompasses the notion of a system of decisions, rules and agreements that involves structural links between existing organizations, and possibly the creation of new organizations, for the implementation of policy. The term refers to the way that the individual rules are arranged and the opportunities and obligations created by those rules among stakeholders and their organizations in relation to the policy issue. Institutional arrangements form the infrastructure of the institutional system (or subsystem) and the venue for the systems dynamics. Similarly, 'institutional setting' can be used to refer to the specific institutional environment or backdrop for an issue, policy or action. 'Institution' should be reserved for rules of various types and their aggregative units.

Examples of high-level formal institutions of governance include constitutions and legislation, and their provisions. Sometimes the distinction between institution and organization can be difficult to draw. For example, Parliament may be viewed as an organization but is, under the view adopted here, an aggregate institution or institutional system. It comprises a set of rules about how representative government is to be carried out, organizational units and processes prescribed by these rules to enable the institution to function, and a range of actors with status and rights of participation also bestowed by the rules. The elected representatives are not thought of as belonging to, or being employed by, the organization of Parliament, but as actors in an *institutional system*, independent and yet bound by a vast array of formal rules, constraints imposed by party affiliation, and norms of social expectation held by the electorate. The Common Law provides a clear example of an important aggregate institution, being made up of a great many individual institutions – principles, decision rules, protocols, precedents and sub-aggregates such as doctrines. However, the Common Law is only one component of the broader legal system – an institutional system of institutions-as-rules, actors, organizations and processes.

Social and cultural norms and their aggregates tend to be regarded as informal institutions, whether or not direct sanctions are applied for breaches of rules. Informal institutions can play a critical role in resource and environmental management in interaction with formal rules, as in many cases the close monitoring of behaviour for breaches of formal rules is not possible. The congruence of formal and informal institutions is therefore an important issue in policy change for sustainability. Wisely handled, with judicious choice of policy instruments and well designed processes, policies driven by urgent ecological imperatives but implying social change should be able to lead compatible normative change, albeit over time-scales that may be politically inconvenient. As North has commented:

> While the rules may be changed overnight, the informal norms usually change only gradually. Since it is the norms that provide legitimacy to a set of rules, revolutionary change is never as revolutionary as its supporters desire, and performance will be different than anticipated. And economies that adopt the formal rules of another economy will have very different performance characteristics than the first economy because of different informal norms and enforcement.[17]

This last statement is directly relevant to the notion of the possibility of learning from other jurisdictions and their institutional settings, and the problem of how to choose appropriate case studies of institutional innovation for sustainability. These issues are addressed in the following section, and in Chapter 2.

## POLICY RELEVANT LEARNING

This section briefly explores what the 'learning' part of an exercise in policy and institutional learning might be about. Four categories of policy relevant learning are drawn from the literature: instrumental, government, social and political learning. All of these are relevant areas from which to draw lessons from the experience of different jurisdictions with sustainable development. In addition the institutionalization of learning – the embedding of purposive learning mechanisms into the institutional system – is something that we undoubtedly need to learn more about. Hence, in its search and evaluation of case studies, this inquiry might look to learn from:

- examples of instruments used
- organizational structures and processes established
- new or different social constructions of problem sets
- strategies used for raising the agenda status of issues
- the mechanisms built into institutional arrangements that have promoted learning and innovation in these areas.

Peter May proposes that policy related learning must involve increased understanding, not just mimicry – the direct transfer of a policy from one situation to another.[18] It follows that, rather than just noting that 'success' has been attained by a certain policy in a given context, evaluation must attempt to understand why the institutional arrangement had the observed effect in its particular social, economic, environmental and institutional context. Further, it is important for analysis such as that undertaken here, as intermediary in a policy learning process, to identify who the appropriate learner might be for each type of lesson. The characterisation of the four types of policy-related learning described here include such linkages, and the later case studies will explore this issue further in context.

## Instrumental Learning

Within government departments and agencies charged with resource and environmental management, in other sectors, and more recently with sustainable development, policy instruments are selected and programs developed to address defined problems with stated intended outcomes. Instrumental learning concerns improving the design of such institutional arrangements to achieve existing policy goals. Evaluation of the 'success' of particular instruments with respect to stated goals might be relatively straightforward if results are conspicuously positive, but generating understanding about why and how particular results were attained in a given context is more difficult. May champions the view that demonstrating instrumental learning requires evidence of increased intelligence and sophistication of thought.[19] We must ponder how to assess, in these terms, whether the present enquiry, or any such analysis, results in real learning. The so-called 'goal trap' of policy evaluation must also be kept in mind: there may be positive (or negative) outcomes that were wholly unintended from which we can learn as much about the nature of policies and context as from evaluation in relation to intended outcomes. Some policies may fail to achieve their primary aims but have unintended side effects that are just as beneficial, or at least educational.

Most members of a policy community, both within and outside the specific implementing agency, can benefit through better understanding of how the use of particular instruments affects social, economic and ecological outcomes through interactions with contextual variables. Instrument choice may be left to implementation units within government departments based on their previous experience with the issues. Alternatively, where legislation or regulations are required to authorise revenue collection, police powers or enforcement provisions, executive government and possibly cabinet-level decision making may be involved. In some cases particular instruments have been specified in legislation as government policy – for example, in Australia, individual transferable quota (ITQ) in the Commonwealth Fisheries Management Act 1991. It is increasingly the case that the norms of the contemporary environmental policy environment require wide consultation and some form of consensus before new policy instruments are implemented. This process will be driven or at least mediated and strongly affected by the section of the government department responsible for policy development in the area. Therefore these policy analysts and managers must be key learners in instrumental lesson drawing from outside jurisdictions. Depending on the issue, analysts from stakeholder peak bodies may also be important, as a coalition for policy change involving the major industry representative bodies and the responsible government departments, sharing a common policy discourse, can be immensely powerful.

**Government Learning**

Government learning involves some conceptual overlap with instrumental learning. However, government learning has as its focus the organizational structure and processes of agencies and delivery systems as distinguished from the policy instruments used. Where existing departments are restructured for greater effectiveness or efficiency, independently of policy change, and continue to utilize the same set of policy instruments, the distinction is clear. However, reorganization can be a result of the adoption of new policy instruments that require special administrative arrangements. Bennett and Howlett[20] use the same passage from Etheredge[21] as a criterion for judging this type of learning – 'increased intelligence and sophistication of thought' – used by May for instrumental learning.[22] The concept of improved structural intelligence in both instrumental and organizational design may be of some utility, to the extent that it can relate organizational logic and effectiveness to the rationality and discourse supporting the policy approach being implemented. Structural intelligence can be said to increase as congruence of organizational logic and policy rationality is improved.

It is clear that the key learners for this category must be senior departmental bureaucrats and in some cases government ministers. Reorganization (like decimation in the Roman army) is used as a periodical strategic management tool within many organizations for reinvigorating functional units. This presents regular opportunities for government learning, and some organizations, no doubt, become structurally more intelligent as a result. However, such learning is attuned to particular management objectives, and these do not necessarily include the needs and principles of sustainability. Structural models that take these needs seriously could play a powerful role in policy-related learning at the both the instrumental and social levels, acting as effective seeds for wider institutional change. This area may be a fertile one if suitably sophisticated studies of the impacts of departmental restructuring for sustainability exist.

**Social Learning**

The above two categories of learning are both about more intelligently effecting predefined policy goals. Social learning, by contrast, involves the recasting of the policy problematique – the policy problem itself, the scope of the policy, or policy goals.[23] Social policy learning therefore involves the wider policy network that participates in modelling and sustaining the prevailing social construction of the problem. The basic building blocks used in these constructions are (according to May):

- beliefs about cause and effect
- preferences concerning desired policy outcomes
- perceptions of policy targets
- beliefs about the ideas that undergird policies.

Changes resulting from a new social consensus about one or a combination of these fundamental aspects of a problem, and therefore the policies in place to address it, comprise social policy learning, according to May. It is clear how this conception of problem framing or social construction is related to Dryzek's notion of policy discourses.[24] Each discourse has its own construction of the problem based on beliefs and preferences for particular outcomes. 'Social consensus' in the above statement relates to 'dominant discourse' in Dryzek's view – the construction of the problem that actually gets supported in policy.

Generalized normative change regarding the environment has an important part to play in social policy learning as it affects preferences for outcomes and beliefs about policy ideas in particular. Normative change involves shifts in individual beliefs and the social consensus over fundamental values. Without normative change at some level social policy learning would be rare. Normative change can occur in different ways, including through diffusion of ideas and values from other cultures, conflict between opposing groups, or persistent deviation from existing norms by subcultures. Certainly, with respect to environmental issues, normative change has been rapid over the past four decades. Science has played a large role in informing these changes, particularly through creation and modification of models of cause and effect relationships and the collection of data on the state of the environment. Improved information has shifted values over preferred outcomes for the environment, but the consequent thirst for more information has exposed pervasive uncertainty with regard to many issues. Perhaps one of the most significant currently incipient normative changes involves the dethroning of science and technology as exclusive providers of solutions to environmental problems. This is bringing more attention to institutional aspects of problem solving, and hence to the institutional construction of problem definitions, with a resulting extension of peer communities and broadening of the range of inputs to policy.

As we have seen in the foregoing discussions, how and to what extent belief systems or worldviews are embedded in cognitive institutional systems, such as policy subsystems, and how durable or adaptable they are are a subject of contemporary theoretical and empirical study. There exists a range of conceptual approaches to the issue with a common language yet to emerge,[25] as we have seen is also the case with the issue of the nature of institutions themselves. However, 'problem framing' is commonly recognized as being of fundamental importance, along with the fact that the framing varies with the worldview of the problem framers. This in turn affects conclusions about what information is required for policy making and management and therefore what research is undertaken or funded by agencies. Walsh provides an example of this in her case study of the Inter-American Tropical Tuna Commission, where the dominant central policy idea (Walsh calls this the 'embedded epistemology') has been replaced successively over several decades.[26] First came conservation (of tuna), then preservation (of dolphins), and then ecosystem management. Each successive central policy goal controlled the research agenda for the period of its dominance and therefore what knowledge was generated by the agency. These goals were formulated by an influential 'epistemic community', in this case mainly comprising marine biological scientists. In other resource management policy subsystems the originators of new problem frames may be biological-ecological or physical scientists, economists or other social scientists, or they may originate in integrating processes drawing on a range of disciplinary and lay inputs. It is new framings of the latter type that are most likely to lead to sustainable policy pathways.

Through the current project we might learn about different social constructions of a particular common natural resource management (NRM) problem, or the processes through which social learning has occurred or been promoted in other jurisdictions. Instrumental and government learning are able to occur at the agency level without elected politicians becoming involved in decision making. However, social policy learning requires political decision makers to either lead community normative change or to respond to it. The greatest opportunity for social policy learning is probably at the point where elected governments change, as different ideological values and beliefs are brought into play and new administrations introduce and search for policies that demonstrate leadership and differentiate them from the prior incumbents. Circumstances where resource issues flare into overt and politicized social conflicts, or where resources and their exploitation systems are in crisis, can also promote a rethinking of attitudes, ideas and policies that have remained stable for extended periods. Conflict can bring information and alternative logics to the attention of policy makers and the public that can result in redefined objectives, changed target groups and redistributed rights. The deeply embedded nature of many of the values that underpin particular framings of policy problems means that there is likely to be a generational aspect to social policy learning. Early adopters of new problem constructions in the sustainability field may well be younger policy analysts with specific education and training in natural resource and environmental problems. However, the key actors in policy decision making are senior bureaucrats, politicians and economic stakeholders, often with long-term investments in current problem definitions, and this is part of what makes for stable institutions. North states: 'Political institutions will be stable only if undergirded by organizations with a stake in their perpetuation.'[27] The same may be said for policies. Rapid change may be dependent on conflict or political opportunism or both, otherwise we may need to rely on long-term social normative change.[28]

**Political Learning**

Political learning involves political actors constructing more effective strategies for getting their concerns on to the policy agenda, countering opposition to their proposals, and eventually getting their preferred policies adopted by decision makers. This type of policy-oriented learning occurs within advocacy coalitions, composed of people from various organizations who share a set of normative and causal beliefs (a discourse) and who often act in concert.[29] These coalitions, in turn, occur within 'policy subsystems,' that is, the interaction of actors from different agencies and organizations, politicians, and so on, interested in a policy area.

How relevant political learning is to the current project is a question that requires further consideration. This aspect of policy-oriented learning is undoubtedly important to effecting policy change, even where substantial normative change has already taken place. In the area of resource and environmental policy for sustainability, powerful advocacy coalitions for defence of status quo policies may be well entrenched on some issues. The question arises as to whether it is appropriate for this project to research issues of political strategy and tactics that may assist policy change. Investigation of policy change that is seeking to explain causation in significant detail, arguably, must attend this issue, as differences in strategies brought about by political learning may explain why policy change occurs in one situation and not in other similar circumstances.

## CONCLUDING COMMENTS

Both the above conceptual discussions offer some insight into the nature of the policy and institutional systems and structures that will be the focus of this study as it attempts to draw lessons from experiences of policy and institutional change for sustainable development. There are distinctive synergies between the systems view of institutions and the policy learning framework, but there are some disjunctions as well. The learning framework, in its attempt to separate categories of learning, under emphasizes the interactions between the levels, conveying a view of a rather linear one-way cause and effect process of policy formulation and subsequent implementation. The systems model developed here, reinforced by standard approaches to policy analysis structured by models of policy cycles and subsystems,[30] reminds us that life is not that simple. For example, whether a particular policy is sold and/or perceived as a change of instrument or a reframing of the problem can depend the political tactics used in the development of the 'policy event'.

The introduction of market instruments is a case in point. These are billed in policy debate as more efficient, with the implication left unspoken that they are more efficient at achieving what we are all trying to achieve anyway. This can be viewed as instrumental learning. However, in many cases the introduction of the efficiency objective actually displaces an existing policy objective of distributional equity. By replacing the instrument the policy problem has been redefined. This can pass relatively quietly, or it can blow up into a confused public debate and protest. The introduction of such 'instruments' usually involve legislative change and the creation of some form of implicit or explicit legal property right – a fundamental institutional building block – and may involve the creation or reorganization of government agencies for implementation and administration. We discuss the property rights instrument example in the last of the case studies in Chapter 7.

Thus there appears little hope of clear-cut and simple categories of policy and institutional initiatives even at the conceptual level. In Chapter 2 we add into this broth the operational ingredients of the specifics of what it is we wish to learn about. This will bring us toward a richer appreciation of the nature of the choices required to select objects for analysis (case studies), but it seems this issue is set to become more complex, not less.

## NOTES

1. North (1990).
2. Goodin (1996); March and Olsen (1984).
3. Henningham (1995).
4. Dovers (2001a).
5. Ibid.
6. North (1990).
7. North (1994).
8. North (1990).
9. For an example of the diversity just within sociology see Scott (1987), and Goodin (1996) provides an accessible summary of institutional interests across a selection of social science disciplines.
10. Simon (1986).
11. See, for example, Howlett and Ramesh (1995).
12. See, for example, Dovers (1997), Dryzek (1997).
13. Dryzek (1997).
14. Dryzek (1996).
15. Dryzek (1997).

16. The use of the term 'institute' in reference to or naming a research, teaching, professional or other organization will not be discussed here other than to suggest that this is generally intended to convey the impression of a distinguished, not to say critical, component of the intellectual establishment.
17. North (1994).
18. May (1992).
19. Ibid.
20. Bennett and Howlett (1992).
21. Etheredge (1981).
22. May (1992).
23. Ibid.
24. Dryzek (1997).
25. For example, see Apthorpe and Gasper (1996).
26. Walsh (2001).
27. North (1994).
28. This analysis suggests that structural change in policy agencies (government learning) may promote social policy learning. For example, shallow hierarchies that support innovative policy cultures, promote policy entrepreneurs, encourage challenge of dominant policy discourses and ongoing theoretical education of staff.
29. Sabatier (1988).
30. For example, Howlett and Ramesh (1995), Bridgman and Davis (2000).

# 2.   Operationalizing learning

## INTRODUCTION

The discussion in Chapter 1 provides a workable definition of institutions and an approach to policy and institutional learning. This chapter proposes avenues for applying this understanding in a more sharply focused way, in terms of what we might wish to learn about and from where the lessons might come. The objective is to trace the rationale for the selection of case studies and examples of institutional change explored in Part II, and, in so doing, further develop the substantive themes of the study. In particular, the following section asks what it is we want to learn about and from whom. It explores the meaning of 'sustainable development' and how policy and institutional systems might, and do, respond to its imperatives, using Australian institutional responses as examples.

The chapter then puts forward a set of criteria for the selection of a handful of case studies from the myriad possibilities and, arguably more importantly for the study, develops a matrix of analytical targets for the study. In working over this methodology we hope to offer not merely a justification for our choices, but also an aid both to understanding the nature of the questions being asked, and therefore the answers produced later, and to the development of further studies of institutional change in this area. Finally the chapter briefly discusses the case study topics chosen, along with some that might have been but were not, explaining how the criteria were applied in the choices made.

## LEARN ABOUT WHAT?

There are several ways in which one could proceed to learn from other countries, depending on the specific jurisdiction that seeks to learn. For example, individuals and groups in Australia interested in institutional change for sustainability might identify countries that are similar and assess their recent experience. Similarity might be defined socially and institutionally (Western, English-speaking, liberal democracies, and so on) or environmentally (dry, variable, high biodiversity, extensive primary production, and so on). The problem with this approach is that a set of 'similar' countries only captures a small and perhaps inadequate sample of potentially relevant experience. Another warning against it is that it would echo the habit of seeking policy and political lessons only from instantly comparable jurisdictions.[1] In a complex and evolving arena such as sustainability the net should be cast of wide as possible. However, the institutional framework prompts us to think about this in terms of tensions and trade-offs. Innovations developed in similar institutional contexts would have greater probability of being supported appropriately, on transfer, by existing legal and organizational configurations. However, mechanisms developed under weak institutional systems may be more innovative and resilient, particularly for issues requiring local action, precisely because there is little external support for enforcement of rules.

Another approach would be to identify the substantive issues most high on a country's domestic agenda and then scan the world for examples of institutional responses to those (for example, in the case of contemporary Australia, water allocation, dryland salinity, off-reserve biodiversity conservation, and so on). This would run the risk of only focusing on issues of the moment, of not being open to cross-issue relevance of particular institutional strategies, and of reducing the field of study back to a collection of discrete issues rather than a (possibly) integrated suite of issues. On the other hand it may produce some immediately applicable lessons for current problems.

However, the current project seeks to learn from examples of institutional reform and change in the *policy* field of sustainable development (SD), not necessarily with regard to particular issues that make up that agenda. To do so, we need to establish what sustainable development means.

**The Meaning of Sustainable Development**

Although a highly contestable term, sustainable development is expressed as aspirations and principles in policy and law internationally and in many national and sub-national jurisdictions. These expressions of the meaning of sustainable development have resulted from international consensus, for example at the 1992 Rio summit, and again at the World Summit on Sustainable Development in 2002. Given the many similarities between expressions of the principles of sustainable development we will take one reasonably standard expression – that in Australian national policy – and seek to translate that into terms more meaningful for policy and institutional learning (noting any differences peculiar to the Australian context).

In Australia, the emerging Rio principles were expressed as principles of 'ecologically sustainable development', or ESD principles (see Table 2.1). These were developed as part of Australia's response to the emerging global policy agenda of sustainability in the early 1990s, reflect international discussions and instruments and other nation's statements, are sufficiently broad to cover the key aspects of the modern idea of sustainability, and have been expressed in many hundreds of Australian policies and over one hundred and twenty Australian laws (Dovers 1999; Stein 2000). Thus the ESD principles should encapsulate much of what Australia and other countries might wish to learn about institutionalizing sustainable development; that is, if ESD is where we think we want to go, then ESD can logically also describe what we need to learn about to get there. Pursuing the institutionalization of 'official' policy goals and principles in this way has the added advantage of providing additional strength to any lessons drawn, as opposed to lessons drawn from statements of the problem that do not reflect widespread consensus at government level.

As stated in policy and law, though, ESD principles are summary, vague and not particularly instructive in institutional terms (although they are more so in policy terms). This is not surprising, as they were compromise and summary statements, conveniently stated during a short-term political process – as indeed also were the internationally negotiated Rio principles. However, they do reflect much of the nature of sustainability as a suite of research and policy problems, for example in the following iteration of the attributes of sustainability problems (from Dovers 1997):

- deepened and variable temporal scales
- broadened and variable spatial scales
- possible ecological limits to human activities
- often irreversible and/or cumulative impacts
- complexity within problems, and connectivity between problems (within the environmental domain, and across social and economic domains as well)
- pervasive risk and uncertainty
- poor information base for many processes
- important assets not traded and thus not valued economically
- new ethical dimensions (rights of other species, future generations)
- systemic problem causes, rooted in patterns of production and consumption, settlement and governance
- insufficiently developed and/or contested theories, methods, techniques
- poorly defined policy and property rights and responsibilities
- public/private costs and benefits difficult to separate
- demands and justification for broad community participation in policy discussion and formulation
- sheer novelty as a recently defined policy field.

These problem attributes, especially when encountered in combination, give some meaning and tractability to the widespread perception and common claim that sustainability problems are particularly difficult. They also reconfirm some of the targets of learning that flow from ESD principles (Table 2.1).

These attributes, and the discussion of learning in Chapter 1, can inform a restatement of ESD goals and principles into a more operational statement of 'what we want to learn about'. Table 2.1 adds to the National Strategy for ESD (NSESD) (Australia 1992) iteration of goals and principles, summary comments that define learning targets that would appear to logically flow from those principles, and from the generic attributes of ESD problems, in terms of learning as that concept is constructed in this study. Also in Table 2.1 are summary descriptors of each goal and principle for use in later discussion.

*Table 2.1    Sustainability (ESD) principles as targets for policy and institutional learning*

| ESD goals, objectives and principles | Summary descriptor | Core meaning as target for learning |
|---|---|---|
| *Goal*<br>Development that improves the total quality of life, both now and in the future, in a way that maintains the ecological processes on which life depends | Goal | Too general – see under objectives and principles below |
| *Objectives*<br>1.  To enhance individual and community well-being and welfare by following a path of economic development that safeguards the welfare of future generations | Sustainable economic development | Policy processes and institutional arrangements that ensure longer considerations in economic policy and planning, and the implications of economic policy for individual and community well-being (well-being defined in broad terms, including social, cultural, environmental and economic aspects) |

| ESD goals, objectives and principles | Summary descriptor | Core meaning as target for learning |
|---|---|---|
| 2. To provide for equity within and between generations | Inter- and intra-generational equity | Policy processes and institutional arrangements explicitly targeting the issue of the multiple dimensions of equity over the long term |
| 3. To protect biological diversity and maintain essential ecological processes and life support systems | Biodiversity and ecological processes | Policy processes and institutional arrangements that elevate the importance of biodiversity and ecological processes as matters of policy concern and as social and policy goals, across policy sectors |
| *Principles* | | |
| 1. Decision making processes should effectively integrate both long- and short-term economic, environmental, social and equity dimensions | Policy integration | Processes and arrangements that seek to integrate, encourage or demand policy integration or research and develop methods for such integration |
| 2. Where there are threats of serious or irreversible damage, lack of full scientific certainty should not be used as a reason for postponing measures to prevent environmental degradation | Precautionary principle | Processes and arrangements that explicitly inform decisions in the face of uncertainty, ensure consideration of risk and uncertainty, seek to enhance the information base for decision making in the long term, or research and develop approaches for so doing |
| 3. The global dimension of environmental impacts of actions and policies should be recognized and considered | International commons policy | Processes and arrangements that account for, seek to account for, or seek to establish the nature of international threats to sustainability or opportunities |

| | | |
|---|---|---|
| | | for improving prospects for sustainability through international coordination of policy and action |
| 4. The need to develop a strong, growing and diversified economy which can enhance the capacity for environmental protection should be recognized[a] | Sustainable economic growth | Processes and arrangements that explicitly seek to link economic growth with environment or to establish whether such links can or do exist |
| 5. The need to maintain and enhance international competitiveness in an environmentally sound manner should be recognized | International competitiveness | Processes and arrangements aimed at explicating, reviewing and/or ensuring the environmental (and social) benefits, or avoiding the disbenefits, of international law, trade, policy and interactions |
| 6. Cost-effective and flexible policy instruments should be adopted, such as improved valuation, pricing and incentive mechanisms | Policy instrument choice | Applications of flexible policy instruments, and/or processes and arrangements to research, monitor, select and test new approaches to policy instrument choice and application (including but not only market mechanisms as implied in the principle) |
| 7. Decisions and actions should provide for broad community involvement on issues which affect them | Community involvement | Processes and arrangements that allow or encourage community participation in policy debate, policy formulation and management |

*Note:* [a] This is a central and contested proposal in the sustainability literature, that is, that environmental protection depends on economic growth (for a review, see van den Bergh and de Mooij 1999). Here, the object of learning that arises is defined not around belief or disbelief in this proposal but rather in terms of policy and institutional settings aimed at either establishing such a link in practice or further testing the proposition.

In Table 2.1 all targets for learning are stated in terms of policy processes and institutional arrangements and framed in a broad manner including policy and institutional responses that fulfil, aim to fulfil, or research and develop approaches for fulfilling that objective or principle or part thereof. Such responses may include sustained (as opposed to superficial) policy programmes, organizational restructuring such as portfolio rearrangements, creation of new agencies, information-based initiatives or deeper institutional change such as statutory or constitutional reform. An integrated and concerted institutional and policy response to all ESD objectives and principles is arguably not evident in any country but would equal a rather fulsome and impressive response to the intellectual and policy agenda constructed between 1987 and 1992. In these terms this translation of ESD principles into (albeit broadly framed) targets for policy and institutional learning constructs what may be regarded as an already sufficiently large canvas for this study. With respect to kinds of learning discussed earlier, most possibilities are embedded in the targets in Table 2.1, although perhaps with a less explicit emphasis on political learning.

The principles of ESD adopted by Australia (Table 2.1) strongly reflect the economic growth element of the Bruntland construction of sustainable development. One critical reading of Bruntland is that the 1987 World Commission on Environment and Development (WCED) emphasis on growth as the answer to global maldistribution was the only approach that could succeed in gaining broad consideration of and consensus on the other central issues of sustainability. Australia's ESD principles enthusiastically restate this approach, emphasizing strong growth and international competitiveness as sustainability goals, and incentive and signalling (economic) instruments as means. This is, though, only a more pronounced emphasis on what has been a political trend in Organization for Economic Cooperation and Development (OECD) and especially Anglophone, developed countries. With time this may come to be seen more widely as an overemphasis produced by transient political conditions and policy fashion – given that three of the seven principles are given over to economics.

However, there are things missing from the NSESD version of sustainability that emerge when actual policy and institutional responses in Australia and elsewhere are considered. The following section reviews such directions of reform. Further, consideration of the most complete and consensus-derived global statement of intent regarding sustainability, the 1992 Rio Declaration, adds other, significant agendas for policy and institutional reform. For example, principles 5–6 of the Declaration emphasize poverty reduction and prioritize the needs of least developed countries, while principle 11 states the need for effective national legislation and standards. Principles 20–22 elevate the views and involvement in sustainability of women, youth, and indigenous and local people. Consideration of such principles in a study like this is important given their status as internationally agreed goals, and given that they have been expressed explicitly and thus may have informed the policy and institutional reform agendas of some nations, especially those who have experimented more vigorously with policy and institutional reform.

## Thus Far …

Here we continue with Australia as an example, one not untypical of broader trends. If ESD principles represent the policy challenge agreed to by Australian governments and major interest groups, it is relevant here to consider the style of response to that challenge thus far. This section characterizes the style of policy response, not in terms of the efficacy or adequacy of the response but rather of the policy and institutional directions that the country has chosen.[2] The following roughly categorizes the policy and institutional baskets into which Australia has placed the bulk of its ESD eggs:

- Community-based programmes such as Landcare, Waterwatch, and so on, with an emphasis on on-ground coordination and works and to a lesser extent monitoring, relying to varying degrees on a mixture of volunteerism and government financial and other support.
- Integrated catchment management through informal cooperative initiatives and more formally structured creation of new administrative and statutory arrangements.
- Often less formally structured or supported regional-scale planning initiatives, often explicitly seeking to integrate economic, social and environmental concerns through long-term planning involving community participation or leadership.[3]

  (The above three are often the delivery mechanisms for government-financed policy programmes, such as the National Heritage Trust and the National Salinity and Water Quality Action Plan.)

- Information-based processes (for example, state of environment reporting, natural resource accounting, land and water audits, and so on).[4]
- The application of economic instruments and market mechanisms of various kinds (incentive and signalling approaches), including tradable emission permits, salinity credits, rights markets in fish and water, levies, and so on (noting that the advocacy of such instruments has exceeded their practical application thus far).
- Self-regulatory approaches (codes of practice, corporate reporting, and

so on) in various industry sectors, usually developed cooperatively between government and the private sector.

- Development or maintenance of intergovernmental arrangements such as the Murray-Darling Basin Initiative, management of the Great Barrier Reef, cooperative arrangements for management of the Australian Alps, ministerial councils, and so on.
- Moves towards co-management arrangements with indigenous people, including major conservation reserves and the more recent Indigenous Protected Areas programme.
- (Variable) domestic engagement in the formulation and implementation of international instruments dealing with major resource and environmental issues.
- Sectoral and issue-based policy development, with associated programmes (oceans, forestry, biodiversity, greenhouse, landcare, coasts, and so on).[5] Of all sectoral policy initiatives the Regional Forest Agreement (RFA) process has been by far the largest and most comprehensive. Most major sectoral policies have been developed cooperatively by the Commonwealth and the states/territories (and less often with local government).
- Some significant specific institutional reforms, such as the creation of the (now defunct) Resource Assessment Commission, a proposed Commissioner for ESD in the state of Victoria and the recently established Sustainability Policy Unit in the Premier's department in Western Australia.
- Experiments in the arrangement of resource and environment portfolios at state and Commonwealth level, where various constellations of resources, lands, agriculture, environment and conservation have been constructed (and often deconstructed). While not an apparent or explicit ESD-related policy, this is of interest given the question of where in the public policy landscape environment and resource issues should be located. At state/territory level some of the experiments seem purposeful in ESD policy terms, whereas at the Commonwealth level the portfolio changes appear to have be driven by other imperatives.
- Research and development programmes (and sometimes actual agencies) in the resource and environmental fields.

A feature of the early ESD era in Australia, consensus policy development organized along so-called corporatist lines (drawing major representative groups, not the broader public, into processes to formulate policy) has been less evident in the second half of the 1990s. Also, less prominent, has been the Council of Australian Governments, an occasional heads-of-government grouping which was key to major policy developments such as ESD.

These Australian responses cannot be located entirely in the post-Brundtland or post-Rio era as they build upon and reflect previous responses constructed before 'sustainable development' was adopted as an over-arching agenda or was fully articulated as such.[6] For example, much of what Landcare 'does' draws heavily on the accumulated knowledge and practice of many decades of the agronomic tradition of soil conservation. Integrated catchment management and regional resource management have similarly deep histories. The world famous Murray-Darling Basin Initiative in its modern form was a product of the 1980s, but its origin dates to before the formation of the River Murray Commission eight decades ago.[7] The importance of historical context of institutional and policy change is revisited below.

Each country develops and favours a particular mix of policy and institutional responses, and Australia is no exception. Some of the response categories above are common to many countries, whereas others are particularly Australian. Likewise other countries may have embarked on quite different pathways than Australia. For example, strategic, statutory planning has not been a feature of the Australian experience recently; nor have the sort of detailed, intergovernmental regulatory approaches of the past decade in Europe. This raises the question, in a study such as this, whether the focus should be on institutional reform across suites of countries that have done similar things or on countries that have headed in dissimilar policy and institutional directions. There are obvious benefits either way – to learn how to do roughly familiar things better, or about things we have not thought of doing – but to choose one or other would perhaps be efficient. Alternatively, this demarcation allows explicit recognition of the quite different basis for learning (accepting that the familiar/unfamiliar demarcation is likely in most cases to be a continuum).

**Defining Objects of Learning**

Given the large number of factors and their combinations that could characterize policy and institutional responses to sustainability, some categorization is required to simplify the task of choosing case studies. Here we use the typology of policy learning outlined in Chapter 1 to group potential objects of learning. As might be expected, the least general examples are the most numerous – individual instrument types. The more generally applicable lessons are fewer in type and likely to be scarce as documented examples – for example, the explicit reframing of policy problems through normative acceptance of sustainability principles. However, we must also remain cognizant of the systems view of institutions presented above, which emphasizes the embedded and interdependent nature of different elements of the policy and institutional landscape. This means individual case studies may yield lessons on several levels of the typology.

## 1.   Implementation instruments

*Policy instruments*   are the policy tools applied to deliver defined policy goals. Bearing in mind the previous discussion of potential multiple impacts of certain types of instruments, including on policy goals, instruments may be classified as:

- *coercive*, such as statutory and regulatory proscription, prescription, standards setting, and so on
- *organizational*, such as community coordination and participatory approaches
- *informational*, including research, education, SoE reporting, environmental monitoring, and so on
- *signalling and incentive*, such as market and pricing based approaches, taxes, levies, user charges, subsidies, and so on

Primary learners here would be government agencies implementing policy to which the case is relevant and their stakeholders.

*Policy programmes*   utilize more than one instrument toward a more comprehensive set of goals, in some coordinated fashion, usually targeted at a substantive issue (e.g. salinity) or a resource sector (e.g. fisheries). The design of programmes allows for greater opportunity for building in the flexibility required for most sustainability problems given their complex nature and the uncertainty of the effects of change. Primary learners would be strategic policy analysts in relevant agencies, although specialists in sustainability problems in this class are somewhat thin on the ground. The sophistication of such design tasks begs a real question here with regard to the sufficiency of human capital and organizational configuration in government to address sustainability problems.

*Policy processes*   involve mechanisms and structures dedicated to policy formulation, implementation design, and policy evaluation and maintenance. Processes may be ongoing, lengthy or of short duration. In areas where policy goals are evolving and uncertainty prevails with respect to the current or future state of a resource and impacts of its use – as is often the case with sustainability issues – complex ongoing process 'rounds' are required to assess new information and update policy settings.

## 2.  Organizing government

*Organizing and restructuring within government* where the structures and processes within a tier of government are rearranged in some way to better meet a policy challenge, including such things as management restructuring within agencies, interdepartmental committees and portfolio redesign, or involving the creation of new or substantially altered organizations/agencies within the public sector to undertake new or revised administrative, policy or information-related functions.

*Intergovernmental structures and processes* where sustainability problems are addressed through coordination between different levels of government within a country (e.g. in a federal system), through coordinated policy development, joint standards, joint agencies, ministerial councils, and so on.

*Participatory processes* whether aimed at on-ground management, monitoring, policy formulation or policy monitoring and evaluation.

Depending on the context, a wide range of players may be closely interested in process evaluation and design, with the broadest group being interested in participatory processes.

## 3.  Problem reframing

*Through normative change* where public opinion, possibly assisted by government-sponsored processes, has demonstrably shifted to redefine an existing sectoral issue as a sustainability problem and has flowed on into government policy.

*Through legal change* mostly statutory but possibly also involving the common law. The law in this sense is viewed broadly, including both regulatory policy in the traditional sense, but more so the crucial and often overlooked roles of statute law in expressing social goals (e.g. sustainability or ESD principles), codifying agency objects, creating process, creating organizational structures, defining public access to decision making processes, and so on.

*Through Parliamentary or executive government processes* (e.g. Senate Committees) that allow sustainability issues to be treated in accordance with their attributes and sustainability principles (e.g. temporal scale, integration, and so on).

**4.  Political advocacy**

While relevant and important to the raising of the sustainability policy agenda in political fora, in the context of the current project we think such advocacy a difficult target on its own. It is likely that examples will be picked up incidentally to studies in the other target categories. For example, under organizing government, the creation of commissioners for the environment or ESD or the specification of advocacy roles for agencies may prove worthwhile subjects.

Clearly these categories are not entirely separate, and in any actual case of policy or institutional reform of any significance more than one would be evident. Note that, across all these types, an important variable is the demonstrable or likely longevity of the institutional or policy change. Longevity and persistence are relevant as positive attributes of sustainability policy efforts, but there are the balancing issues of irreversibility in policy and institutional change and of persistence becoming a dominant characteristic at the expense of adaptive learning. Another important variable is where a particular reform sits on the continuum between application or use of existing policy or institutional settings or capacities and creation of substantially new settings.

## FILTERING CASES AND LESSONS

Given that the potential pool of case studies for a study such as this is immense, the cases for more detailed (but still summary) analysis must be selected carefully. Among the factors that might be used to inform selection of cases in terms of their relevance both to a specific jurisdiction that may seek to learn and to the nature of sustainability problems are:

- ecological/biophysical similarities and differences
- substantive issues that are relevant in the 'learning' jurisdiction, or are likely to be so
- comparability of socioeconomic conditions in the case location and the jurisdiction that seeks lessons
- formal and informal institutional context
- political imperatives and policy styles (see further below)
- resourcing requirements and availability (human, financial, informational).

All such factors need to be assessed and interpreted with cognisance of particular historical contexts of institutional evolution. A general principle linked closely to the concept of an institutional 'system' is path dependence.

Institutional possibilities are historically defined – sudden creation is possible but rare, and even sudden change will be dependent on precedent conditions (information, cultural context, legal precedent, politcial norms built up over time, and so on). Transfer of institutional models or ideas therefore should be informed by the immediately apparent suitability of the recipient setting but also by appreciation of how that setting has evolved over time.

Further to these considerations there is the matter of deciding whether or not to have a 'sample' of case studies or thematic areas that cover all of, most of or a selected small number of the variables discussed in this chapter. These include: familiar or unfamiliar policy and institutional responses to sustainable development judged according to what the recipient jurisdiction has done so far or a more extended typology of responses; similar/dissimilar countries and political contexts; differences in the statement of sustainability principles; and types of learning. Clearly not all can be covered, so the basis of selection needs careful thought.

Recognizing the interdependent and nested nature of the institutional system, there may be cases of institutional reform that are both apparently successful and novel in the case location but which on any balanced analysis may be judged very unlikely to be adopted in another setting. Institutional (and simpler organizational) lessons, and the reforms they might lead to, need to be analysed in the context of the political and institutional setting into which they are to be transplanted. In the list of prospective cases provided below there are some which may be, for this reason, judged unlikely to inform actual change in a specific location. To illustrate, we will use the reference point of Australia. For example, sustainable development has been given constitutional recognition in some countries, which would generally be regarded as a significant institutional change and in keeping with consistent but unsuccessful calls for an environmental head of power in the Australian constitution. Leaving aside the eventual impact of such a reform (flowing from the form of expression and the existence of implementation mechanisms for constitutional law), the history of rarely-successful moves for constitutional reform through referenda in Australia would indicate that such constitutional expression would be most unlikely there.

The intent of this study is a positive one – to look at cases of 'successful' institutional reform. This is intended to, first, maximize positive and operational lessons and, second, avoid the tendencies in the environmental and sustainability literature either to be entirely critical and negative or to champion and advocate single examples of institutional (or more usually organizational) change. While this is a useful general tone to adopt, defining 'successful' raises some problems that can be briefly noted here.

The success, effectiveness or worth of an institutional or policy reform will be judged differently by different groups and individuals. For example, major components of environmental policy in Australia in the past decade – such as Landcare or the Regional Forest Agreements process – have been judged very positively and very negatively by different observers and analysts. That situation is the same elsewhere. Who is right? One criterion might be that widespread (but rarely universal) acceptance or support among the broader policy community would indicate successful institutional reform, at least in early years. That highlights another problem: in many cases the impact of policy and/or institutional change in terms of positive improvement in the state of the environment, human interactions with it or in the human condition may take some time to become apparent. Many cases of institutional reform for sustainability are only a few years old and thus 'success' has yet to become assessable. In other cases this will be less of a problem, such as where the policy or institutional reform has as an aim something that may emerge quickly, for example, creating an information stream by including stakeholders in a process. Such strategies can be assessed with respect to their procedural rationality and effectiveness in achieving these short-term goals, independently of the long-term substantive outcomes. One useful distinction in judging success, then, is to separate process from outcome. Finally a case of institutional reform is likely to have sub-components that are more or less successful than others. Indeed, because a multifaceted institutional reform may be brought undone by one poor component, an institutional experiment generally regarded as a failure may provide valuable lessons in process or structure. These considerations are best worked through on a case-by-case scale, but this does raise the issue of how strictly (and indeed just how) to interpret the positive or negative outcomes of a case study.

Note that none of these factors rules out particular kinds of cases or countries but rather may inform or qualify choice, and will be important in both informing analysis of selected cases and in qualifying and contextualizing any conclusions drawn.

**Synthesising: Scoping Criteria**

As forewarned, this discussion of operationalizing learning from one context to another has revealed the complexity that underlies the attractive notion of 'institutional learning'. To reduce the large range of possible avenues of investigation to a manageable level consistent with the tone of the explanation of institutions and policy learning given in Chapter 1, the following section proposes primary criteria for selecting case studies and thematic areas for further exploration in this study.

**1.   What 'parts' of the institutional system?**
It is proposed that, in terms of a hierarchical understanding of institutional

systems, focus would best be placed on cases involving higher-order institutional change where there is evidence of credible commitment by governments to sustainable development principles. This would involve change at statutory level and/or in structures and processes that have transformative impacts on the way policy and management is carried out. This emphasis is chosen in preference to seeking out examples of change happening primarily at the program implementation level. Having said that, the most fundamental and radical forms of institutional change (revolutionary refashioning) would not be a sensible focus given the practical intent of the study.

## 2.  What type of learning?

It is proposed that the focus be on more significant forms of government learning and on social learning, in keeping with (1) above. Instrumental and political learning may become an incidental topic in some cases through this focus, but would not be sought as a primary target for analysis.

## 3.  What sustainability (ESD) principles to explore? And what attributes of sustainability problems?

The five ESD principles (from Table 2.1) with the greatest generic and institutional relevance in terms of (1) and (2) above are: sustainable economic development; policy integration; the precautionary principle; policy instrument choice; and community involvement.[8] These can be reshaped to capture deeper properties of sustainability issues and ESD principles and the spirit of the institutional approach so as to provide a set of targets that may connect with the variety of jurisdictional responses to the sustainable development agenda:

- integration of social, environmental and economic policy and goals
- handling of pervasive uncertainty
- the deep embedding of sustainable development principles in the institutional system, evidencing credible commitment to the long term
- the links between credible commitment to sustainable development, property rights instruments and problem reframing
- community participation in all the above (as opposed to programme delivery through community-based groups not involving deeper or more lasting institutional change).

## 4.  What objects of learning?

The remainder of the book will focus on the following parts of the typology presented earlier:

- substantial policy processes targeting elements of (2) and (3) above
- organizing government (restructuring, intergovernmental, participatory) where the reorganization involves significant and ongoing refocusing of policy activity, information flows, participation, and so on.
- problem reframing (normative and legal change, parliamentary or executive government processes).

Thus implementation instruments and policy programmes would not be a focus, with the exception of instrument classes with the intent or potential to affect (2) and (3) above; that is, significant legislative change, transformative rights instruments and some educational instruments (dealing with reframing the problem rather than specific issues).

This narrows the criteria set to a manageable level but certainly still allows more than ample scope. An additional and important criterion in selecting particular case studies of institutional change is the availability of sufficient existing data and analysis, given the difficulty for a study such as this to engage in substantial primary data gathering. The 'filters' for considering cases from other countries, discussed above, would be applied at a finer level to case study selection and utilized to qualify institutional lessons that might emerge from analysis.

## CASES FOR ANALYSIS

Utilizing the above criteria this section proposes a range of potential case studies and thematic areas that could be examined in this study. The options in the selection below are all viable as targets for investigation and analysis, and it is noted how they address the criteria – in most cases more than one criterion. The following options are divided into two groupings, first those selected for analysis and second those that would be appropriate but not selected. The basis for this division, referring to the scoping criteria above, is provided for each.

### Cases Selected for Analysis

- New Zealand's *Resource Management Act 1991* (RMA), as a major statutory reform in response to sustainability, organized in part on a regional basis, with significant participation by varied policy and epistemic communities and well-described in the literature. As a focus for case study this legislation and its implementation could provide lessons at various levels from devolution of environmental management through nested policy hierarchies, catchment based regionalization of resource and environmental management responsibility (structural logic), to consultative development of policy and legislation. The RMA presents the most well-documented attempt to move from traditional planning schemes towards planning for sustainability. Existing literature containing comparative analysis may allow some extension of this case study towards recognition of similar or contrasting reforms in other countries.

- The institutional context and social, environmental and economic implications of creating and maintaining *rights markets in natural resources*. This will be done via an examination of individual transferable quota (ITQ) in fisheries in different countries. Water rights may be a more obvious choice in terms of wider relevance, but ITQ have been in place longer and have been subject to recent and wide-ranging reviews. Water markets will thus be treated as an adjunct topic to the more tractable fisheries domain. This option addresses a transformative instrument, property rights issues, integration of social, economic and environmental dimensions, and the stated developed world preference for market-based mechanisms.
- Actual and proposed *strategic environmental assessment* (SEA) processes, and proposals for integrated assessment (IA), in different jurisdictions, as responses aimed at extending the tradition of environmental impact assessment beyond discrete projects and on to non-environmental policies, plans and programmes. Depending on particulars and implementation, this addresses integration, whole-of-government mechanisms, and the definition of policy and property rights and responsibilities.
- *National councils for sustainable development* and equivalent bodies, now established in dozens of countries, as national-level, inclusive policy advisory and educational responses addressing (potentially) integration, long-term policy making, reorganizing government and participation. In particular, this theme allows investigation into possible models for whole-of-government/cross-sectoral mechanisms for furthering sustainable development.
- Institutional and especially regulatory and policy *integration in the European community* in environmental policy and standards across national boundaries as the most significant example of transboundary, detailed mixed regulatory–self-regulatory approaches in the world at present.
- *Statutory expression of sustainable development principles* in different jurisdictions, especially those with comparable political and legal

traditions within the suite of developed nations, in terms of the extent to which expression can influence or has influenced the institutional and policy system and decisions made within it. This would of necessity include consideration of implementation of treaties and agreements, specifically the Rio-related set of instruments. This addresses problem reframing, integration, whole-of-government impact and legal change. The role of statute law is observed through the case studies and revisited in the final analysis.[9]

## Cases and Themes Deemed Suitable for Analysis but Not Selected[10]

- *Constitutional expression of sustainability principles.* As discussed earlier, this appears an unlikely prospect in many jurisdictions, and it is noted that recent major constitutional reform for other reasons appears to be the key reason for such expressions in those few countries that have given sustainability such status.
- *Implementation of national sustainable development strategies* in various countries where, at least as can be ascertained, the strategies are whole-of-government. While attractive, this would demand detailed and repeated analysis of specific national policy-making contexts beyond the scope of this study.
- *Parliamentary or executive government processes* whereby bi- or multipartisan agreements on policy directions are developed, removing some aspects of sustainability problems from rapid and perhaps unthinking change following elections or changes in political fashion (nevertheless accepting the rights of governments to make and change policy and priorities). Again, while attractive this would demand detailed understanding of the political context in a range of countries.
- *Implementation of international instruments*, focusing on inclusiveness of processes (community, and within federal systems), translation of principles to domestic law and policy, and monitoring of implementation. While the impact of especially the Rio set of instruments is a significant issue, this would require considerable effort and the lessons generated may be of limited transferability across legal systems. The favoured option of exploring the role of statute law across case studies will offer some insight into this.
- *Participatory policy and management processes* (not specific programmes) that enable lasting and/or significant transfer of power to stakeholder groups, to provide a contrast to a more common emphasis on the programme level of participation. This addresses participation and reorganizing government. This would require substantial research

and scoping to select particular cases, given the great number and fine scale of most cases. Also, it is probably the case that participatory arrangements have received more attention than other options, given their prominence in practice and in research in recent years, and efforts would best be directed elsewhere.

- *State of environment reporting* in a sample of jurisdictions, emphasizing the institutional setting for SoE and the institutionalization of linkages between the reporting process, long-term environmental and policy monitoring, and policy formulation. SoE is but one science–policy–communication mechanism in the sustainability arena, and examined alone may be of little interest in the absence of consideration of other mechanisms (resource accounting, corporate reporting, and so on). However, a fuller, comparative examination of science–policy–community information transfers would be a large task. To be effective it would also require assessment of the impact of SoE systems as opposed to the production of reports and, while an issue deserving of close attention, this would be beyond the scope of the current study project.

The favoured five options are considered to offer a balance between sufficiently well-defined avenues of enquiry and the need to consider a range of kinds and degrees of institutional change, in particular the constraints and opportunities to be found within the institutional systems in which these reforms have taken place. In this way it is the intention to not simply or even primarily document these cases, but to utilize them as vehicles for increasing the sophistication and operational usefulness of discourses around institutional change for sustainable development.

## CONCLUDING COMMENT

These first two chapters have established the scope of this enquiry and framed the sustainability problem in a manner suited to its intent. The core notions of institutional systems, the nature of change within these systems, and policy and institutional learning have been set out. The issue of selection of case studies and themes appropriate to analysis for lesson drawing has been discussed, and cases and themes selected. This background provides not only a logic and explanation for the ensuing chapters but also a framework of enquiry for the issue of institutional change for sustainable development more generally. The next five chapters deal with the five cases and themes, with sufficient descriptive content to support the final discussion of transferable lessons.

# NOTES

1. For instance, in the Australian case, mainly seeking policy lessons from Anglophone, developed liberal democracies, a recent example being the applications of neo-liberal political and neo-classical economic theory most vigorously in the English-speaking world (Castles (1990); Bell (1997); Orchard (1998)).
2. Reviews of both kinds of reforms and their adequacy can be found in Productivity Commission (1999); Yencken and Wilkinson (2000); Dovers (1999, 2001b); State of Environment Advisory Committee (2001); and especially the comprehensive set of reviews in Dovers and Wild River (2003).
3. For examples see Dore and Woodhill (1999).
4. See Venning and Higgins (2001).
5. Note that some of these policy initiatives, and Oceans Policy in particular, cut across traditional sectors (fishing, coastal management, shipping, marine conservation) and are attempts at integration over the broader sustainability policy concerns, using ecological rather than economic parameters as primary criteria for defining the policy sector.
6. For a potted history, see Frawley (1994).
7. For a critical history, see Connell (2002).
8. While important, it is proposed that the principles of international policy and competitiveness not be a focus as this would require a massive and impossible widening of the project to consider issues of development aid, trade policy, and treaty negotiation and implementation. The focus here is on domestic policy and institutional settings at national and sub-national scales.
9. This case was selected for a study at the start of the enquiry but not pursued as a discrete case due to the paucity of comparative or review material available. However, it was pursued as a cross-cutting theme in later analysis.
10. These are recorded here for methodological clarity and to identify later possibilities, and noting that some observations on these are made occasionally in the course of analysis.

PART II

Case studies in institutional change

# 3.  Environmental policy in the European Union

## INTRODUCTION

This case study is more substantive and broader than some subsequent ones investigated in this book. The justification for this is that Europe doubtless represents the most advanced, complex and sustained example of integrated policy and institutional development between nations in the history of modern government, in the environmental and other domains. Europe has in many ways provided the lead in the conceptualization and operationalization of sustainable development, whether or not actual achievements are judged as sufficient. As such it deserves close attention and also serves to raise more specific themes that are developed further in the other cases and the synthesis in Chapter 8.

The environmental policy of the European Union (EU) provides a rich example of a federalist institutional system[1] from which to draw lessons for other jurisdictions in resource and environmental policy and in the pursuit of sustainable development more broadly. The EU is in fact an international regime, with several member states themselves being federated. The EU federalist context encompasses not only sovereign nations but, moreover, different languages and legal traditions. This deepens system complexity but yields more points of entry and opportunities to learn, and a number of levels of linkages with other, comparable contexts. This complexity, including institutional, political and historical complexity, makes any attempt at comprehensive coverage well beyond the scope of this study. Here we therefore sample the field of relevant topics and available material and identify aspects of the institutional system and change processes that are generally instructive. Of particular relevance, especially to other federal or inter-jurisdictional situations, are: the reiterative processes of policy development and associated network building and evolution of skills within and outside government; the connection with economic policy development via the creation of a European market; and the constitutional embedding of environmental concerns.

In addition EU environmental policy and the associated body of legislation has evolved over the life of the regime, and this covers the whole period of the emergence of environmental policy (and more recently sustainable development) as an issue on national and international political agendas. Therefore we here describe first the rationale and the history and development of the policy together, consistent with observation made earlier that institutional change – and transfer of lessons from the analysis thereof – demand appreciation of historical context.

## REGIME DESCRIPTION

### Evolving Policy, Evolving Rationale

The rationale for EU environment policy emerged, and has changed in parallel with the substance of the policy itself, in several major steps over the more than four decades since the Treaty of Rome was signed in 1957 establishing the European Economic Community (EEC). The guiding rationale for the EEC itself, which built upon the prior Coal and Steel Community, was to enmesh national economies to the extent that war (particularly between France and Germany) became impossible. This focus continues to have an influence on the reasons for expanding the EU today. There was no recognition in the Treaty of Rome of a need for separate environmental policy, and the environment was not recognised as a significant policy arena until after the UN's 1972 Stockholm Conference on the Human Environment. Up to this point, actions affecting the environment can be regarded as pragmatic measures rather than policies and were incidental to economic objectives. The overriding objective of the EEC at that time was to harmonize national laws in order to reduce trade impediments between member states.

Despite the introduction of an official environmental policy for the Community from 1973 through the first Environmental Action Programme (EAP1), the removal of impediments to the working of the single market remained as the key legal basis for legislative action on the environment right through to 1987. During this period three key factors stimulated progress on environmental measures. First was rising public concern over the state of the environment and destructive impacts of economic activities; second was the occurrence of several major environmental disasters; and third was the concern of member states that uncoordinated national environmental legislation was creating intra-community trade distortions.[2]

The legal basis for action during this period lay in reference to and interpretations of Article 100 – on establishing the common market – and Article 2 (via Article 235), which sets out the objectives of the Treaty as:

the task of the European Economic Community is to promote … a harmonious development of economic activities, a continuous and balanced expansion, and increase in stability, an accelerated raising of the standard of living and closer relations between the states belonging to it.[3]

A generous reading of this statement is that it supports as a goal an increased quality of life, as well as higher incomes, and that environmental quality contributes to this quality of life. In addition negative external costs imposed on the environment through pollution can be argued to be counter to harmonious economic development. Thus in the opening statement to EAP1, the Council of Ministers declared that the task of the EEC as stated in Article 2 (above) 'cannot now be imagined in the absence of an effective campaign to combat pollution … and an improvement in the quality of the environment'.[4] Despite this evolving sensibility within the EC institutional system solid legal foundation for community-wide action was only to be found with reference to harmonization of markets. But as normative change drove legislative change at the national level the issue of differences in environmental protection laws among member states made harmonization action necessary at Community level.

**The Environmental Action Programmes**

While harmonization was the underlying goal, EAP1 (1973) set out basic principles for environmental action and established the notion of shared competences in environmental matters – that some measures would be carried out by member states while others would be carried out at Community level. The principles for environmental actions included early reflections of the ideas of sustainable development:

- Prevention of pollution is better than cure.
- Environmental impacts should be taken into account at an early stage in planning and decision making.
- Overexploitation of resources should be avoided.
- Scientific knowledge should be used to inform policy.
- The polluter pays principle.
- Need to control trans-boundary pollution.
- Need to take the problems of developing countries into account.
- EEC should take a role as an international actor in the environmental area.
- EEC should assume a role in dissemination of information on environment.
- EEC should decide the appropriate level for action.[5]

The second EAP, 1977–81,[6] consolidated by confirming the basic principles laid down in EAP1 and declaring the improvement of the quality of life and protection of the natural environment as fundamental tasks of the Community, thus requiring an explicit environmental policy. EAP2 directed particular attention to non-damaging use and rational management of land, environment and natural resources, and the need for measures to encourage the growth of public awareness and personal responsibility for environmental protection. It emphasized the need for preventative measures and the concomitant need for monitoring and assessment (EIA), the protection of flora and fauna, and the use of environmental labelling.[7]

EAP3, 1982–87,[8] strengthened the commitment to harmonization further to make the most economic use of natural resources. In the face of questions regarding the priority that should be afforded environment in times of economic difficulty, EAP3 made the point that environmental policy is a structural policy that must be carried forward regardless of cyclical conditions. In this regard EAP3 gave special attention to the issue of integration of environment into other areas of policy. This programme also made important advances in support of the polluter pays principle, reduction of pollution at source, and the application of the principle of subsidiarity, which states that each type of action should be carried out at the most appropriate level.

EAP4, 1987–92,[9] was introduced at the point that the first renegotiation of the EEC Treaty was finalized in the Single European Act (SEA), and this inserted an Environment Title into the constitutional base of the now rebadged European Community (EC), providing the first solid legal foundation for environment policy. EAP4 reaffirmed principles established by the other programmes, with particular emphasis on policy integration, shared competence and avoidance of market distortion. The period of this programme was coincident with that of the broader agenda set by the SEA, to complete the internal market by 1992. The internal market was defined as 'an area without internal frontiers in which the free movement of goods, persons, services and capital is ensured'.[10] The growing understanding of environmental policy as having profound implications for the economy was reinforced through the emphasis on integration and by positive linking with employment prospects – environment could be good for jobs. EAP4 produced an important change in pollution control strategy from media-based regulation (water, air, land) to substance based controls and targeted the chemical industry. It also recognized the growing implementation deficit with regard to application of Community environment policies at the national level, and proposed an education and information strategy to open up the policy process.

EAP5, 1992–2000,[11] was subtitled 'Towards Sustainability'. This document acknowledged the significance of the body of environmental law established by the EC (now EU) to date and the positive affect of this, but again emphasized the implementation deficit regarding existing measures. It turned attention to the search for new instrumentalities to protect the environment, driven by the galloping global environmental policy agenda and the expectation of a rapid increase in EU GDP due to the completion of the internal market. Existing measures needed to be fully implemented and new measures put in place in a more effective manner using a wider range of policy instruments, including greater emphasis on market instruments and incentives and on education, information and citizen/group/firm participation and responsibility. EAP5 had a longer tenure than previous programmes and succeeded over time in establishing acceptance of sustainability as a process rather than a goal to be reached in a given time-frame. It also targeted five sectors as key polluters (industry, agriculture, transport, energy, tourism) and seven themes for action.

EU environment policy in the shape of EAP5 was given new force by the signing of the Maastricht Treaty on European Union in February 1992. This built on the legal foundation for environment policy established in the SEA, introducing sustainability language, a requirement for a 'high level of protection' for the environment, and the precautionary principle as a fundamental tenet of policy. Maastricht also clarified and extended the existing requirement for policy integration and introduced a power for the European Court of Justice (ECJ) to impose fines on member states for non-compliance with prior court orders to implement Community environmental law. The political contest on subsidiarity was intense but resulted in a reformulation of the principle which is arguably less clear for environmental policy than that of the SEA.

The Maastricht Treaty made several institutional changes that have made progress on environmental policies easier, prompted largely by the prospect of enlargement of EU membership.[12] Voting systems in the Council of Ministers and decision-making pathways have been changed in light of expectations that full agreement of member states on particular measures would become less likely as membership expands.[13] Greater involvement of the European Parliament in codecision-making partnership with the Council is intended to make the process more democratic and accountable but adds considerable complexity to the system. As it happened things did not go quite to plan with the Danes voting by referendum not to ratify Maastricht, and the French were split down the middle. The reforms to decision making thus were still not quite settled by the time of the 1996 meetings on the Amsterdam Treaty – the third constitutional change, and intended to prepare the EU for monetary union and further membership expansion. However, the Amsterdam Treaty further extended codecision making to environment policy among other areas, and agreed to simplify some parliamentary procedures.

Amsterdam built on a number of previous initiatives to consolidate environmental policy. It enshrines sustainable development as a fundamental objective of the EU at constitutional level (Article 2). The new Treaty also brings the objective of integration out of an obscure environmental section (Article 130r) and into the headline articles (Article 3d) to require that 'environmental protection requirements must be integrated into the definition and implementation of Community policies and activities ... in particular with a view to promoting sustainable development'. The Commission also declared that it will prepare environmental impact assessment (EIA) studies whenever any policy proposals may have significant impacts on the environment.[14] These are significant changes in bringing the environment to the top rank of policy issues for the EU and give the environment Directorate considerably more authority to take a direct approach to ensuring integration of environmental concerns occurs across the full range of EU policy.

The sixth EAP, 2000–10,[15] re-emphasizes and extends the issues identified in previous programmes and assessments. It identifies five elements of a strategic approach to the full range of environment policies:

1.  improving implementation of existing legislation: using legal action through the ECJ and an information strategy of 'name, fame and shame'
2.  integration: all policies to be assessed and progress monitored through indicators and benchmarking
3.  working with the market: penalties and incentives for business to perform better and eco-modernize, information for informed consumer choice, and public subsidies to promote environment friendly practices
4.  individual citizens: better information on choice and environmental consequences of individual actions to change views
5.  land use planning and management: use of Structural funds to promote best practice.

In addition four issue areas have been identified for priority action:

1.  climate change
2.  biodiversity protection
3.  environment and health
4.  sustainable use of natural resources and management of wastes.

Finally the new plan reiterates the values of the EU as a major player in international environmental policy and the participation of stakeholders in the policy-making process.

## Structure and Administration

A basic institutional triumvirate lies at the heart of the EU – the elected European Parliament (EP), the Council of Ministers, and the Commission of the European Communities (CEC). These decision-making bodies are supported by the European Court of Justice (ECJ), the Court of Auditors, and several committees attached to the Council and the Parliament. The purpose of this institutional system is to make, implement and administer policy and legislation over all the areas of concern for the EU, including the environment.

The Council of Ministers[16] is made up of ministers of the governments of the member states, representing their national interests. Constitutionally the Council is a unitary body, but in practice several councils meet at various intervals to deal with policy on a sectoral basis.[17] For example the foreign ministers of the EU states meet as the General Affairs Council, and the finance and economics ministers as the Council of the Economic and Finance Ministers (ECOFIN Council). Environment ministers meet as one of several technical councils, and some cross-sectoral joint councils have met to consider policy integration, such as for energy and environment. Decision making in the Council has historically been by unanimity, but qualified majority voting[18] has gradually been introduced to an increasing number of areas including the environment.

The Commission is made up of a political arm and an administrative arm. The political arm, the College of Commissioners, comprises an executive appointed by the member states, who are generally ex-politicians (currently 20 in number). They are supported by offices with private advisers and a large bureaucracy organized into Directorates General (DG) – equivalent to government departments or ministries. There are currently 24 DGs, one of which deals with environment, nuclear safety and civil protection (DG XI).

The seats of the European Parliament (there were 624 in June 2002) are allocated to each member state on the basis of population and have been elected by universal suffrage since 1979. They do not form national groupings but affiliate to one of about ten political party groupings or separate European parties, with the largest of these holding about one-third of the seats. The largest party from 1989 to 1999 was the Party of European Socialists, with their close rival the European Peoples Party taking the lead in 1999. By 2002 these two parties held 179 and 232 seats respectively. A further six parties won between 18 and 53 seats each, with the Green Group increasing its numbers from 25, prior to 1999, to 45 in 2002. Non-attached candidates hold 32 seats.[19]

Power is shared among the three key constitutional bodies through a primary division of roles that is blurred somewhat by a set of constitutional checks and balances. The Council of Ministers is the primary decision making body, but it shares this responsibility to some extent with the EP, which has the power to reject or amend legislation, acts jointly with the Council as the budgetary authority, and participates in codecision-making procedures on specific issues. The members of the EP are the direct representatives of the EU citizenry,[20] while the Council members are representing national interests as defined by current member state governments. The EP has been quite influential in pressing for more effective and extensive environment policies.

However, it is the Commission's prerogative to initiate legislation and propose policy, although the Council primarily controls agenda priorities. No major development in the EU has occurred without being discussed at summit meetings of the Heads of Government. However, the Commission has a great deal of power in the system and participates in what can be intense contests with the Council in agenda setting and refining policy. The Commission acts as a mediator among member national governments, ensures the interests of the EU are paramount and that the process of European integration is advanced, and acts as external negotiator in international negotiations and treaties. The Commissioners attend all sittings of the EP and are expected to defend their actions and decisions in that forum, providing an accountability link back to the electorate. The administrative arm of the Commission manages the EU's financial resources, ensures that legislation is implemented and enforced and administers the Council and EP.[21]

Environmental Action Programmes set the general agenda and ethos for action through three main binding legislative instruments – regulations, directives and decisions. Regulations have rarely been used in the environmental area, being generally binding on all states and specific in their effect. Decisions are binding on those to which they are specifically addressed, and in the environmental area are used mainly for international matters and for some procedural issues. Directives are the most commonly used in environmental policy, being binding as to the result to be achieved, but it is left up to each state to decide the means through which they will comply.

Once legislation is in place the Commission works with member states to implement the intent of policy by translating it into national-level legislation and action programmes. There is a monitoring role for the Commission in assessment of, first, the degree to which directives have been translated and adopted into national law and policy and, second, the degree to which they have been implemented on the ground. They are assisted in this task by the Court of Auditors, whose task it is to audit national legislation for compliance with the intentions of EU policies and directives. This transposition of directives into national legislation is particular (situation specific) with respect to the aspects of, and degree to which, the issues addressed by the policy are operative in the member state, as well as with respect to interactions with existing legislation. It is also subject to differences in interpretation of legal language and translation between national languages of terms into inexact equivalents.

The Commission may bring a legal case against a member state for non-compliance with EU legislation. This is done through the European Court of Justice (ECJ). The Maastricht Treaty authorised the ECJ to levy fines on members for non-compliance with prior Court rulings. Thus, where the Commission has won a case against a member state and the state has subsequently not addressed the problem, the Commission goes again to the ECJ and the Court can impose a fine.

## Other Recent Institutional Developments

As part of the 'Shared Responsibilities and Active Participation' approach of the EAP5, consultative networks and groups were encouraged and established. These included the Green Forum, the Network for Implementation and Enforcement of Community Law (IMPEL), and the Environment Policy Review Group.

The Green Forum began as a group of 32 members in 1993 and was formalized by the Commission in 1997 to become the European Consultative Forum on the Environment and Sustainable Development. The group brought together independent experts from across the EU representing industry and business, consumers, NGOs, local and regional authorities, trade unions and academia. The forum produced a stream of policy analysis and advice to the Commission reflecting the broad membership. The tenure of the formalized forum was four years, and in 2001 it was closed following the introduction of EAP6 and the new Strategy for Sustainable Development (SDS).[22] The forum itself, in its final advice, urged the Commission to take an initiative to implement a wider participatory regime in support of the SDS as well as to work for greater coherence in the effort to integrate sustainable development in all policy sectors.[23] The Forum has been replaced by a new Sustainable Development Round Table reporting directly to the Commission. It is not clear at present whether this represents a significant institutional change or merely a rebadging of the existing form.

The other two consultative groups comprised mainly staff from member state agencies responsible for the corresponding area at national level. This network policy model brings together those dealing with the national manifestations of the problems being addressed at the Community level for discussion and input into the policy and legislative processes, and to share ideas and experiences in implementation. In theory this should serve to ground supra-national policy, bring the experiences of policy leaders into the process, and promote greater commitment of national bureaucracies to new legislation by giving them a channel through which to contribute to its formulation.

The Network for Implementation and Enforcement of Community Law (IMPEL Network), like the Forum, began informally. Discussions among senior environmental regulators and policy makers in the late 1980s made clear to them that networking would be beneficial in facing the challenges of implementing EU environment policies. A Dutch study of EU environmental enforcement agencies in 1991 recommended the creation of a network among member states to focus attention on developing common enforcement standards and approaches. Given the degree of concern among states about the centralization of power in the EU, an informal organization with voluntary participation seemed appropriate. IMPEL remains informal in this sense, but was brought into partnership with the Commission in 1997 through the creation of a DG-XI based secretariat and cost sharing. The original structure had been of four working groups, each dealing with different aspects of permitting, compliance monitoring and enforcement. The early years of the network were spent in a slow-paced cross-cultural learning process whereby the participants got to know the structures, rules, processes and regulatory culture of the other states. This paid off after the more direct affiliation with the Commission, when work was restructured on a task-oriented basis into project groups. These were coordinated by two standing committees, one dealing with legal policy and legal implementation issues and the other with practical issues of enforcement and management, and the original work programme comprised some eighty projects. Six-monthly plenary meetings of the network have continued, and after some experience with the new structure the standing committees were abandoned, with supervision carried out directly by the plenary meetings.

A major achievement of IMPEL is formation of a successful inter-jurisdictional policy learning process. This has made new policy at the Community level more practical in its orientation and has promoted the modification of member state machinery to utilise best practice and to better harmonize across the EU. Harmonization of implementation and enforcement at the practical level is important as the final stage in reducing the market distortions created by differing environmental standards among states. At the level of structure and process in institutions it is important to the efficient and consistent application of new standards and directives promulgated by the EU. IMPEL continues to be supported by member states as a valuable policy learning exercise and is appreciated by the Commission and EU policy makers as a supplier of information and analysis. A key lesson noted is that 'voluntary participation is the way to make progress in contentious or unfamiliar areas'.[24]

Another network that has increased its direct involvement with EU policy making is the European Environment Bureau (EEB). The EEB is a federation of 141 environmental citizen organizations based in all EU member states and most accession countries. The organization first set up offices in Brussels in

1974. It has consultative status and working relations with the Council, the Commission and the EP, The Economic and Social Committee of the EU, OECD and the UN Commission on Sustainable Development.

The European Environment Agency (EEA) is the key information provider to the EU on environment in support of the commitment to sustainable development. The agency was established in 1990 following a five-year experimental project to determine information needs on the environment: the Coordination of Information on the Environment initiative (CORINE).[25] However, the EEA did not become operational until late 1993, as the Maastricht processes delayed decisions on the EU agencies. The EEA is theoretically independent of the policy-making process and the DG XI, with its own autonomous management structure and organization. However, the information sensitivity of environmental issues and the role of the agency in evaluation of policy alternatives in producing State of the Environment (SoE) reports make it an important component in the institutional system. In 1998 the scope of the SoE reporting was extended to include the identification of future trends and prospects.

The agency is the centre node in an information network that includes all the national-level agencies of member states responsible for gathering environmental data. This is the European Environment Information and Observation Network (EIONET). Again the network model has been applied to provide a structure not only for the exchange of data on the environment but also for sharing of knowledge and experience in methods and organizational management of the process of environmental monitoring and information collation. Such exchange accelerates learning and promotes confidence among smaller member organizations as well as ensuring that monitoring methods across the membership of the EU converge to make environmental data more directly comparable and relevant to decision making.

The EEA produces several series of technical topic and environmental issue reports, a series of indicator-based environmental reports by sector (for example, agriculture, energy, tourism) and an annual environmental assessment based on an agreed set of indicators for sustainable development. This latter assessment was only initiated in 2001 but preliminary outputs summarise progress made on big-ticket items such as GHG emissions, renewable energy and waste reduction. Regulations, particularly on fuel quality and vehicle emission standards, are shown to have been effective, keeping increases in major pollutants under control. However, increasing incomes have increased car ownership and use, and the single market has produced significant increases in inter-state trade and road freight per capita, making Kyoto targets unlikely to be met without further policy action.

The new Sustainable Development Strategy (SDS) and EAP6 are the institutional vehicles for taking the action agenda on environment forward. The SDS arises from the commitment, in 1992 reaffirmed in 1997, of signatories to the Rio Declaration to complete strategies for the World Summit on Sustainable Development in 2002. The EU strategy focuses on a small number of what are believed to be the most urgent issues and takes what is fundamentally an eco-modernization approach. The aim is to decouple environmental degradation and resource consumption from economic and social development, requiring a major reorientation of public and private investment towards new, environmentally friendly technologies. The SDS is proposed to be a catalyst for policy makers and public opinion and a driving force for institutional reform and changes in corporate and consumer behaviour. It argues for clear, stable, long-term objectives to shape expectations and give investors confidence. In other words, a key objective of the strategy is to provide leadership for normative change. The primary issues identified for focus are:

- greenhouse gas emissions and global warming
- public health threats – particularly antibiotic resistant disease, long-term effects of hazardous chemicals and food security
- poverty and social exclusion
- problems associated with the ageing population
- biodiversity loss, renewable resource depletion (particularly fish and soils) and waste management
- transport congestion.

The strategy calls for committed political leadership, a new integrated approach to policy making, widespread participation, and for the EU to take an internationally responsible role with regard to the impacts that European policy has on the potential for other nations to implement sustainable development.[26]

Notably this list of issues represents an integrated view of sustainability, as opposed to a merely environmental view. It recognizes social issues such as poverty as significant threats to sustainability along with global warming and biodiversity loss, acknowledging fundamental links between these seemingly disparate policy areas. These are major policy commitments in such a significant institutional platform as the SDS of the EU, given the constitutional commitments already in place to pursue sustainable development.

The strategy has three parts: a set of cross-cutting proposals to change the way policy is made across all sectors; a set of headline objectives and specific measures; and a set of steps for implementation and monitoring. The most relevant to our current purpose are the cross-cutting proposals. These are concerned with:

- improving policy coherence
- getting prices right
- investment in science and technology
- improving communication and mobilization of citizens and business
- taking EU enlargement and the global dimension into account.

In mid-March 2002, at the Barcelona EU leaders summit, the time had seemingly come for environment to finally take its place as a fully integrated partner on the socioeconomic policy agenda, as the leaders considered progress on the SDS for the first time. However, despite many positive signs and the imperative of the approaching World Summit on Sustainable Development (WSSD), the leaders largely ignored the sustainability issue, distracted seemingly by more immediate political issues. Whether the EU will be able to provide firm leadership in the years beyond the 2002 WSSD in Johannesburg is open to question.

The irony of this situation is indicative of the difficulties in pursuing sustainable development through political channels subject to short-term incentive changes. In terms of the rationale and insights explicit in the SDS, the events of 11 September 2001 should have underlined the urgency and priority of moving forward on the sustainability agenda. The SDS emphasizes poverty and social exclusion in both domestic and international spheres as key obstacles to sustainability: seemingly among the root causes of the international conflict and insecurity.

However, as we shall see in the more analytical sections of the study, the EU sustainability policy system is built on more durable foundations than just political leadership. The institutionalization of sustainability has progressed to the stage that, although short-term political concerns may displace issues such as the SDS from particular meeting agendas, the longevity of the sustainability policy agenda has been secured.

## EU INSTITUTIONS: ADAPTING FOR SUSTAINABILITY

What we can observe in the EU response to environmental policy issues over three decades can be characterized in a number of ways. It can be viewed as the birth and development of an institutional subsystem to address an emerging set of new issues; alternatively, we can view this process as the beginning of the adaptation of the greater system of governance institutions to the realities of a finite and full world – the sustainability imperative. Where this transitional process is perceived as both essential to long-term welfare and long-term in itself – perhaps taking sixty or more years in the wealthy countries – judgements of success or failure at this stage are not of much value. However, the EU may well be judged to be one of the most interesting cases available for study and learning. It is rich with institutional innovation in general due to the development and expansion of the Union, and this provides a fertile ground for experiment and adaptation for sustainability.

Rather than a response to the sustainability agenda set by UNCED and the WCED, EU environment policy has been and continues to be an integral part of the generation of that agenda. Key elements of 'sustainable development' were part of the EAPs as far back as 1973. However, 1992 did bring significant change in the approach to environmental policy within the EU, in unison with Agenda 21, through the emphasis of EAP5 on fundamentals such as policy integration. Although founded on sound principles – later to become fundamental to the sustainable development concept – previous EAPs had tended toward being wish lists for the legislative program, reacting to the issues of the moment.[27] The peak of sustainability policy debate and activity realised through the UNCED processes provided extra impetus for the EU, but the embedding of the principles of sustainability in the constitutional Treaties had already, and finally, provided solid legal foundations for action on the environment.

The evolution of EU environment policy and the associated institutions and organizations provides numerous examples of innovation in policy processes and in the organization of government. The story also demonstrates an interactive process of normative and institutional change. Changing social attitudes to, and values for, the environment supported the expansion of the environmental policy agenda, while the information and analysis produced by the policy process fed back into social debate to drive further normative change.

When the EEC was established in 1957 the arena of environmental policy did not exist. Beginning incidentally, but then in earnest in 1972, and driven by the twin imperatives of removing impediments to the common market and changing social values for environment, environment and latterly sustainable development have risen to become central to the policy agenda of the EU. Agents of change within the institutional system have gradually built an increasingly solid set of principles and legal foundations for sustainable development policy. These are embedded institutionally through the constitutional Treaties and the body of relevant legislation, and organizationally in the Council, Parliament, the Commission's bureaucracy and associated agencies, and through the consultative fora. During the 1990s these foundations were used strategically to apply real pressure on policy makers across the key sectors affecting the environment, to integrate ecological concerns into policy. [28]

The means for normative change in civil society to influence policy are multiple: the main direct route perhaps being through the European

Parliament. Here, direct citizen participation allows Europe-wide political parties and coalitions of interests to provide some counter to the political bargaining processes among heads of state on the Council. Less direct paths may be at least as important: through national governments via the Council and through networks such as the Green Forum, but also through the knowledge and idealism concentrated by specialist environmental bureaucracies such as the DG XI. The Europe-wide collection, collation and publication of environmental information by the EEA not only informs the policy process but also the wider social perception of environmental problems and the efficacy of policies. This completes a critical feedback loop for any environmental decision-making process.

The EU case illustrates the development of 'credible commitment' in institutional systems over a considerable period of time as opposed to commitments being merely espoused by a particular executive. The notion of credible commitment necessitates a deep institutional embeddedness such that it is very difficult for an executive government to revoke.[29] The EU's set of complimentary institutional arms and democratic system of constitutional checks and balances has allowed the logic of sustainability to take hold. This has produced an environmental policy complex that is currently grappling with the practical application of some of the most difficult and fundamental issues for sustainability – particularly policy integration. This includes recognition of the need for coordination, monitoring and enforcement of policy integration – a process that necessarily still occurs within traditional areas of sectoral responsibility – and 'vertical policy integration', a process of policy learning through assessment of experiences of actual implementation.[30]

On the other side of the ledger the policy process itself has some tendency to lapse into bargaining mode due to large number of veto players, and this is exacerbated by the lack of sufficient resources for proper analysis of policy problems (in the DG XI). The Commission tends to pick up on policy ideas from member states so as to be assured of a basis for support in the decision-making processes, rather than following an agenda developed through analysis and priority setting.[31]

Despite these problems the policy-making situation still looks fairly healthy, but the wider institutional system has not been as successful with implementation.[32] The implementation problem has several institutional levels, the key ones being the adequate translation of Community policy intent into the national law of member states and that of compliance of citizens and businesses with those laws. The 1990s saw positive institutional developments in both areas – such as the consultative forums and networks like IMPEL and powers for the ECJ to impose fines on states – but serious issues remain, particularly in terms of heterogeneity of context. The expansion of the EU in Central and Eastern Europe is exacerbating the problems inherent in attempts to apply common standards across economies in disparate stages of economic development.[33]

Policy action was taken to address the implementation deficit in the early 1990s, but the results are not yet clear. New emphasis has been placed on the use of framework directives that allow greater adaptation in the translation of Community policy into state legislation to suit local circumstances and to adopt least-cost methods of achieving the desired environmental outcomes. The EAP5 also mandated the use of signalling and incentive instruments in place of standard regulatory approaches. Little evidence is apparent as to the success of these strategies to date. However, the lack of specificity of framework directives can make translation into national level legislation more demanding and compliance audits more difficult. One of the roles taken on by the IMPEL network is to support states in these functions, but clear pay-offs may be some way off. Other changes interact with these elements, such as the greater use of the Court to pursue contention over whether states are obliged to act or not and for the Court to impose fines for subsequent inaction. Even among the core states of the Union, lack of commitment by national governments under local political constraints is still inhibiting implementation of agreed Community policy.

Thus we see that the development of an institutional system for sustainable development has quite a long way to go. However, the environmental policy subsystem has come a long way since 1972 and is working its way towards establishing a credible institutionalization of sustainability as a fundamental principle of governance, at least on paper. The implementation problems should not be underestimated, and it seems that another decade or two might not be an unreasonable time-frame for working solutions to these issues to develop. We cannot know if all this effort will result in 'success' or even what such a success might look like. Hence there is certainly no case for mimicry of EU structures or processes. However, an examination of some of the underlying principles of the processes that appear to be moving the system in the right direction may well yield some valuable lessons for other jurisdictions.

## KEY PRINCIPLES OF THE EVOLVING INSTITUTIONAL MODEL

The institutional arrangements for environmental policy in the EU are still actively evolving and may be significantly transformed in the future decades. However, recognizable principles are at work in the development of the system. The key structures of the EU institutional system, such as the Council, the Parliament and the Commission, are of course fundamental to the way in which environmental policy is made in the Community. However, within this general system environmental policy has established an institutional subsystem with some significant characterizing features. Here we use three important features to lead the analysis toward lesson drawing for other jurisdictional contexts. These are: the general iterative framework; the use of semi-formal voluntary networks; and the use of a combination of top-down and bottom-up approaches – particularly in dealing with the important issues of policy integration and subsidiarity.

## General Reiterative Framework

The environmental policies of the European Union have been built on a long-term, ongoing iterative process (the periodic EAPs) through which policy commitment and institutional structure have been formed. Principles are stated and restated over time, assessed and amended. Although some additions of principles have been made, mostly this has been a process of coming to understand the meaning and importance of the principles more profoundly, testing the practicality of different modes of implementation, and adjusting approaches according to experience and increased potential derived from institutional change. Thus policy learning has been greatly facilitated by the long-term reiterative framework.

Indeed it is arguable that an adjustment in policy so profound as the move to sustainability could only be feasible as a staged transition and, given that there is no consensus on what the sustainable society will look like institutionally, the 'sustainability transition'[34] seems impossible without such a cyclical process. From the point of view of institutional design for sustainability, reiterative processes appear to be fundamental to a systematic approach. The cycle time of the EU planning and review process is interesting as an indicator of the potential time-scale of the overall sustainability transition. This will not be accomplished within the life of any government – indeed each cycle is longer than most. The phase length of this policy cycle in the EU is supra-electoral, not so much transcending electoral cycles as ensuring that each successive regime and each generation of elected representatives is presented with fresh opportunities to contribute to progress in the transition.

There has been a reiterative interaction between institutional and normative change, building commitment to sustainable development at both the social normative level and at various institutional levels, including the constitution of the EU. Institutional capacity has developed as a consequence, facilitating the generation of further information on the state of the environment and further developing policies. Such capacity building in policy areas of social concern is standard stuff, but the iterative framework provides regular opportunities through which this (normative–institutional) interactive process can be revitalized during certain parts of the cycle, and necessary lower-profile policy work may be carried out at other times. This contrasts with open-ended linear policy processes that may lose public and political attention after an initial period and never make it back to the top of the agenda for want of a formal procedure. The requirement for new EAPs to be adopted at the highest level of governance ensures regular refrain of the key issues and principles in the ears of the whole EU institutional system, and has served to deeply embed, in stages, commitment to sustainable development into the institutional system.

The way in which the EU has dealt with the issue of harmonization of environmental standards has also produced a reiterative process whereby minimal standards have been gradually ratcheted up. The underlying rationale for the EU, represented in the goal of the common market, is the key driver for harmonization. Allowing different environmental standards to apply would only have created pollution havens, distorted the market and promoted descent into regulatory laxity all round in a competitive struggle to attract and retain industry. Setting standards equivalent to the least stringent would have achieved nothing, and setting them at the highest level would have been impractical to implement. Once the principle of bringing all states up to intermediate minimum standards was accepted, the northern 'green leader' states (or early adopters) fought for and won the right to maintain their own higher standards. They did this against the objection that such higher standards reintroduced the differentials harmonization was trying to eliminate, and thus erected barriers to the single market.

The compromises were made at Maastricht, moving in both directions toward a variable-speed Europe. For the green leaders, the right to maintain higher standards was confirmed in Article 130t, after a Court of Justice ruling on a Danish law requiring the use of returnable bottles established the precedent that environmental considerations could prevail even at the expense of trade distortions. For the so-called cohesion states, the new Treaty introduced (Article 130s(5) provisions for temporary derogations from requirements of EC environmental measures where the cost is prohibitive, and/or financial assistance from a new Cohesion Fund to implement environmental measures.[35] The new arrangements acknowledged the reality that a range of standards exists across member states and set in place mechanisms whereby reiteration over time can raise up both the bar of best practice and the target minimum standards.

The effectiveness of the regime in dragging standards up has been less than could be wished for but is picking up momentum, particularly since the ECJ began imposing fines for non-implementation. Another major factor in getting the cohesion states up to standard is the integration of environmental policy into conditioning of the allocation of the huge Structural and Cohesion Funds, discussed further below. Last, it is clear that the accession states (those conditionally accepted for future membership of the EU) are making significant progress with addressing the improvement of environmental standards as part of satisfying minimum conditions of entry under a fixed timetable.

## The Use of Networks

The EU itself is a formalized network of states with common interests. In environmental policy the network model has been used to effect in bringing together actors from the disparate social and governance cultures of the states on a voluntary basis. The network strategy was launched with EAP5 in 1992 as part of that program's attempt to change the approach to, and increase the effectiveness of, environment policy.[36] The need to involve the full range of stakeholders in policy formulation in order to improve implementation and compliance on the ground drove the establishment of the Green Forum, IMPEL and the Environmental Policy Review Group. The IMPEL network clearly illustrates the benefits of semi-formalized networks in shedding light on the nature of inter-jurisdictional problems (in this case implementation of environmental policies) and in facilitating the learning required to solve them. This has been recognized formally by the system, with the mandate and roles of the network being expanded to provide direct advice to central policy-making processes. Based on this positive experience the Council has invited member states to encourage the creation of national coordination networks involving the main relevant authorities at different levels of public administration.[37]

On the policy level, the Green Forum – latterly the European Consultative Forum on the Environment and Sustainable Development – did so well that it has become formalized as part of the Commission system, while retaining its broad community representation. This group has been advocating extension of the network model as part of the institutional route to sustainability through 'multilevel constitutionalism'. This seeks to apply the subsidiarity and participation principles to develop systems of networks taking greater local responsibility for contributing to policy, dealing with implementation and being accountable for outcomes. This includes everyone – governments at all levels, commerce and the general public. National offices of a 'sustainability ombudsman' are suggested as the link between civil society and public authorities, taking responsibility for monitoring the implementation of environmental legislation. The ombudsmen would collectively form the European Sustainability Council, advising the EP and the Council on the sustainability of proposed legislation.[38]

Another aspect of the network strategy in the early 1990s was the

Commission's requirement for all DGs to designate integration correspondents to be the contact point for DG XI, and to monitor and report on progress to integrate environmental concerns into sectoral policy. This internal networking was not so effective. It tended to create capacity to defend 'business as usual' rather than to encourage cultural and procedural change within the DGs. Reports concentrated on highlighting cases of 'no regrets' policies (good for the environment, but happening to be the best option regardless of environmental considerations as well) and did not report on how environmental considerations shaped policy.[39]

The wide availability of internet technology has greatly facilitated the network approach and has served to validate for many people the notion of informal international networks for discussion of issues, exchange of information and development of projects. The officially recognized voluntary model, exemplified here by IMPEL, allows the terms of participation to be those of the participants. This means that the real-world problems affecting the participants are the issues dealt with, and the lack of externally defined output requirements allows the network to concentrate on the job of clarifying understandings and developing new approaches. The voluntary nature of participation means that if the network is not providing value to the participants they will drop out. This contrasts sharply with the familiar institutionalized inter-departmental committee that ritually meets for years and produces regular reports but achieves little of value to anyone.

**Top-down and Bottom-up Approaches to Change**

Beginning from a weak base in terms of power relations with respect to other policy subsystems within the EU and those of the member states, environmental policy interests have had to tread carefully. This has meant attempting to educate other interests about environment issues, particularly of the need to integrate environmental concerns into sectoral policy and to take initiatives to develop both environmental institutional capacity and legal clout as the opportunities arise. An important distinction can be made between the bottom-up procedural approach used in the main to try to educate and inculcate sustainability values and make sectoral departments more aware of the environmental consequences of their policies, and the top-down imposition of conditions through constitutionally defined power relations.[40] In the development of EU environment policy both approaches have been required. Institutionalized structures and processes – the old regime – impede change, in part because established practices become important for organizational and individual identity and for ritual reasons beyond functionality. The system is resistant to change despite the recognition of the importance of doing so by insiders (through the bottom-up process), and hence top-down muscle is required. This is illustrated in the campaign to integrate environmental concerns into broader sectoral policies within the EU and in member states.

## Policy integration

Policy integration is fundamental to sustainability but is extremely difficult to achieve as sectoral policy subsystems are mostly long established and are powerful primarily due to their economic significance. Where integrating environmental considerations is perceived as a cost these sectoral interests will seek to deflect initiatives at policy integration. Apart from costs to the sectoral client group interests, any change to organization and procedure within regulators and other agencies imposes costs. The longer organizations exist the more tasks tend to be defined to minimize costs to staff, making the costs of change higher and creating resistance to change.[41] The bottom-up approach seeks to educate and influence the process of cultural change within both regulators and their client groups in business and the community so that environmental issues are gradually taken more into account in policy and planning. However, this strategy can reach a point where the normative change has progressed but procedural change is resisted due to budgetary and cultural costs. This is where top-down methods may be needed to facilitate change.

Direct top-down approaches such as imposed structural reform or binding procedural frameworks across sectoral departments require political muscle. Strategic alliances between DG XI and the EP Environment Committee successfully applied such top-down pressure in the mid-1990s by threatening to block 50 per cent of the finance for the huge Structural and Cohesion Funds. These funding mechanisms, established by the EU to assist those states with lower per caput incomes to develop stronger economies, comprised about one-third of the total EU budget in 1995 (ECU29 billion).[42] The substantial environmental impacts of development of the large infrastructure projects financed under these schemes had generally been ignored in their planning and in the funding approval process. The primary problem identified by DG XI was the lack of environmental policy integration within the DG responsible for project approval and fund allocation. A secondary issue was inherent in the funding process under which applications were required to be developed, which did not allow time for thorough investigation of potential environmental impacts and encouraged the funding of large projects in order to disburse funding before it was lost to the budget cycle. During the 1995–6 budget process, the EP Environment Committee threatened to block funding if environmental impact was not made an integral consideration in project appraisal for funding decisions. The relevant DG was required to produce a code of conduct for the use of the funds that required environmental appraisal of each project, continuous monitoring and evaluation of environmental impacts and regular reports to Parliament and the Council.[43]

This example shows the Environment DG starting to flex the institutional muscle built up in the constitutional treaty. The Amsterdam Treaty strengthened this existing commitment considerably and should lead to wider application of such top-down power to invoke change in structures and processes of bureaucratic organization in the EU. Other top-down instruments include rolling national sustainability planning and sectoral action plans requiring annual reports on progress by sectors and review of reporting by the Parliament. Intermediate strategies on the top-down–bottom-up continuum include the application of strategic environmental assessment (SEA) and environmental auditing and reporting. A type of SEA was mandated in 1993, as part of a package of internal arrangements within the Commission. This mechanism is discussed further in Chapter 6, which focuses on SEA.

All of these strategic elements are important in an overall effort at continuous improvement of the integration of environmental principles in sectoral policy making.

**Subsidiarity**
Subsidiarity – the principle that action should be taken at the level within the institutional hierarchy at which it can be most effective – is an important driver within EU policy debate and is another example of the tension between top-down and bottom-up approaches to environmental policy. The tension and debate over what is the appropriate level for action on particular issues, energised by member state concern over loss of sovereignty to the 'Monnet Method' – integration by stealth – ensures greater attention is given to the nature and severity of environmental problems and possible solutions.

During discussions leading up to the signing of the Maastricht Treaty in 1993 the constitutional principle of subsidiarity was seized on by politicians to reassure constituents that the Treaty secured their interests. Its use as a rhetorical device has left the meaning of the term now more fluid. On one view it was meant to ensure less interference by the EU policy makers in national affairs (sovereignty) of member states and to provide an opportunity to roll back imposed policies, including environmental policies.[44] On another, the raising of the prominence of the principle means that the level at which particular issues should be dealt with needs to be more carefully justified than it has been in the past, with the burden of proof shifting to the EU to show that centralized action is justified. Arguably this can bring democracy closer to the citizen. However, it also holds the potential to strengthen obligations for member states to implement Community policy when it has been justified and scrutinized more openly.

Unfortunately it could be argued that the debate over preferred allocation of competences has not taken place.[45] This can be viewed as the core issue of subsidiarity and the essence of (con)federalism itself. Prior to the early 1990s the Monnet Method had been the key methodology for the establishment of the common market, but this met increasing resistance in the run-up to Maastricht. Despite an outbreak of nationalistic rhetoric and the change of emphasis in the Treaty, existing environment policy was shown to be one of the most strongly supported by the public, and the Monnet Method continues despite being checked. This is cited as support for new institutionalist views of path-dependence in institutional development, with the implication that roll-back of environment policy is unlikely.[46]

Sustainable development in a highly connected and complex world arguably implies the necessary application of the subsidiarity principle, within a nested hierarchy of governance institutions. Many impacts on the environment are best monitored and regulated at the local level, but the cumulative and spillover impacts of local activity on broader-scale environmental parameters are better assessed at a broader jurisdictional level. The subsequent decision making about allocation of resource use and means of regulation of local action creates the political tension in the debate. A key factor in subsidiarity for many policies in the EU affecting the environment is economic and cultural heterogeneity among member states, yielding differences in values and expectations in organizational structures of government and in path-dependency effects in institutions. Such diversity increases with the expansion of EU membership.

**Coping with diversity**
The impact of this diversity within the federalist system is illustrated in a comparative study of the implementation of EU agri-environmental regulations in Germany and Spain.[47] This study used a mixed top-down–bottom-up bargaining analytical model to help explain variance in implementation outcomes. This model allows recognition of a degree of negotiation between regulators and the regulated such that outcomes can reflect stakeholder preferences through the implementation process as well as in policy formulation. In the study four sets of relevant variables are recognized:

1. character of the policy formation process prior to implementation
2. organizational and inter-organizational implementation behaviour
3. street-level bureaucratic behaviour
4. response of target groups.

This case study emphasizes two key areas of interest: government and organizational structures; and normative views of the 'problem'.

The contrast between Germany and Spain is instructive. The fundamental issues of contrast are, first, in ethos – the characteristic spirit and beliefs of the community; second, in bureaucratic culture and capacity; and third, in available funding. Germany's agricultural sector (more so in the West) has developed a post-productivist ethos following a post-war tradition of supporting small family farm units. As the nation's industrial productivity made it affluent, European agriculture produced large surpluses of traditional commodities but at an increasingly uneconomic cost. The rationale for social subsidy of producers has changed with social values and is now seen as the purchasing of countryside management services – or paying farmers for environmental stewardship as well as for production. These income support schemes for farmers, tied to improved environmental management practices in agriculture and land management, are referred to as agri-environmental policies. Efficiency in use of land for commodity production is no longer the first priority for farmers, who have a range of sources of income assistance available to them tied to improving environmental management. By contrast, Spanish agriculture sees itself as behind in the modernization of farming practices and in need of catching up with the rest of Europe. The development of farming from peasant agriculture toward export-oriented growth is part of a broader productivist aspiration in post-Franco Spain.

In terms of bureaucratic organization, Germany generally has a well-organized and skilled public service, with staff motivated primarily by task achievement. On the other hand, Spain's bureaucracy is characterized by political appointment of many senior posts, with status and security in employment being related to patronage rather than performance, and low skill levels and organizational capacity leading to officials being swamped by administrative paperwork. Lines of communication with Brussels over EU policies and programmes are much more open for Germany than for Spain.

These differences are amplified by the relative lack of financial resources in Spain, both for the support and improvement of organization and for matching funding for EU programmes. Germany has had a long-term commitment to farmer support schemes in general and specifically to agri-environmental schemes. Both farmers and local-level bureaucrats are aware of the range of options available and work to match these to individual farmer circumstances. This long policy experience and Germany's centrality to the EU policy machine means that the EU schemes have been heavily influenced by the German model, which makes it a natural extension of previous institutional development. Spain has had no prior experience with agri-environmental policy. Post-Franco regionalist inclinations in the young federation tend to devalue policies and programmes originating from central government. Relatively low standards of education among farmers in many areas and poor vertical communication of information on schemes offered by the EU and their requirements have led to a very low uptake of the programmes.

The contrast in conditions applying in these two member states serves to remind us of policy sensitivity to historical contingency, institutional path dependence and specific contextual factors. But despite these differences the Wilson et al. study found common factors influencing the distribution of scheme take-up in the two countries. A key problem area is the lack of consistency in government structures within the member states' own federal systems. For example, some regional governments have separate departments of agriculture and of environment, others have them combined. The allocation of responsibility for agri-environmental schemes to one or other department or division varies, and the mission and ethos of administrative units responsible at this level for the EU scheme therefore also varies widely. This can have a strong effect on the general level of enthusiasm and promotion of the schemes and thereby the take-up rates as well as horizontal communication between adjacent administrations and wider coordination of programmes. Disparities in budgets at the local level can also affect implementation and take-up rates, and this is particularly evident in the contrast between the West and East German areas, as are differences in ideology and the structure of the industry, particularly in the size of farm units. The structural conflict between agricultural and environmental administration of the EU programmes means that, even in Germany, the environmental benefits of much of the implementation are questionable.

This example highlights a generic structural issue in the (re)organization of government for sustainability: the conflict between economically defined sectoral interests represented in established policy and administrative units, and the broadly encompassing public interest in environmental outcomes. In response to environmental concerns, common practice has been to establish government departments or ministries for environment modelled as a new sectoral interest competing directly with the others for resources and influence on executive government. The EU's DG XI has been conventional in this regard. Other institutional models include broad inter-sectoral (umbrella) policy initiatives such as, for example, Oceans or Biodiversity policy initiatives in a number of countries. This model internalizes the issues but establishes itself as a policy process over the top of a range of established interests, with the legal jurisdiction and implementation links to be made down the track once the policy framework has been agreed. A more radical style of reform takes a comprehensive approach, restructuring governance from the start with environmental or sustainability concerns at the centre of the structural and process rationale. An example of this approach is examined in the next case study, Chapter 4, on the New Zealand Resource Management Act 1991 (RMA).

The EU's DG XI, in the conventional mould, has been rather toothless by itself and is often ignored or dismissed by other sectors. However, it provides the anchor for environmental policy initiatives within the wider EU institutional system, with at least some permanent staff capability to provide both specific problem analysis and a more strategic outlook. A group of environmental institutional initiatives forms a linked cluster with the DG, providing some security against political action against any one agency.

Taking the view of the 'sustainability transition' – the inter-generational time-frame for institutional adjustment to this new fundamental principle of governance – there is no general answer to the question of the best first (or second) step. Current arrangements should in general be viewed as interim, with institutions needing to evolve through a series of steps or reforms. What might follow on from any particular step will be determined by the specific context – existing institutional conditions, current political proclivities, available information, including examples of working institutional models and new proposals – with all these being preconditioned by history. What is likely to be critical to a successful and smooth transition is the ability of the institutional system to learn effectively.

There may well be long-term problems with the 'competing sector' model for environmental governance as much of the adjustment to policy for sustainability must occur within mainstream sectoral activities, not just as add-ons or stop-gap measures such as conservation reserves or end-of-pipe pollution control. The need to make profound structural changes to energy use patterns, for example, cannot be addressed without a more integrated approach. How far the 'environment agency as policy police' approach can go in affecting integration is questionable and under test around the world. It is well that the EU has not relied solely on this approach, having applied a goodly proportion of available resources to diversifying the institutional basis for action and in particular having embedded commitment to sustainability at the constitutional level.

## LESSON DRAWING

In keeping with the intent of this study – to instruct thinking about the nature and possible directions of policy and institutional change rather than to collect specific and probably non-transferable templates – the following seeks to draw out of the EU experience themes of relevance to other contexts. The lessons identified are generic and broadly applicable, although we will use the Australian and Western developed contexts as points of reference. This is undertaken under the headings of the key principles identified in the previous section.

## Reiterative Framework

The EU case can remind other countries that the idea of sustainable development did not come out of nowhere. The principles expressed in the EAPs were an important articulation of the emerging sustainability ethic before it was brought to prominence by the WCED in 1987. By the time of Rio, EU environment policy was the expression of more than two decades of developing concern over the degradation of environment and the realization that a positive approach, integrated across the economy, was required to address sustainability.

The model of the EAPs as the backbone of a long-term approach to sustainability policy has relevance. The 1990–92 ESD policy process in Australia – and similar efforts in many other countries – can be viewed as a one-off EAP-type effort, seeking to define both the principles by which sustainability policy should be pursued and a sectoral analysis of specific problems. The EU model suggests that other countries could benefit by a reiterative process that periodically revisits the achievements of sustainable development policy, reconsiders the principles, frameworks, objectives and mechanisms developed, and seeks reaffirmation of these from current governments and the policy community more broadly. Setting a time-frame for further review and specific objectives for the period (five- to ten-year scale) would provide a firmer guiding framework for action than what can become an increasingly distant, dusty and in some details dated document set.[48] For those working in policy, timely 'generational' reminders and refreshment of the agenda, and government commitment to it, may help to maintain momentum. It would also help to develop deeper conceptions of 'sustainability as process' and 'sustainability as core principle of governance' rather than 'sustainability as one-off policy event'.

Through the long-term reiterative approach taken from the early 1970s, the EU's EAPs and the subsequent policy and legislation ensured that the basic principles of sustainability became embedded in the institutional fabric over time. This has occurred to the extent that, although still able to negotiate new proposals and amendments, governments of particular individual member states are not able to threaten the underlying basis of the Community's commitment to sustainability. This slow process of embedding has seen co-evolution of institutional and normative change within the broader policy community, with each country and policy sub-communities undertaking this evolution at different rates.

However, the case also instructs that constitutional commitment on its own is not enough. This applies also to the bare statutory expression of sustainability principles. Agreement to principles does not mean much if there is no implementation. In this regard the initial driving force behind environmental regulation in the EU – economic integration – brings free-market theory and ideology increasingly under the spotlight. It is clear to see that reluctance to clamp down on nitrate pollution of ground-water by intensive feedlot farming in France, for example, has both national economic and political underpinnings and should be addressed from both environmental and competitive free trade perspectives. However, it is not so clear that, for example, incentive packages for farmers to change agricultural practices introduced under the McSharry reforms of the Common Agricultural Policy – modelled on problems and policy solutions in West Germany – are equally applicable in some of the newer states of the EU, particularly the Mediterranean countries and Eastern European states. This is discussed further under policy integration below.

A critical attribute of the reiterative framework in the EU is that it has, over time, evolved to provide a supra-electoral continuity to environment policy. That is, although short-term changes of government and thus policy preference are important, such changes are attenuated, often muted, and the impacts negotiated. In that the temporal disjunction between electoral and political processes on the one hand and sustainability problems on the other is commonly viewed as a deep and serious issue, this possibility is interesting.[49] Differences in the political system are relevant here: the European Parliament does not produce a central, majority government, and the 'states' are more numerous than in most 'federal' situations and moreover are equivalent sovereign nations rather than provinces. So perhaps the translation to more typical federations (e.g. the USA, Australia, Malaysia, South Africa) would not be wholly effective, but the creation of mechanisms to protect broad policy evolution from numerous and unpredictable changes in political preference is a desirable goal.

## Networks

A critical part of a reiterative approach is the supplementation of institutional and policy 'hardware' with human and information 'software' through networks. While networks within and across policy communities occur as a matter of course, for a long-term and complex policy challenge like sustainability, more purposeful and explicit use of networks is desirable. The EU has created and utilized policy networks of different yet interrelated forms, inclusive of varying players according to the role envisaged for the network. Furthermore, these networks have evolved over time, changing function, membership and formality, while maintaining their overall purpose. Of particular interest is that, collectively, the EU networks encompass and serve to connect (whether sufficiently or not) the executive, bureaucratic, professional and non-government domains. While largely positive there have been less successful network experiments, such as the Integration Correspondents in other DGs reporting to DG XI. In answer to such weaknesses the existence of multiple, interrelated networks provides a fail-safe towards maintenance of purpose and momentum. Perhaps if there is a lesson from this last example it may be that reliance on networks involving only bureaucrats could be a mistake. Wider membership brings a greater chance of stalemate-breaking initiatives emerging when required and greater accountability for inaction.

Australia and the USA can provide illustrative contrasts. While it is also the case that multiple networks occur and at times operate influentially in Australia, it is our judgement that, despite this, networks in Australia have not displayed the depth, pervasiveness or continuity as in the EU case. More crucially, the maintenance of policy discourse and evolution of ESD as an inclusive, cross-jurisdictional and cross-sectoral problem set is notably lacking. By and large, inclusive policy development and implementation networks in Australia have been event- rather than process-driven – for example, the ESD working groups – or have been located within subsidiary parts of the ESD field, that is, resource sectors or substantive issues. Cross-sectoral linkages and succession planning are not well catered for. This appears to hold also in the USA, although that has not been a focus here. In Chapter 5, the failed promise of that country's Presidential Council on Sustainable Development is discussed, indicating again the problem of networks created for a short-lived policy purpose and not embedded in the institutional system.

Why some jurisdictions favour embedded networks and the slow process of cooperation they demand is not an issue that can be considered in detail here. However, apparent changes in policy style can be noted. Illustratively again, the 1980s saw a semi-inclusive style of national-scale policy making emerge in Australia, known and sometimes denigrated by the term 'corporatism'. This began with the consensus-driven National Conservation Strategy for Australia (NCSA) and reaching its peak through the ESD process and related subsidiary policy development such as the biodiversity and rangelands strategies.[50] In the 1990s and to date this style has been replaced by, on the one hand, a return to a more selectively inclusive, traditional public sector 'white paper' process and, on the other, district community and regional or catchment-oriented policy processes and programmes. These tend to have discrete foci, not serving to connect the ESD policy field. Headline policy programmes in recent years – for example the National Heritage Trust and now the National Salinity and Water-quality Action Plan – although sizeable, are discrete in time and inclusive of only some subsidiary issue within the ESD field. An apparent decline in inclusion and network building and maintenance at higher policy levels has been concurrent with increased activity at smaller spatial scales in management activities rather than policy development. The situation at the former scale is discussed with respect to national councils for sustainable development in Chapter 5.

Frustration with the lack of whole-sustainability approaches by national government may spur endeavours at state or provincial government level or by coalitions across non-government groups. For example, several Australian state and territory jurisdictions have – albeit belatedly – initiated structural and policy responses to sustainability, including sustainability strategies, offices of ESD in premiers' departments, sustainability commissioners, and so on. One outcome of the World Summit on Sustainable Development has been an emerging international network of sub-national initiatives. On the civil society side, it is from outside government that more ambitious, whole-field endeavours are now emerging in Australia, such as the Australian Collaboration, involving peak groups representing conservation, development aid, consumer, welfare, indigenous and religious interests, and the more recently emerged WA (Western Australian) Collaboration.[51]

It is notable that in many countries, but to a significantly lesser extent in Europe, broader policy discourses are retarded when different policy sectors and substantive issues remain compartmentalized. The effect is that lesson drawing across policy problems (say, regarding community engagement, regulatory implementation or design and function of rights markets) is rendered difficult and rare. This can be viewed largely as a result of the relative lack, in many places, of a whole-of-policy-field focus enabled by central capacities and mechanisms for policy integration (see below).

The conclusion from this section must be that it is only when the sustainable development policy field is united by event, process or policy that the necessary discourse and networks emerge. The sustainability transition requires sustained discourse and policy activity and activism, and the lesson from the EU is that this requires a mandate in the form of generalized driving policy objectives and programmes that affect all relevant sectors.

## Top-down, Bottom-up

The EU experience of mixing top-down approaches – regulatory, imposed and uniform – with bottom-up approaches – educative, voluntary and differentiated – is pertinent. The EU case also allows for observation of the coordination and evolution of the two approaches. It has been observed already that such a mix was necessary politically as well as being perceived as desirable. The mixed approach is closely associated with the broader reiterative EU style.

Against this, it is unclear whether there are sharp differences with the Australian approach over the past two decades, given a broadly similar mix of top-down and bottom-up approaches, and this applied generally across the developed world. In Australia, different styles of interaction between the federal and lower tiers of government are evident over time. Negotiation rather than forceful use of Commonwealth Constitutional power (which was used in the 1970–80s) became dominant from the early 1990s, with greater emphasis on consensus-driven standards and policy and, more recently, the tying of programme funding to defined goals. A clear basis for these shifts in style is hard to determine. However, the centralized regulatory and policy development capacity in the EU case is qualitatively different from that in typical federal systems, a function of the presence of supra-national institutions and the maintenance of effort through reiteration over time. No single country has developed anything like the range and specificity of EU policy directives in the environmental protection arena. Thus the lesson from the EU is not that the mixed approach is necessary – all developed economies have pursued this path – but that sustained coordination of top-down and bottom-up approaches is more likely to result in improved performance over time than a more haphazard style. That in turn depends on the existence of institutional settings favourable to persistent, joint efforts.

**Policy integration**
The top-down–bottom-up mixture has been particularly evident in attempts to integrate environmental with social and economic policy. Such integration, as opposed to the more traditional 'balancing' of conservation and development, is the absolute core of the sustainability idea. And it is supremely difficult, due to the impermeability of traditional, non-environmental policy subsystems and communities, and a lack of procedures and methods for integration. The EU achievements, such as they are, have been slow and partial, but certainly notable on international comparison and all the more so given the multi-jurisdictional context. Critical to these achievements has been the slow permeation of the institutional system by environmental and, more latterly, sustainability ideas, matched with an equally slow evolution of stricter requirements.

Policy integration is probably the most crucial missing link in national-level sustainability policy, with little explicit institutional or procedural development. Given this, two dimensions of the EU experience are most relevant. First, as well as bureaucratic and political mechanisms, the EU has (albeit only recently) taken the international lead in adopting the most well-developed operational tool for policy integration, strategic environmental assessment (SEA) (see further discussion in Chapter 6).

Second, in the EU sustainability imperatives have been linked closely with pre-existing policy rationales. The leveraging of the Structural and Cohesion Funds represents the most singular and sharp instance of insertion of environmental concern into mainstream policy in the EU thus far (if not anywhere). However, it is unlikely that this would have been possible had not considerable sensitization taken place beforehand. Central to policy integration in the EU is the single market imperative, the overriding policy goal of the entire European endeavour, which has evolved to incorporate environmental concerns. Reduction in investment distortion through common standards, plus the right to maintain higher standards, can iteratively shift the environmental protection bar higher. In so far as some might see the 'Federal problem' in countries such as Australia, and perhaps to a lesser extent the USA given its stronger role for national government, as favouring lowest common denominator standards and processes, this has some relevance. It is more relevant when it is considered that the most powerful arena of federalist policy theory and practical impact across the world in recent times has, like in Europe, been the neo-liberal, market reform one. Why economic integration in the EU has been coupled far more with environmental policy and sustainable development than, for example, National Competition Policy in Australia bears close investigation.[52] One area where environmental performance and economic efficiency and competitiveness are most explicitly joined is in the use of rights markets, explored further in Chapter 7.

The EU also evidences a multiple approach (even if born of unsurety) to the place of 'environment' as a policy entity in the panoply of portfolios and agencies. Sustainable development as an integrated agenda has accelerated rather than caused the move from separate agency for environment to a mixture of 'environmental police' and 'environment in other departments'. The jury is still out on the efficacy of either model, and the logical mix and balance yet to be achieved. Australia has, collectively across jurisdictions, experimented with all sorts of portfolio mixtures over the past two decades, even if this experiment has not been well documented or even intentional. Structured investigation of the efficacy of the various arrangements should be possible. Whatever the administrative and portfolio arrangements, however, without central commitment to sustainability policy and institutional development, integration is unlikely to occur.

## Subsidiarity and diversity

As a complex of nation states, sub-national regions and supra-national institutions and processes, the EU illustrates both the necessity and difficulty of creating the nested hierarchy of governance institutions commonly understood as necessary for sustainable development. Australia has in recent times, like many other countries, experimented extensively with new (or rediscovered) spatial and administrative scales of governance, policy and management for resource and environmental management: regions, catchments, inter-governmental processes on specific issues, and so on.

However, it is commonly perceived that connections between these scales, all of which have good justification and are necessary, are far from sufficient; nor is there clarity of division of responsibilities and power. It is also relevant that Australian experiments have been largely in natural resource management (that is, non-urban, not including energy or manufacturing sectors), have largely ignored local government, and have rarely invested actual legal, financial or policy-making power at these levels. Certainly, the experiments in most countries do not constitute a nested, interdependent institutional hierarchy – as is at least becoming evident in the EU – and do not appear likely to in future in the absence of reform.

The underlying feature in the EU case is the principle of subsidiarity – mutually acknowledged as crucial even while its meaning in application is hotly contested – coupled with the presence of shared, central nodes of political power and bureaucratic capacity. The latter condition – shared, central capacities – is worthy of separate comment (see below). Regularizing comprehensive debate and decision on the best scale for different responsibilities is not an easy path but appears a crucial one. Not that this is settled in Europe either, but the widespread recognition of the subsidiarity concept forces debate to focus on longer-term policy effectiveness and appropriateness as opposed to convenience or shorter-term political considerations, just as the acceptance of 'sustainability' as a core policy imperative does.

**Shared, central capacity**
A feature of the EU story is the presence of central political and bureaucratic capacity to engage in and persist with policy experimentation. That this combines a democratic element (the European Parliament), a law-making dimension and an administrative rationality and mandate, is worthy of note. Within most federal systems this tends to be lacking, and is enabled in the EU through the partners' status as sovereign states as opposed to, elsewhere, subsidiary parts of a single nation. The central bureaucratic capacity and democratic fora are interactive and serve to connect different forms of policy learning across a range of situations.

The tensions between national/central and state/provincial loci of powers that bedevil inter-governmental policy development elsewhere has been constructively refocused to at least some degree in the EU. Even while tensions between the individual nation states and a federal Europe are hugely significant, the institutions of the emerging federal system have been mutually built and will continue to be mutually determined. Member states negotiate and accept the authority of Community policy and law over aspects of their sovereignty.

The EU indicates the potential for inter-jurisdictional policy systems that are, if not free of conflictual politics and lowest common denominator tendencies, then at least somewhat closer to the 'bounded conflict' that Lee defines as useful politics for the environment.[53] The contribution of reiteration and networks within this framework allows for a dynamism and evolution more suited to a problem set like sustainability, involving as it does a long-term, integrative strategy, than is a tendency to seek closure on issues of responsibility, power and jurisdiction. The existence of a central bureaucratic capacity – far more substantive than any 'part-time secretariat' model more typical of inter-jurisdictional arrangements – has been important in the development and survival of policy ideas and lessons across time, despite electoral shifts in member states.

## CONCLUDING COMMENT

Evident in the above discussion of pertinence to other settings of environmental and sustainability policy and institutional development in the EU over the past three decades is the fact that there are few independent lessons or factors emerging. That is, the apparent causes of what might be categorized as 'successful' (or at least interesting) EU experiences are tightly linked. Reiteration over time has been both a cause and an effect of the development of centralized political and bureaucratic capacity, of the existence of durable networks, of the use of top-down–bottom-up approaches, and so on. This warns against the lifting of singular ideas or settings from the EU (or any other) situation, and reinforces the importance of a core idea developed in the conceptual background to this book – the complexity and interdependence of institutional systems and the co-evolutionary nature of normative and institutional change. This has both positive and negative connotations. Negatively, it weighs against swift and simple transfer of improved institutional models and thus of swift achievement of substantive outcomes. Positively, it indicates that, if sensitively conceptualized and implemented, institutional change can be progressive and moreover to some degree irreversible in trajectory.

## NOTES

1. The EU is not a federal system as such but a confederation of separate nation states.
2. Hildebrand (2002).
3. Article 2, Treaty Establishing the European Economic Community, Rome 25 March 1957 (Treaty of Rome).
4. CoM (1973).
5. Adapted from Barnes and Barnes (1999), Fig. 2.1, p. 30.
6. CoM (1977).

7. Barnes and Barnes (1999), p. 35.
8. CoM (1983).
9. CoM (1987).
10. Article 8a of the Treaty of Rome as inserted by the SEA 1987.
11. CEC (1992).
12. See Wilkinson (2002).
13. See next section and note 18 for comment on qualified majority voting.
14. Jordan (2002a), p. 56.
15. CEC (2001a).
16. Otherwise known as 'The Council of the European Community' and referred to in the text as 'the Council'. Citations of Council publications use the acronym CoM.
17. Barnes and Barnes (1999), Ch. 3.
18. Qualified majority voting (QMV) removes the requirement for unanimity in the Council and therefore the ability of one state to hold out and demand concessions or changes to legislation otherwise agreed. This becomes more of an issue as membership expands, and so QMV has spread in several stages to apply to a greater number of issue areas in EU decision making. QMV is weighted by the size of states and requires a 71 per cent majority to carry (ibid, p. 56). Thus even the large states cannot individually block measures supported by all other members. QMV still does not apply to all areas of environmental policy – for example it does not apply to fiscal measures as some states fear having policies such as carbon tax imposed against their will.
19. Web source: http://www.europarl.eu.int/home/default_en.htm
20. The nature of this direct representation must be understood in the context of generally low turnouts for, and lack of interest in, EP elections. However, this is not a reason to abandon the mechanism, and for the purposes of this study it is arguably the potential of it that is of significance.
21. See Barnes and Barnes (1999), Ch. 3.
22. CEC (2001b).
23. CEC (2001c).
24. Duncan (2000).
25. Barnes and Barnes (1999), p. 112.
26. CEC (2001b).
27. Wilkinson (1997), p. 158.
28. Ibid.
29. North (1993), explains 'that a commitment is credible in either of two senses, the motivational or the imperative. A commitment is motivationally credible if the players continue to want to honour the commitment at the time of performance. In this case it is incentive compatible and hence self-enforcing. It is credible in the imperative sense if the player cannot act otherwise because performance is coerced or discretion is disabled'. There are, of course, trade-offs between commitment and flexibility, but institutions develop essentially through a series of step-lock commitments that establish the long-term framework of rules.
30. Wilkinson (1997, 2002).
31. Weale (2002), p. 209.
32. Demmke (2001); Barnes and Barnes (1999); Jordan (2002b).
33. Wilson et al. (1999).
34. O'Riordan and Voisey (1997).
35. Wilkinson (2002), p. 46.
36. Bohm-Amtmann (2001).
37. CoM (1997).
38. CEC (2000).
39. Wilkinson (1997), p. 163.
40. Wilkinson (1997), p. 155.
41. See, for example, Meyer and Rowan (1977).
42. Wilkinson (1997), p. 166.
43. Ibid.

44. Jordan (1999).
45. Ibid.
46. Ibid.
47. Wilson et al (1999).
48. For a review of the Australian ESD policy and of the role of discrete policy processes within the institutional system, see Dovers (2003).
49. It is perhaps relevant that in much of Europe cohabitation and shifting coalitions or minority governments are an accepted norm rather than being viewed, as in, say, the United Kingdom or Australia, as unfortunate if increasingly common aberrations. The differences in political culture and discourse produced by familiarity with jointly shared as opposed to single-party defined government may be significant in terms of the likelihood of persistence with policy ideas over time or the definition of bi- or multipartisan positions on long-term issues.
50. Note that both the NCSA and ESD process were responses to international policy development.
51. On the former, see Yencken and Porter (2001).
52. Curran and Hollander (2002).
53. Lee (1993).

# 4. Sustainable management of natural and physical resources: The New Zealand Resource Management Act 1991

## INTRODUCTION

This chapter examines New Zealand's Resource Management Act 1991 (RMA) as an early and substantive example of a major statutory reform in response to sustainability. The purpose here is not to propose the RMA as a model to adopt but to attempt to understand what the New Zealand experience has been both in the policy development process and in over a decade of implementation. From this we hope to learn about sustainable development policy and the institutional structure and process necessary to bring such policy to bear on the real world. The RMA experience directly addresses the two key types of policy learning – social and government – and all three objects of learning defined in Part I of the book: substantial policy processes, organization of government and problem reframing.

The Resource Management Act was passed into law by the New Zealand Parliament in July 1991 and came into force on 1 October of that year, following four years of intense development work. The RMA remains an important example of a comprehensive and integrated approach to resource management law reform based on sustainability principles. The legislation enjoyed bipartisan support in the Parliament, having been conceived and developed by the Labour Government but passed into law by the conservative National Party that gained power in 1990.

The RMA replaced some twenty major statutes and fifty other laws related to the environment, some dating back as far as 1889. It provides a mechanism for managing the quality of land, air and water under a single law. The key exceptions to its coverage are fisheries management and minerals, which are dealt with under their own separate legislation. During the development of the RMA a concurrent review of legislation empowering local government presented the opportunity for the redefinition of structures and function to facilitate the implementation of the new resource management regime.

The RMA places environment at the centre of the policy and functional concerns of local government in New Zealand. It provides a hierarchy of authority that allows central government decision makers to impress national priorities on the system while at the same time attempting to ensure that planning and management functions are delegated to the lowest public authority consistent with effective action.[1]

Given the comprehensive nature of the reforms and the context of the emergence of sustainable development on to the world political agenda through the Brundtland Report[2] in 1987 the four-year process involved may seem like a virtually instantaneous response. Beginning at the time of the publication WCED report the reforms were legislated and operative before the UNCED conference. However, as we shall see, the RMA was part of a broader historical shift in governance in New Zealand during the 1980s which, while largely following global trends, was pre-conditioned by a particular historical political economy.

The first part of the chapter examines the context, origins and provisions of the RMA, adopting a primarily descriptive stance. It dedicates sections in turn to historical context, coverage of the Act, the Purpose and Principles clauses, and the policy and planning framework. The Purpose and Principles are considered crucial drivers of both changing attitudes and practice with respect to the environment and the ongoing sustainability debate in New Zealand. Thus close attention to the detail of these provisions is repaid in later analysis. The last section explains the main governance framework established by the Act to deal with sustainable management of natural and physical resources through statutory planning.

The second part of the chapter provides an analysis of the RMA in practice and attempts to draw some thematic lessons for other jurisdictional contexts. First it provides a preface to the analysis of the nested hierarchy of principles, policies, plans and processes through which the RMA is implemented. It then proceeds to examine the development and meaning of the critical purpose of the Act – sustainable management. The following three sections examine the key strengths and weaknesses of the roles played by central government, local governments and the Environment Court respectively.

The third part summarizes some general thematic conclusions from the New Zealand experience.

## ORIGINS AND STRUCTURE OF THE RMA

### Historical Context

New Zealand has a high rainfall temperate climate and geologically young and fertile soils. Combined with its convenience as a harvesting base for seals and whales, these characteristics have been the foundation of its prosperity as a resource colony for Britain and latterly as a member of the OECD club of economically advanced nations. Low population base, generally rugged terrain and geographic isolation meant central government has played a crucial role in the provision of infrastructure services to the modern New Zealand economy for the one hundred and fifty or so years since its establishment. New Zealand earned a reputation as a leader in social policy, pioneering universal suffrage and provisions of the Welfare State. In natural resources, a centralized development-oriented bureaucracy developed, as did a wide range of government-run, resource-intensive enterprises, including hydroelectricity generation and supply, forestry, coal mining and construction. This structural mentality of hands-on involvement – of government as resource development entrepreneur – strengthened in the post-Second World War period and peaked in the late 1970s under the Muldoon National Government. In response to the oil shocks, this administration embarked on a portfolio of new large-scale projects aimed at making New Zealand self-sufficient in energy. These so-called 'Think Big' projects ranged through high-dam hydroelectricity, offshore gas exploration and development, gas and oil fired electricity generation, a synthetic methanol-petrol plant, natural gas reticulation infrastructure and oil refinery construction.

The New Zealand environment movement was first galvanized to popular protest by the massive Lake Manapouri hydroelectricity project of the 1960s, and in the mid-1970s matured in taking on the government over its logging of native forests. Environmentalists were incensed by the 'Think Big' energy projects and their disregard for both environmental impacts and any form of public participation in planning processes. The Government passed special legislation allowing them to bypass the limited legislative protections that did exist, in the national interest.[3] These projects were the last straw for a struggling economy, and the National Government exited in the midst of a fiscal crisis. The neo-liberal reformists waiting in the wings wasted no time in delivering their prescriptions for deregulation of the closed economy to the incoming Labour Government. Government debt required serious reduction, prompting a rash of asset sales and the corporatization and privatization of government enterprises, including the resource production areas of mining, forestry, lands and electricity. The new philosophy was to retain only the core roles of government in public hands and to concentrate on correction of market failures.[4]

The new government began its environmental reforms by disestablishing major state resource agencies – the New Zealand Forest Service (state loggers) and Ministry of Works (dam builders) – and creating the Ministry for the Environment, the Parliamentary Commissioner for the Environment and the

Department of Conservation through the Environment Act 1986 and the
Conservation Act 1987. Thus a large chunk of the development and resource
development bureaucracy was transformed (at least officially[5]) into one
concerned with conservation and environmental protection.

New Zealand was catching up fast with the sustainability agenda. Following
its establishment and the 1987 re-election of the reformist Labour Government
the new Ministry for the Environment was tasked with the comprehensive
reform of the existing corpus of resource management legislation, the
Resource Management Law Reform process (RMLR). The key Cabinet driver
of this reform process was Geoffrey Palmer, the then Deputy Prime Minister,
Minister of Justice, Attorney General and Minister for the Environment, who
had a background as a legal academic. His Associate Minister, Philip
Woollaston, 'brought a steely operational toughness as well as a sharp mind
and local government experience to Palmer's driving legalistic zeal for
reform'.[6] Palmer also credits Woolaston as his mentor on environment issues.
The other strength of this partnership was a commitment to equity and
principles of process both in the reform and the subsequent legislation. This
threw open the reform process to wide public consultation, participation and
debate, albeit constrained by the tight three-year electoral cycle. The reform
process provided the venue for the New Zealand public convergence of
several strands of ideas, summarized by Frieder:[7]

> The RMLR was an enormous and impassioned effort. Its conceptual influences
> were Maori ideas about stewardship and sustainability, the 1986 [*sic*] Brundtland
> Commission Report on sustainable development, *Our Common Future*,
> international trends toward deregulation, decentralisation and community
> empowerment, existing New Zealand resource law and public reaction to
> deficiencies within those laws, as well as the ideas of efficiency and accountability
> that were at the heart of the economic and state sector reform.

In the event time ran out for the Labour-driven RMLR. The Bill was
introduced to the House in late 1989 but was not passed before the
government changed twelve months later. Somewhat ironically, the Labour
bill was 'an efficiency model rooted in economic rationalism, tempered by an
emphasis on public participation', while the final Act was made 'greener' by
the incoming conservative National Government under influence of their
Hayekian Minister for the Environment, Simon Upton.[8] Upton himself was
heavily influenced on the matter of the RMA by the ideas of Guy Salmon, the
leading New Zealand environmental lobbyist of his generation. Salmon was
appointed to a panel to review the bill for the new government. He had already
been pressing Palmer for changes to the critical definitions of sustainable
management away from the existing principle of balancing interests of
conservation and development to set environmental bottom lines:

development should be carried out within set environmental constraints.[9] This was achieved, although some of his other aims were not, notably greater emphasis on the use of economic instruments.

The final result has been called a 'statutory framework for a relatively more holistic and integrated approach to environmental planning based on ecological and democratic principles.'[10] Young says of the RMA:

> its integrating power can still deliver a gestalt effect (greater than the sum of its parts). It is, primarily, about principle, processes towards community-agreed goals, about dialog rather than dictat, mediation rather than confrontation … The RMA is about a new order; for the first time in our history we are being asked to put the environment first, this in a country so recently of the backwoodsman, now largely gone, having taken so much that was uniquely indigenous with him.[11]

## Coverage of the Act

The resulting legislation was substantial, running to 382 pages with 433 sections and eight schedules. The key components are:

- Part II: Purpose and Principles – discussed in the following section
- Part III: Duties and Restrictions – This part sets out restrictions on land use and activities affecting the environment that generally apply unless specifically permitted under a policy, plan or by a resource consent. The key duties, essentially established for the entire New Zealand population, are to avoid unreasonable noise and, crucially, the duty to avoid, remedy or mitigate adverse effects on the environment
- Part IV: Functions, Powers and Duties of Central and Local Government
- Part V: Standards, Policy Statements and Plans – This part establishes the key hierarchical operating framework for policy and planning for land and resource use. This is discussed below
- Part VI: Resource Consents – This sets out the processes for resource consent application, consideration and appeal, and is discussed briefly in a following section
- Part VIII: Designations and Heritage Orders and Part IX: Water Conservation Orders – These sections empower Ministers of the Crown and local authorities to designate specific areas of land for special purposes such as public works, and to issue heritage protection and water conservation orders to protect natural and cultural heritage values.
- Part X: Subdivision and Reclamations
- Part XI: Planning Tribunal – This part re-authorizes the existing Planning Tribunal as a Court of Record (in 1996 renamed the Environment Court). This is discussed further below.

Remaining sections of the RMA deal with enforcement and penalties, administrative and transitional matters. As Part II of the Act encapsulates the thrust of the legislation as well as providing the basis for much ongoing debate over its future, key sections are set out in the following section.

**Purpose and Principles**

Section 5 of Part II of the RMA declares the stated purpose of the Act is to promote the sustainable management of natural and physical resources. For the purposes of the RMA, 'sustainable management' means:

> Managing the use, development, and protection of natural and physical resources in a way, or at a rate, which enables people and communities to provide for their social, economic, and cultural wellbeing and for their health and safety while
> (a) Sustaining the potential of natural and physical resources (excluding minerals) to meet the reasonably foreseeable needs of future generations; and
> (b) Safeguarding the life-supporting capacity of air, water, soil, and ecosystems; and
> (c) Avoiding, remedying, or mitigating any adverse effects of activities on the environment.[12]

This purpose and definition are crucial sources of statutory ambiguity for the promotion of an ongoing sustainability discourse. The use of the language of sustainable management rather than sustainable development was a deliberate attempt to constrain the scope of the Act, while the definition in some ways opens the door again to a broader debate. The definition of environment in the Act is crucial to interpretations of what should be admissible in contention over permitted activities, as is the definition of an effect.

> 'Environment' includes –
> (a) Ecosystems and their constituent parts, including people and communities; and
> (b) All natural and physical resources; and
> (c) Amenity values; and
> (d) The social, economic, aesthetic, and cultural conditions which affect the matters stated in paragraphs (a) to (c) of this definition or which are affected by those matters.[13]

Thus sustainable management includes avoiding, remedying or mitigating any adverse effects of activities on not only people and their communities but also the social, economic, aesthetic and cultural conditions that are affected by natural and physical resources. In addition the definition of 'effect' is broad, and the particular importance of the scope of the term is recognized by a special section of the Act devoted to its meaning.[14] It includes positive, adverse, temporary or permanent effects occurring at any time, any cumulative effect that arises over time or in combination with other effects, and potential effects of high probability or low probability but with high potential impact.

To help decision makers and others in achieving the RMA's purpose of sustainable management a number of explicit principles are set out that must be recognized and provided for in the everyday operation of the Act. These principles are split into Matters of national importance; Other matters; and Treaty of Waitangi.[15]

Matters of national importance identify parts of the environment that New Zealanders hold in particularly high regard, including:

- the natural character of the coastal environment, wetlands, lakes and rivers, and public access to those resources
- natural features and landscapes
- significant indigenous vegetation and habitats
- the relationship of Maori and their culture and traditions with their ancestral lands, water, sites, *wahi tapu*, and other *taonga*.[16]

Decision makers must also 'have particular regard' to a number of other matters that include:

- *kaitiakitanga*: the exercise of guardianship by the *tangata whenua* of an area in accordance with *tikanga* Maori[17] in relation to natural and physical resources
- the ethic of stewardship
- the efficient use and development of natural and physical resources
- the maintenance and enhancement of amenity values
- the intrinsic values of ecosystems
- the recognition and protection of the heritage values of sites, buildings, places or areas.

Last, the RMA requires that those making decisions under the Act must 'take into account' the principles of the Treaty of Waitangi. The Treaty is now considered to be New Zealand's founding constitutional document and establishes the relationship between the Crown and Maori as *tangata whenua*.[18] Other recent New Zealand legislation requires that consideration be given to the Treaty's principles. The principles of the Treaty of Waitangi are an interpretation of the Treaty's text. Their definition, while continuing to evolve, has been assisted by their consideration by the Court of Appeal and the Waitangi Tribunal. In the broadest sense the principles of the Treaty are:[19]

- The right of the Government to govern and make laws (*kawanatanga*)
- The right of *iwi* and *hapu* to self-management and control of their

resources in accordance with their tribal preferences (*te tino rangatiratanga*)

● The principle of partnership and a duty to act in good faith (partnership)
● The duty on the Crown to actively protect *tangata whenua* in the use of their resources and *taonga* (including the provision of redress for past injustices).

The requirement to take into account the principles of the Treaty of Waitangi means that those with statutory functions under the RMA should be informed of, and actively consider, the concerns and needs of *tangata whenua*. Given the need to take these principles into account it is deemed wise for virtually all planning and policy making by government to involve consultation with Maori. Very often this is the case, but it is not compulsory under the Act and for Maori this is a key disappointment in the Act as it stands.

## Policy and Planning Framework

### Three levels of governance
Concurrently with the RMLR process of the late 1980s the New Zealand Government overhauled the system of local government in 1988 and again in 1989 through amendment of the Local Government Act 1974. This substantially reduced the number of local and regional units of government. Thirteen regional councils, 74 district councils and seven special-purpose boards were created to replace 625 existing units of local government which had included authorities, united councils, counties, municipalities, districts and special purpose boards. Many of the special purpose boards that were abolished, such as catchment, drainage, river and pest destruction boards, had significant environment-affecting missions.[20] Hence many development proposals had involved multiple consent processes with different agencies, often involving long delays. The rationalization of resource management administration was an attempt to reduce costs and duplication as well as clarify and integrate environmental and resource management responsibilities and decision making.

The new regime divided the country into 13 regions delineated by major watersheds, and the new regional councils were to some extent created by conversion of existing catchment boards. This move was advocated by the leadership of the New Zealand Catchment Authorities (the umbrella organization for catchment boards) and a group within the New Zealand Federated Farmers opposed to the prevailing fiscal absolutism but frustrated by the existing complex set of multiple overlapping jurisdictions.[21] Existing territorial planning authorities were amalgamated and redefined so as to match the regional boundaries. This delineation by catchment equals arguably the most pervasive example of watershed governance in the world, at least in principle.

Under the new system a further structural option is possible for local government – the Unitary Authority – that assumes the responsibilities of both regional and district councils. The current system has 12 regional councils and 74 territorial local authorities (TLAs), including four unitary authorities.

The system created through this reorganization of the units of local government, combined with the principles, duties and responsibilities imposed by the RMA and the earlier reorganization of the central government environment agencies, represented a massive change in the framework of environmental governance in a five-year period. In fact the system was acknowledged by its authors to be merely an enabling framework – not a comprehensive scheme covering all bases. Within the conceptual framework of principles and duties to consider the effects of activities on the environment, and through the organizational structure of the three tiers of government – central, regional and district – the main operational institutional structure is the hierarchy of policies and plans.

## Policies and plans

The land use planning process under the RMA developed and transformed the British Town and Country Planning model already in place. It introduced a nested hierarchy of authority, policies, standards and plans. For example, district councils develop land use plans within an environment defined by the legislation, central government policy statements, environmental standards and regulations, and policy statements and plans promulgated by the relevant regional council. The fundamental decision rule is that actions, decisions, policies, and so on should 'not be inconsistent with' the overarching framework.

As described in the previous section, the RMA itself lays down substantive issues as 'matters of national importance', as well as a set of principles and duties, and its singular objective of the sustainable management of natural and physical resources. A further key element of the policy and planning schema at the central government level is the provision for National Policy Statements (NPS),[22] National Environmental Standards (NES) and statutory regulations. These allow central government to provide leadership on issues of national importance where a coordinated approach is desirable, or on technically demanding issues. They are binding on both regional and district councils. One NPS was prescribed by the RMA as compulsory: the New Zealand Coastal Policy Statement, to be developed and recommended by the Minister of Conservation within a specified time-frame. This in turn requires the development of regional coastal plans by regional councils. Interestingly no other NPS or NES has yet been gazetted. The reasons for this and the implications for the operation of the RMA framework are discussed later.

Regional councils are elected authorities, and each must prepare a Regional Policy Statement (RPS) setting out policies for integrated resource management in their jurisdiction. The RPS provides an overview of the region's resource management issues and facilitates an integrated approach to dealing with them. Responsibilities include control of:

- taking, use, damming and diversion of surface and ground-water
- maintaining and enhancing water quality and quantity
- land, air and water contamination or pollution
- land use with respect to soil conservation
- the introduction of plants into water bodies.[23]

The regional policy statement sets out the expectations of the Council for the way the issues identified will be addressed, through the establishment of objectives, policies and methods for implementation, and how these intentions will be monitored and reviewed. In addition regional councils must prepare a regional coastal plan that is not inconsistent with the national coastal policy statement, and may prepare other regional plans to address any issue relating to their functions under the RMA.

Hence district or city councils, the elected territorial local government bodies, carry out their planning for land use and resource management within a framework constrained by an RPS in terms of overall impacts of activities on the environment but at the same time have the ability to permit any activity that is not inconsistent with these rules. The emphasis of the RMA is firmly on managing the effects of activities on the environment rather than proscribing or prescribing particular land uses or activities. District and city councils are responsible for controlling:

- the effects of land use (including hazardous substances and natural hazards)
- subdivision
- noise
- the effects of activities on the surface of rivers and lakes.

District and city councils are charged with preparing district plans that describe the district's significant resource management issues and set out objectives, policies and methods to address these. They must outline the environmental results expected from their implementation and how they will be monitored and reviewed.[24] For both regional and district councils policy statements and plans must undergo full review at least every ten years.[25]

**Resource consent processes**

Both regional and district councils administer processes for issuing resource consents. Under Part III of the Act a resource consent is required for any use of land contrary to rules in district plans or for any activity with effects on air or water not expressly permitted by rules in regional plans.[26] All plans include specification of activities and conditions for which resource consents must be obtained. For example, a regional plan may set standards for discharges into a water body from a particular activity, or a district plan may set out concerns for the preservation of the visual character of an urban precinct. Where a proposed activity may exceed the standard or affect the specified environmental value, a resource consent must be sought before the activity can proceed. Plans must include specification of the information required to accompany a consent application. Where resource consents are required from both district and regional authorities for the same development activity, a joint process is arranged so that all issues are considered together. All consent applications must be accompanied by an assessment of environmental effects (AEE), and conditions may be attached to a resource consent in order to avoid, remedy or mitigate any adverse effects.

Resource consent applications must be publicly notified unless exempted under S94 of the Act, which applies a dual cumulative test. The adverse effect of the proposed activities must be minor and written consent must be obtained from all parties that may be adversely affected. Notification is important in that it opens the door to public participation in the decision-making process. Therefore, how consent authorities exercise the discretion they have to require notification shapes the nature of local democratic practice. Where necessary, a hearing may be held by the consent authority for consideration of an application.

**Appeals to the Environment Court**

Where resource consent applicants or other parties are dissatisfied with a decision of a consent authority they may appeal to the Environment Court, but to do so they must have been a party to the consent process. This underlines the significance of decisions over public notification of consent applications.[27] Appeals may also be made to the court on other decisions made by councils, such as aspects of proposed regional policy statements or regional or district plans, heritage orders or other designations.

The Environment Court, formerly called the Planning Tribunal, is constituted by the Resource Management Amendment Act 1996. It is a Court of Record consisting of Environment Judges (who are also District Court Judges) and environment commissioners, appointed by the Governor General.[28] Except for the hearing of enforcement proceedings that involve questions of law, sittings are usually constituted by one Environment Judge and two Environment Commissioners. The Court has a central registry at Wellington and holds sittings throughout the country. Parties before the Court are usually represented by lawyers, but anyone may appear in person or be represented by any other agent. The Court is not bound by the rules of evidence and the proceedings are often less formal than the general courts. Most of the Court's work involves public interest questions. Because of the gravity and complexity of the subject matter of the proceedings, oral decisions can seldom be given and decisions are usually reserved – meaning that a written judgement is delivered at a later date.[29]

A resource consent applicant may appeal different parts of the decision on a consent, such as the level of administrative charging, and decisions of the Environment Court may be further appealed to the High Court, but only on matters of law.

Of note is the fact that Judges of the Environment Court are, or become, specialists not only in the applicable body of law, but also in natural resource management and planning issues. Consent appeals are generally heard *de novo*, considering all of the facts of the case anew, rather than reviewing consent authority decision processes. In contrast to having such issues heard by general tribunals, this arrangement can only assist with resolving cases so that outcomes are not just in compliance with the law, but are environmentally sound as well.

**The call-in procedure**

Sections 140 to 149 of the Act allow a resource consent application for a development of national significance to be 'called in' by the Minister for the Environment, which takes the consent proposal out of the hands of the local consent authority. An independent Board of Inquiry then considers the matter and a decision is made by the minister. Such a decision can be appealed to the Environment Court in the same way as other consent decisions, but the process allows intervention where the Minister believes the national interest is at stake.

# THE RMA IN PRACTICE

## A Nested Hierarchy of Governance

The resource management law reform process was ambitious in setting out to comprehensively address the impacts of resource use and development on the environment under the rubric of sustainable management of natural and physical resources. The concurrent restructuring of local government and the assignment of new mandates to the resulting authorities provided a real opportunity for dramatic changes. The result is a sophisticated and subtly complex institutional system – a combination of ideas, principles, rules, structures and mandated processes – dependent, perhaps more than has been widely appreciated, on the interaction of a range of critical components.

The RMA represented a major shift in direction for the New Zealand planning and resource management establishment, and it should be no real surprise that there have been some problems in making the adjustment to practice. There is now a widespread view that the framework has not performed as well as was hoped, but there is considerable dispute over what is wrong and how it should be improved, with alternate suggestions pulling in opposite directions. Some believe the ambiguity in the Act, particularly in the purpose and principles, has led to confusion and promoted dispute.[30] Others believe the Act is fundamentally sound but that problems have occurred in implementation for a range of other reasons.[31] The following sections look at some of the problems with the RMA in practice, opinion on what the causes of the problems are and views on what should be done to address the situation.

At the heart of the RMA lies the 'Purpose and Principles'. This part is intended to animate the schema, to drive and underpin all responsibilities conferred and actions carried out under the Act. All other sections of the legislation are intended to carry out the fundamental purpose of sustainable management. Although there is much detail included in the Act about what must be done by whom, and how it should be done, the intention was to allow adaptation driven by the purpose and principles. The mechanisms of the Act that provide its ability to be adaptive are, first, the fact that it adopts what is a contemporary dynamic discourse at its heart – the very meaning of 'sustainability' is the subject of vigorous debate in the community. Having sustainable management as the purpose of legislation that eventually directly affects the majority of citizens promotes interest in and discussion of this vital global conversation, attempts to focus individuals on the environment, the values that they and others hold for it, and how their actions affect those values. This should promote behavioural change and social policy learning at all levels in the governance hierarchy – what might be termed 'normative push'. Such learning was very much a part of the development of the legislation, and the development of the Purpose clauses – Section 5 – is examined in some detail in the next section of the chapter.[32]

A second component of the adaptive framework is the provision for National Policy Statements and National Environmental Standards. These are, or arguably should be, the central ongoing coordination signals for the system. The elaboration of national policy on matters of national importance already recognised in the Act, or on emergent issues, can not only coordinate to provide desired levels of collective outcomes but can also save much duplication of effort at the local level and reduce dispute. The fact that these mechanisms have been left largely inactivated deserves some investigation and analysis, and this is provided below.

The coalface of adaptation is in the policy and planning processes of the local authorities. The institutional hierarchy of statutory rules, policies and plans provides procedural form and guiding principles, but territorial authorities must cope with decision making in unique and complex social, economic and environmental circumstances. The new planning system is constraining only in identified areas, rather than permissive only in them, as in the older regime, placing a greater burden on local authorities to be proactive and fully informed. Hence it might be predicted that local authorities would require proactive and dynamic support in making a cultural change to work under the RMA, and to establish new functionality and protocols. The issues of applying the Act at local level are discussed under the heading 'Local Government Roles'.

The development of jurisprudence based in the RMA is carried on by the Environment Court. How this has coped with interpreting what the Act sets down, as well as with what was not anticipated, may yield some valuable insights into the practicality of the framework and its strengths and weaknesses. The final section of this chapter looks to the experience of the Environment Court.

**Purpose and Principles**

Part II of the RMA, Purpose and Principles, has become something of a battleground both in legal and ideological terms. One view is that this section is muddled and ambiguous, particularly in conjunction with supporting sections such as definitions in the interpretation and matters set out in the schedules to the Act. This makes legal challenge all too easy on the grounds that decisions under the Act are inconsistent with the intent as expressed in this part. To attempt to understand the underlying issues, this section will delve back into the process of the development of the purpose and principles sections of the RMA.

Although hailed as an attempt at comprehensive and integrated reform of the environmental administration,[33] the New Zealand reforms were at least partially incremental in that the RMLR process was first conceived by MfE staff.[34] Hence without the prior reconfiguration of agencies the possibility of the RMA may not have arisen – an example of institutional path dependency. As might be expected, a range of key actors perceived different sets of opportunities presented by the RMLR exercise. For example, the Minister saw an opportunity to consolidate a plethora of legislation into a landmark Act, while MfE officials saw a chance to rationalize and integrate environmental administration. Initially the RMLR was to serve these two main purposes, but the contemporaneous publication of the Brundtland Report[35] and the strong presence of antecedent lines of thought in New Zealand environmental politics had planted the sustainability idea firmly inside the reform policy process.

As part of the RMLR a series of essays on sustainability and related concepts was produced,[36] and a discussion was directed at the potential use of sustainability as the pre-eminent objective for the legislation. The key planning Act being replaced had such a general and all-embracing description of the purpose of planning as to arguably provide no guidance at all.[37] In sum, it promoted the wise use and management of resources for the benefit of the people, admitting virtually any action to be justified as wise. The declared purpose was underpinned by no guiding principle. For the new RMA, sustainability was to provide the principle to guide decision making affecting the environment. Reasons for having a pre-eminent objective included the reduction of uncertainties about the intent and philosophy of the legislation and the provision of guidance and criteria for decision making and judgement of the effectiveness of the legislation. But most deliberately it was to make a fundamental value judgement to avoid the obscure and uncertain business of weighing competing objectives.[38] It placed an ethical governing principle over all the actions carried out under the Act. In a contribution to the consultation on the issue, the Department of Scientific and Industrial Research stated: 'Sustainability is a general concept and should be applied in law in much the same way as other general concepts such as liberty, equality and justice.'[39] Simon Upton, the Minister for the Environment presiding over the final passage of the legislation, argues in retrospect that sustainable management should be seen as the guiding principle of the RMA, rather than its purpose as stated in the Act, and this seems reasonable. The precise elaboration of that principle was something of a last-minute affair, with final authorship of section 5 being claimed by the then new Minister, although, as we shall see, the concept had a long gestation period and deep roots. However, at the point of the change of government in 1990, with the bill in the House, it still bore the distinctive dirigiste flavour of the prior regime.[40]

In the earlier development of the bill under Geoffrey Palmer, the primary debate over the purpose of the legislation was between a Treasury-supported view that the task was simply to allocate resources to their highest valued use, and the traditional planning view of wise and balanced use. Both held that all values – economic, social and environmental – should be weighed against each other on a case by case basis, the difference being in how such a reckoning should be achieved – by 'wise men' or through the market and cost–benefit analysis. Consultation on the first bill tended to support the elevation of the overriding principle of 'sustainable development', as elaborated by Brundtland, on the view that this integrated all these values. The confusion over the meaning of this newly emerged principle promoted the idea of converting it to become the purpose of the Act, namely 'sustainable management'.[41] Parts of the wording of the standard WCED short definition of sustainable development were actually included in the draft bill, declaring a direct lineage: '"sustainable management" means managing the use, development, and protection of natural and physical resources in a way or at a rate which enables people to meet their needs now without compromising the ability of future generations to meet their own needs'. The general caution with which the idea was treated is indicated by the amendments made by the Parliamentary Select Committee considering the initial bill, which included, among many changes, softening the above statement by replacing 'now without' with 'without unduly'. Such word smithing of the drafts introduced discretionary language in an attempt to ensure the ball was passed back to the 'wise men'.

However, electoral fate intervened and the government changed in 1990. The new Minister commissioned a review of the bill by a group of specialists who argued for the purpose of the RMA to be constructed as a constraining rather than balancing section. Their view was that sustainable management, as a subset of the Brundtland 'sustainable development', was essentially about safeguarding the options of future generations in making use of natural and physical resources. They set about redefining the concept to increase certainty and workability, particularly with respect to present versus future use of resources, and development versus protection of resources. They felt a need to define the relationship between biophysical and socioeconomic considerations, and eventually the definition was shaped by the conception of the biophysical characteristics of resources as a constraint on resource use, characterized as 'the environmental bottom line'. This was a key development in the fundamentals of the legislation.[42] The issue is one that is critical to the sustainability transition in general: the acceptance that we live in an ecologically constrained environment and that it is imprudent to continue ignoring these constraints. In fact the Minister of the time, Simon Upton, made it clear that this was his intent both in his third reading speech to the House[43] and subsequently.[44]

Another important element contributed by the review was to emphasize in this section the required major shift in practice that the Act signalled, from the direction and control of development, to the control of the effects of development on the environment. This was already built into the bill but deserved more explicit notification, in their view, as fundamental to the new regime. This heralded a major shift in planning practice from a presumption that property owners were not allowed to do anything unless they gained permission first, to a situation where any action was allowed unless specifically prohibited on the grounds of its impact on the environment.

The final drafting and review process overseen by the Minister, with the fingers of Cabinet, the Select Committee, the Review Group and various lobby groups all in the pie to some extent, introduced some refinements and subtle changes, but the key elements worked out by the Review Group for the Purposes and Principles remained intact.

To some extent Upton's retrospective rationalization of the intent of the RMA has a revisionist tone to it. In his commentary he emphasizes the old regime planning culture as something that needed to be done away with. In referring to the notion of sustainability, he writes:

> The RMA was undoubtedly ahead of its time in institutionalising this way of thinking. But it remains backward-looking in other respects. I do not for one moment believe that we have yet developed allocation mechanisms to match the progressive policy thrust of the Act. We are still stuck with planning mechanisms that better fit a world of direction and control.[45]

The former Minister likes to align 'sustainability' with the 'progressive' neo-liberal 'thrust' of decentralization of decision making through market-based instruments and reduced government intervention. Despite the potential contribution of such approaches to sustainability, there are many aspects of modern urban development activity that have negative external effects on others, not of a biophysical nature, for which markets do not exist. An open and consultative planning process seems still to be a reasonable means for coordinating interested parties to make decisions on these issues.

The planning tools are written into the RMA – perhaps, at the time, the Minister was too focused on the principles, or perhaps the realization that the change in operational approach was not that profound came later. The rather tortuous definition of 'environment' that supports the inclusion of all aspects of social, economic and cultural life, as well as natural and physical resources, provides the foundation for the continuance of social and economic planning activity that Upton and like-minded critics seem to despise.[46] The crucial difference between the old and new regimes in this regard is that the RMA privileges biophysical environment in weighing costs and benefits. Social and economic impacts of actions are to be considered as part of the broadly defined environment, but the natural environment must not be traded off against socio-economic gain. This is the 'environmental bottom line'.

This definition of environment allows scope for development proposals to be blocked, using the resource consent process, on the grounds that intended activities will have a purely social, cultural or economic adverse impact. According to the detractors of town planning it also allows those planners with a 'global mission', or mere control freaks, to impose their subjective values on the community through statutory plans. The definition of environment is not alone in opening the door to objection to planning provisions or consent applications on social or cultural grounds. Section 7 dealing with amenity values provides strong support, as does the statutory support for Treaty principles. The second schedule to the Act sets out matters that may be provided for in policy statements and plans, and the fourth schedule enumerates matters to be considered in preparing Assessments of Environmental Effects, both of which provide support for the expression and protection of community social, cultural and amenity values. As Grundy points out:

> The requirement for the avoidance, remedying or mitigation of adverse socio-economic and cultural effects on people and communities resulting from resource use is logically consistent with the provision of their social, economic and cultural wellbeing. ... Social, cultural and economic concerns are intimately part of any resource use. Indeed, social, economic and cultural factors are involved in the very definition of a particular feature of the environment as a resource.[47]

Apart from such logical conceptual linkages residing in foundations of the sustainability concept, two other factors are operational. One is that pointed out by Upton above: better mechanisms for dealing with regulation of resource use have not been developed, hence the existing ones must be relied upon. The second is that there is still support in the community, it seems, for the general function of local governments in regulating economic and infrastructure development and associated social and cultural impacts, independent of the impacts on the biophysical environment. That is, there is still support for group input into, and ultimate veto power over, decisions to carry out actions that are considered to have social, cultural and economic externalities. This has been a major role for the local government planning sector in the past, and the elevation of the priority of the biophysical environment in decision making does not somehow negate the rationale for this function. This is further demonstrated, as several authors have pointed out, by a growing trend with councils, having been somewhat restricted in their mandate within the planning instruments of the RMA, to develop a range of other planning documents, supported in part through amendments to the Local Government Act. These extra-RMA initiatives include growth strategies, strategic plans, asset management plans, structure plans and codes of practice.[48]

Grundy and Gleeson[49] argue that the RMA embodies the conflicting political agendas of neo-liberalism and environmentalism, and that this is the source of the confusion and conflict in both the Act and the resulting implementation. They conclude:

> The political intent (underpinned by neo-liberal ideology) of the legislation is to limit intervention in resource allocation decisions and to curtail the role of planning in regional and district affairs in preference to market processes. Paradoxically, however, the general wording of the legislation, and the concept of sustainable development in particular, requires increased intervention and more comprehensive

planning by the state in the interests of the common (environmental and social) good.

Although the observation that both these ideological positions recognized the RMLR process as a critical opportunity to advance their agendas is a valid insight, it seems that in formulation of the Purpose and Principles clauses at least, environmentalism won some vital ground, but neo-liberalism failed to impress. Despite the switch to regulating effects from regulating activities and land use directly, and the general thrusts of rationalization and decentralization of decision making, little of the neo-liberal made it into the core of the RMA. For example, greater emphasis on market-based instruments was rejected by Cabinet.[50] However, just quietly it seems, a recognition that a total separation of biophysical considerations from the social and cultural is neither possible nor desirable, is woven all through the fabric of the Act.

What has happened since the enactment is that a neo-liberal intellectual argument, supported by some business and economic development interests, has called for removal of all powers of local governments to regulate development on any grounds other than biophysical effects on the environment. The (rather spurious) logic seems to be that because the RMA is about protecting environmental bottom lines, therefore local government – the key authorities empowered by the Act – should be restricted to that function only. The proponents of this position generally fail to address the issue that community social and economic planning has been around for a long time and has a rationale that is little to do with protecting the environment – one of the key reasons for reform. These functions are legitimated through community support and the democratic process as well as in legislation. The preparation of district plans and consideration of development proposals is now more open to public input than prior to the reforms. This is also a concern for the detractors of planning. Their position is ultimately more libertarian than neo-liberal in that it is really aimed at reducing group interference in individual action. In the context of the RMA, libertarian advocates recognize only explicit quantifiable biophysical externalities as relevant social concerns, not impacts on social and cultural values. This very selective view emanates from a property rights idealism not likely to take the New Zealand public by storm any time soon. However, this position has always had a strong appeal, as an elegant simplification of messy situations, to decision makers with only a loose grip on its subtleties and hence remains something of a danger to the existing structure of the RMA.

One important issue that is overlooked in the debate over how much state and local government activity is warranted, and the costs, is the fact that reforms such as the RMA not only attempt to make systems more effective and efficient but also raise the level of functionality required from the system. If we require 'sustainability', it must be admitted that this is unlikely to be simple or easy to achieve. It is a high goal and will take a big investment in human resources, organization and complexity. But if it works, the savings in terms of the costs of unsustainability will be very high. Pointing at the new system and saying 'we went in to rationalize and we ended up with a system that is more complex, therefore it didn't work' is to miss the point that the new system is trying to do a much more difficult task. This requires substantial social investment, not only because it is likely to be more costly to run due to its complexity but also, and particularly, due to the costs of transition in the first years or decades.

McShane, for example, in asserting the number of complaints he has received in correspondence from citizens as an indicator of how well councils are administering the Act, points to Waitakere City Council as 'a clear winner in creating anger and grievance among its citizens and professionals'.[51] He says 'there are no economies of scale in the civil service. The largest cities have the most bureaucrats per head'. However, a systematic study has identified this same city council, Waitakere, as being a stand-out in terms of plan quality, having had a real crack at implementing the objectives of the RMA.[52] In his commentary to McShane's review, Nixon (a planner himself) comments:

> I solemnly swear that (good old?) activity based plans are simpler and easier to understand, and are more certain than effects based plans. Of course they also have major disadvantages. However, this is an awful truth that those administering the Act must come to terms with.[53]

The development of the purpose and principles of the RMA had an impressive array of influences. They included political opportunism, bureaucratic pragmatism and ambition for a greater MfE influence, the intellectual traditions of sustainability arising in Stockholm in 1972 and developing strongly in the early 1980s World Conservation Strategy era – reinforced by the Brundtland Report, neo-liberal and libertarian preferences for rationalization of government and reduced intervention, organized and influential sets of rural and industrial interests, a significant body of existing environmental legislation and a well-established town and country planning tradition and bureaucracy. And yet the bill passed unanimously. It is little wonder that some of this seeming consensus can be attributed to statutory ambiguity – the framing of the key principles in such general language that multiple views of the Act's implications for future governance were possible. And yet it is this same ambiguity that has kept the sustainability debate alive and kept at least some looking for improved conceptions of what it might imply in practice.

An alternative interpretation of this ambiguity and non-traditional structure of the legislation is given by the eminent QC Royden Somerville:

The RMA allows for a public law process to enable law, policy, cultural considerations, economics and science to work together to meet its legislative goal of sustainable management which is based on environmental values rather than human rights. The RMA highlights the importance of the new public law concept which goes beyond the traditional understanding of public law, which was about the distribution and exercise of power by the state, or public power. The focus of the new public law is on how the law can influence policy outcomes. The RMA in the main provides for a decentralised environmental administration and decision-making system, and for a more pluralist approach, rather than a formalist (Diceyan) approach. In a pluralist system of environmental law and administration, power is decentralised to enable better bargaining between interest groups. These interests, as well as individuals' interests, are involved when deciding what policies and legal rules should be in place.[54]

The parliamentary system in New Zealand at the time of the passage of the RMA into law was an example of the very concentrated power of unicameral two-party Westminster systems. This enables rapid law making, although this was balanced in this case by an unprecedented effort to consult the public and draw relevant expertise into an open debate. This direct power of executive government has now been moderated by the new mixed member proportional electoral system, but the small scale of New Zealand society means that statutory principles, such as those embodied in the RMA, remain vulnerable to the influence of individuals or focused groups with ideological agendas. This same issue of relatively small numbers of participants in the policy debate can tend to polarize the debate and result in a first-past-the-post policy war rather than a crafted series of compromises or consensus on the issues. Perhaps this is one reason why New Zealand has been able to take such a bold step so early in the general sustainability transition.

While developed under a social reformist – albeit neo-liberally influenced – Labour Government, the RMA has languished under the conservative National and National Coalition administrations, arguably due to a stronger laissez-faire preference for the role of government. It also came perilously close to having radical reduction surgery on its fundamentals, only to be redeemed by the return of Labour to the Treasury benches in 1999. The following sections look more closely at the problems associated with implementation of the RMA in the three main spheres of action: central government, local authorities and the Environment Court.

**Central Government Roles**

If there were problems with the interpretation of the meaning of Act itself, then central government was empowered in various ways to address such failings. It has not been shy to amend the RMA, which has had five amendment Acts totalling 191 pages and 369 sections.[55] None of these, however, addressed the core issues disputed in Part II of the Act. The Amendment Bill 1999, proposing to simplify critical sections, was not passed before the government changed. Many of the key changes have since been abandoned, and the remainder of the Bill has yet to be passed.[56]

As to the role of central government in the implementation of the RMA, several major criticisms have emerged since enactment. Almost universal is a condemnation of the lack of application of National Environmental Standards and National Policy Statements.[57] The RMA is clearly an example, enabling legislation,[58] 'thus reposing in the decision maker the responsibility of determining how best to promote the Act's purpose in the particular circumstances'.[59] Somerville comments:

> The RMA itself has very few rules for the management of natural and physical resources. Instead it provides a framework for the making of environmental policy statements and plans by central and local government. It is this sequential system of subordinate instruments which is intended to give legislative effect to the purpose and principles of the RMA.[60]

A different view put by one of Young's commentators (Clive Anstey) is that:

> The RMA is all about process; for me it's all about spelling out the context and spelling out the process to the people who are going to get engaged with it. It's not about an NPS spelling it out for them.[61]

This latter view seems another case of retrospective rationalization and perhaps wishful thinking. Somerville has more the measure of the Act as written. In the absence of the central government's contribution to the sequential system of subordinate instruments, the framework is missing a vital link between helm and rudder, leaving local authorities to flounder. This is at great cost of duplication of effort and inconsistency of rules across jurisdictions. Individuals are forced to litigate environmental standards on individual applications on a local basis. Williams comments:

> The inaction of central government has made implementation of the 1991 legislation the more fraught and its results more uncertain. The Government's course may in part be explicable by the procedural requirements attending the development of standards and policy statements. But Government has long known of this problem, and has only recently begun steps that may overcome it. Meantime a significant vacuum remains.[62]

In a major recent study of local government performance under the RMA, Ericksen et al. found that the only existing example of an NPS – the New Zealand Coastal Policy Statement – linked to regional coastal plans had considerably lessened the problems of identification and conflict in council planning on the coast.

It was a reasonably easy task for planners, in consultation with their scientific advisors, to align local policies with national policies. The consensus about values, which the New Zealand Coastal Policy Statement (NZCPS) expresses, meant that these were not re-litigated region by region. Rather the focus shifted to methods by which the objectives and policies of the NZCPS could be implemented.

Our research shows serious impediments common to many local councils searching for solutions to local problems that relate to a lack of clear national policy on other key principles in the Act.[63]

NPS and NES mechanisms are a central and clear set of policy levers for central government to direct implementation of the Act. The fact that they have not been used at all points to several strands of explanation including, lack of understanding or deliberate disregard of the RMA mechanisms, ideological opposition to 'intervention', and lack of resources for the Ministry to carry out its mandate. These are briefly discussed in the following paragraphs.

*Lack of understanding or deliberate disregard*   At the time the RMA was passed into law, the National Party Government was only about eight months old and was in a determined cost cutting mode with a eye to reducing taxes. Simon Upton was surprised to be given a portfolio and had not been shadow spokesperson on the environment prior to the election. That position had been filled by Rob Storey who was opposed to the whole idea of the RMA. Perhaps it was thought prudent not to overturn the significant reform efforts made to date, especially since the local government reforms to support the RMA were already in place. Starting again would be costly. But it seems the heavyweights in the new government may not have been too interested. Upton was the junior Minister in more ways than one, being the youngest member of the Government, whereas Labour had had the Deputy, later Prime Minister, as the Bill's sponsor. Whether understood or not, the fundamentals of the RMA were rejected from the start by at least one senior colleague of the Minister for the Environment. Some have accused Upton and Storey of both being opposed to the use of NPSs, but Upton deflects the accusation on to the Ministry, arguing that they had counselled against their use, for example to regulate landfills.[64] Commenting shortly after the passing of the RMA, Buhrs and Bartlett have this to say:

> The Resource Management Act is not self-implementing; its ultimate influence on environmental policy development and environmental quality is not predetermined by the language of the Act only. Should environmental policy become a high priority agenda item of some present or future Cabinet or influential Environment Minister, the opportunity will exist for policy entrepreneurs to contribute to significant policy development *under* the Resource Management Act, in addition to the usual statutory route.[65] (emphasis in the original)

*Ideological opposition to the mechanism*   Upton's ideological credentials were clearer than most having 'already espoused his Hayekian philosophy in *The Withering of the State*', as Young comments, 'displaying his wariness of government involvement in matters not, according to strict economic rationalist theory, its business'.[66] Hence it is a reasonable speculation that the new government may have proceeded with the legislation in the belief that it should work without central government 'interference' (read 'involvement'), that it was (or should be) devolution of power and responsibility to local government, not just (as it was written) mere delegation. The RMA as part of deregulation and responsibility shedding – leave it alone, and if it goes wrong, blame Labour, then fix it up or dump it altogether. To some extent the Ministry may have adopted 'the attitude of the day ... that local government should be left to fend for itself'[67] as a justifying defence mechanism, given its inability to do much else without funding.

Another twist on this theme is the case made by Buhrs and Bartlett that the RMA represents a shift towards the further privileging of business interests in the planning process. They describe three ways that the Act alters the balance in this way from the old regime, including the strong presumption favouring private property rights with respect to land use, the discouragement of preventative anticipatory policy, and the requirement for assessment of costs and benefits of policies. They then state:

> There is, of course, the potential for this bias to be counterbalanced by the active, assertive involvement of central government in this process, notably through the significant powers of the Minister for the Environment to issue national policy statements, to set national environmental standards, and to issue guidance for the implementation of the Resource Management Act.[68]

The fact that these are the things that the Minister has consistently failed to do tends to support the prediction of this 'do nothing' option as a deliberate policy stance to favour development interests under the new regime.

*Lack of resources*   The new government turned off the budget tap to the Ministry for the Environment. Upton admits he subsequently failed to secure increased budget for MfE.[69] Without staff capacity and operational funding the MfE could not effectively research and develop proposals for NPSs and NESs, nor could it provide education and training, to councils or the public, that would address issues causing concern in implementation. The process set out in the Act for NPS development has been criticized as overly complex and costly – involving a board of enquiry comprising three to five members and an extensive public submission and hearing process.[70] Again, this smacks of retrospective rationalization attempting to justify the government's lack of financial commitment to the policies of its own – albeit adopted – legislation.

The Act's requirements in this regard could have been amended at any of several legislative opportunities and were not; and in any case, cost here is only relative to the overall budget of the Ministry voted by the Government. In terms of process and the sequential or hierarchical structure of policies, cutting costs at this primary level doesn't make much economic sense. In the same terms the logic of the system for NPS demands both full public participation – for legitimation of their impact on local policies and plans – and a 'difficult' process – to ensure such policies are not subject to change at the whim of executive government. Once in place the NPSs are designed to have a formative impact on policy statements and plans at both regional and district levels – instruments with a lifetime that will exceed a decade.

Over the decade since enactment there have been continuous calls for the development of NPSs on a range of topics, including the interpretation of the purpose and principles, greenhouse emissions, forestry, biodiversity, the relationship between section 8 of the Act and the provisions of the Treaty of Waitangi, rural subdivision and landscape values, subdivision and development of coastal land, mining on conservation land, and sustainable (farm) land management. Uniform standards for 'environmental bottom lines' to be established for such matters as air and water quality are obvious candidates for NESs. However, presumably in order to avoid both the cost and the loss of executive control over content implied in the prescribed processes for development of statutory instruments, the Government has opted instead for the development of sets of guidelines on a few topics, for example on water control in 1992 and 1994 and air quality in 1998. In January 1999 it was announced that an NPS on biodiversity would be developed to explain section 6c of the RMA.[71] Momentum has now finally picked up on this issue with the Labour Government carrying this initiative forward and looking at other possibilities.[72]

Another serious criticism of the role of central government in implementation of the Act is its lack of effort in outreach. For such a profound change to both philosophy of governance and the practice of planning and resource management the Ministry has generated little public information, let alone an active public education programme on a scale commensurate with the impact of the Act. MfE has also conspicuously failed to provide support for local government with capacity building, training and technical expertise. Critics have put this failure down to the funding issue[73] but it can be safely assumed that there were some firmly held views that underpinned lack of action, either in Cabinet or at MfE, or both. An example of essential public education on the RMA, the Ministry publication 'Your Guide to the Resource Management Act' was accessed as a PDF file from the MfE website in early 2002.[74] This document is well prepared and the only one of its kind found – a practical reference in lay language – but is marked 'Draft Only' and dated January 1999, more than seven years after the legislation was passed. To give the Ministry its due, they have produced other guides to the Act and public involvement in it, but the strategy has hardly been proactive, with the appearance of most of these occurring since 1998, even the simplest of information pamphlets aimed at the general public.

On the role of public education and advocacy, Young writes:

> The funds shortage that characterised the implementation of the RMA was so severe that the MfE was forced to drop most of its statutory obligations to educate the population into the new ways of thinking. ... As Minister, Simon Upton wrote some fine speeches and newspaper and website pieces, but the real financial commitment to ensure an informed populace and their newly decentralised councils never took place.[75]

This criticism regarding outreach by the Ministry may, however, be missing a key issue of strategy. A relatively large research and development funding mechanism, administered by MfE and established to generate more information about how to do sustainable management, has been in existence since 1994. This is the Sustainable Management Fund (SMF). The stated goals of the SMF are to support, through co-funding, practical environmental management initiatives that have a significant public good component. Such national benefit may be derived, for example, through a project's role as a model of management practice for wider adoption, in the dissemination of information, in the development of protocols for monitoring, or in the provision of training for Councils.

This funding mechanism may to some extent have been the destination for much of the funding that might otherwise have been used by the Ministry in outreach, and may represent an outsourcing strategy. Considerable sums have been allocated through the SMF. Some 361 funded projects are listed on the SMF website,[76] with grants ranging in value from $2500 to over half a million (NZ) dollars. Contractors include local government, *iwi* and other community groups, producer organizations and private consultants. However, the programme took several years to ramp up, with most activity being post 1998. No documentation was found evaluating the effectiveness of the SMF. This certainly should be a priority if it has not been carried out before, both in terms of the effectiveness of projects in delivering national benefits in a cost-effective manner and the coverage of needs for outreach provided by the programme.

**Local Government Roles**

Regional councils have responsibility for management of key regional resources such as rivers, air and water quality, and soils. Although the presumption about permitted land use prevailing before the RMA – that you can't do anything without permission – has been reversed, for these major (mainly common-pool) resources, managed at the regional level, the old rule still effectively applies. This makes explicit the public interest in the use of these resources and recognizes the fact that many such uses produce environmental externalities. Hence regional councils need to survey and maintain an inventory of the natural resources of their region and produce policy statements and management plans that both recognize the concerns expressed in the Act and subordinate national-level instruments, and provide guidance for integrated management by territorial local authorities (TLAs – city and district councils).[77] This places integrated management at the core of the operational administration of the RMA.

### Integration and efficiency: confused imperatives?

In the absence of any NPSs or NESs that address the meaning of integrated management in a more specific way than in the Act itself, it is left to the councils to define it through their policies, plans and practices. However, the Act does provide for a range of mechanisms to enable integration, as summarized by Frieder:

> Some of the mechanisms are: transfer of powers, delegation of functions, an integrated planning hierarchy for making national and local policies consistent and for coordinating RMA plans with other plans (eg iwi management plans and annual plans), combined planning, cross boundary matters, consultation, assessment of environmental effects, notification, pre-hearing mediation, joint hearings, combined hearings and coordinating consent processes.
>
> In sum, the RMA provides for integration of the biophysical environment. It provides for integration of institutional responses. It recognises the existence of various and competing resource values and provides for a public process to establish community objectives and goals. In nearly every function, duty and power conferred on local government there is an opportunity for integration.[78]

In one of only a handful of published empirical studies of council performance found, Frieder looked for evidence of integration both in regulatory areas, such as statutory instruments, processes and duties, and in non-regulatory areas, such as organizational structure and process, communication and coordination. She found that in general the concept of integrated environmental management was not well enough understood at a conceptual or applied level by front-line practitioners for significant benefits to be derived from it. It was construed as meaning 'one stop shopping' for development approval (resource consents), with the key benefit being cost saving for both the applicant and administration. Mid-level managers had a better understanding of the ideas but viewed the concept of integrated management as abstract and not useful in helping them with what they define as their primary concern: fulfilling their statutory obligations under the Act.

This is a retreat from sustainability as the animating idea of the RMA. Frieder identifies the failure of the Ministry to communicate or provide leadership and clarity in the realm of either the concepts or applied objectives. In her words, 'without well defined outcomes, the notion of IEM [Integrated Environmental Management] is daunting, even threatening, to the resource manager who is unaccustomed to looking across borders, sectors or disciplines'.[79] In a broader and more detailed systematic study of council performance (the PUCM study[80]), Ericksen et al. concur that lack of clarity in the mandate for councils, combined with the failure to provide resources for capability building in central and local government, badly compromised the institutional system created by the RMA. They make the point that failure at the centre of the system, such as lack of clarity in the Act or in official interpretation, weakens all councils' ability to produce quality planning documents. Results from the study show that a majority of council planners found key provisions in the Act unclear, particularly in Part II, Purpose and Principles, and also in the sections setting out council functions. Neither was the issue of the relationship between councils and Maori well understood. All these sections could be subject to clarification and interpretation through NPS or even amendment of the Act.

**Planning culture and capacity**
Such confusion about the nature and boundaries of the mandate of councils reduces the ability of councillors and staff to develop commitment to their role and tasks and creates consequent selection pressures on staff, staffing levels and demand for training. In these circumstances the retreat to focus on efficient production of measurable outputs, such as resource consent processing times, is understandable. And the MfE reinforces this to some degree. A key annual feedback document provided to local government by the Ministry is the report on their annual survey of local authorities.[81] This reports quantitative statistics on Council performance in resource consent processing. The emphasis is on numbers of consents processed, the time taken, percentages of consents appealed and notified, and so on. This focus on easily measurable performance has not gone unnoticed by the current Minister for the Environment, who takes the opportunity to remind practitioners in her Foreword to the 2001 report that such statistics are only one indicator of performance under the RMA.

Greater attention and emphasis at the council level on understanding the legislation and on discussing and resolving locally appropriate interpretations of mandate can make a difference. Frieder noted in her study that a council where a member of staff had had a prior role in central government development of the legislation had a much more developed view of their mandate and role and a better understanding of integrated management.

A recent study of urban planning issues under the RMA[82] makes the point that the reforms to the Local Government Act 1974, carried out in concert with the RMLR, contributed greatly to the culture of efficiency and accountability to statutory obligations noted by Frieder. The amalgamation of local authorities, the requirement that they adopt more business-based administrative practices and re-badging of officials as managers and CEOs, all contributed to reshaping the local government work culture. Many older staff resigned and some senior managers were recruited from the private sector. Annual strategic plans were made mandatory and in 1996 further amendment introduced ten-year strategic and capital works plans. These business planning practices, apart from focusing council planning and producing more transparent results, have opened up new avenues for urban design and social and economic development planning, to some extent displaced from the RMA framework.[83]

So it seems that the dual emphases of the reforms – efficient administration and integrated effects-based resource management – have to some extent brought about a separation of urban design and economic development planning from resource management. Within councils these are now being dealt with in many cases by separate work groups without much cross-communication. In the planning process itself Frieder found evidence of recognition of the need for integration of a sort. This is most well understood in terms of complex resource systems such as water, but also in cross-media linkages and at a policy level in recognizing the need to integrate Maori values into planning.[84]

At the TLA level change from the entrenched Town and Country Planning regime has been slow and patchy.[85] Neglected by central government on policy, extension, education and training for capacity building, some council staff took on the role of salvaging what they could of the old regime. This certainly seems to be reflected in the current criticisms of local authority performance as overly controlling and anti-development. Prominent critics have played up the 'command and control' mentality of supposed planning zealots, and McShane has asserted that they generally dominate over the views of elected councillors.[86] Nixon, in a practitioner's response to this accusation, says:

> I can assure Mr McShane from experience that the role of elected representatives and other professionals is as important in the formulation of plans by councils as is that of planners. Council planning staff are frequently the target of attack both from within and outside councils for alleged failure to promote greater intervention.[87]

It seems that professional planners whose job description is in part written into the RMA would be likely to be at least as well appraised of its provisions as would local politicians or the public at large. However, the PUCM findings are not very reassuring that these levels of understanding are adequate. The findings on organizational capability in policy and planning development are salutary and serve to remind us that skills and resources are often difficult to come by 'out there', particularly in smaller units of local government. Erikson et al. note:

> When capability is strong, the quality of plans is significantly greater. (Capability is: commitment, i.e., dedication of councillors and staff to plan; and capacity, i.e., quality and quantity of resources available for planning.) We found many troubling gaps throughout the local government planning process.
>
> - Generally, effects-based planning and the plan quality principles were not understood well enough by plan makers.
> - Inadequate time was devoted to strategic thinking about the mandate and to project management.
> - Authors of plans often failed to write policy in a rigorous fashion and appeared to lack the technical skills to conduct research as indicated by the weak fact-base in plans.
> - There was too little emphasis on research and too much on consultation at the start, and too little consultation at the end when methods and rules needed community testing.
> - Many councils placed a bare minimum staff in core planning groups, with about 50% of district councils having less than one full-time planner.
> - Councillors, most of whom had little knowledge of the mandate and plan-making principles, set unrealistic deadlines, often aimed at notifying plans ahead of elections.
> - Many councils committed relatively large amounts of resources to making plans, truncated the consultative process where it mattered most, then had to conduct substantial plan variations in response to strong public reaction following notification.
> - Just over half of councils understood the mandate with respect to the Treaty of Waitangi and Maori interests philosophically, but failed to follow through due to lack of political commitment and capacity.[88]

Section 35 of the RMA requires councils to monitor the effectiveness of plans, including the exercise of resource consents. Further preliminary results from the continuing PUCM study found little attempt by councils to measure the quality of plan implementation. This part of the study investigated links between plan quality (as assessed by earlier research referred to above) and plan policies, and mitigation techniques used in consent conditions (specifically for dealing with issues of stormwater, urban amenity values and *iwi* consultation).[89] The results found little direct relationship between plan quality and the number of techniques used in consents. For example, although most policies in plans called for new and innovative techniques to be used for stormwater, most consents specified the use of conventional 'pipe it' techniques. The study's assessment of the state of planning practice found:

- that the quality of information required for similar resource consents varied greatly between councils
- little evidence of consent monitoring (4 per cent)
- costs of consent process varied greatly as well as the allocation of costs between public and applicant
- minimal public involvement in consent process (3 per cent notified)
- issues of concern to Maori not well addressed through consultation
- conservative techniques favoured over best practice
- contextual factors highly influential in implementation processes.

As explanatory factors the study again found that commitment and capacity were important to both plan quality and implementation.

> We found that smaller councils, especially rural ones, do not have the capacity to implement their plans effectively … In these councils, and some of the larger ones, the political commitment is more likely focused on promoting growth and development than improving environmental quality. Overcoming this implementation gap in district councils so that improved environmental outcomes are promoted requires capacity building initiatives by central government and regional councils.
>     Our study found that the quality of plan implementation [ie environmental outcomes] may be less influenced by the quality of plans than by socioeconomic and organisational factors. It is, however, still important to continue improving plans and their implementation because, among other things, plans set out a consensus of community values about the environment. Further, the process of plan development helps to clarify goals and build commitment to those goals. Perhaps the most important observation is that, in the short term, building council capacity and commitment, rather than focusing on plan quality, may be more likely to lead to better environmental outcomes.[90]

These findings serve to remind us that change takes time, especially in smaller communities. Despite the seeming rational-comprehensive approach taken to reform, the enabling nature of the RMA means that change can (and in many cases must) be incremental. But such change does not proceed inexorably in a coordinated and somehow predestined manner just because the law has changed. As both of the key studies used here have argued, we must look to incentive and accountability structures, as well as educative processes and policy leadership from the centre, to encourage change.

**Environmental assessment and monitoring**
A critical area stressed by both Frieder and the PUCM study is the weak fact base. The RMA requires councils to conduct assessments of the state of the

environment, to select and prioritize issues and to develop the best policies for meeting objectives. Although an initial national state of environment report was produced in 1997 there is no structured programme of data collection in place involving local authorities. This means data formats and what information is collected will vary from one authority to another. TLAs are also required to monitor both consent compliance and the performance of their plans in terms of environmental outcomes, but few have developed the capacity to do so adequately.

The PUCM study found that, of all their eight principles for assessment of plan quality, Quality of Fact Base scored lowest for both regional policy statements (1.2 out of 10) and district plans (0.62 out of 10).[91]

> These results indicate the absence of analytical rationales for defining and prioritising issues and selecting policy alternatives. The weak fact base also partially explains the generally lacklustre scores for the principles of issue identification and monitoring. Without a strong fact base it is difficult to clearly define issues and to set up appropriate monitoring of environmental outcomes for evaluating plan performance.

At a national level there are grave deficiencies in knowledge of the state of the environment, and at local level it is worse. At the time of Frieder's study in late 1997 less than 10 per cent of local authorities had reported baseline knowledge of environmental quality. The study noted that adequate feedback mechanisms in planning processes were also lacking, so that even if data were available the pathways to bring new information into a process of plan improvement do not exist.[92]

The development of the annual survey of local authorities (mentioned above) since Frieder's report may have answered some of the need for feedback mechanisms. In addition the development of regular monitoring and reporting of the state of the environment, and of monitoring of resource consent conditions and plan performance under section 35 of the RMA, will provide information essential to planning under the Act. The question is, when will the system come up to speed in this regard? The Ministry's 2001 survey report[93] stated that 'many local authorities are still in the early stages of state of the environment reporting' with only 13 of 70 TLAs producing state of the environment reports in 1999–2000. The same document reports that TLAs have spent an average of $2.1M producing their district plans, but spend only $56 000 per annum, on average, on section 35 monitoring. This includes (or should) the state of the environment, the suitability and effectiveness of policy statements and plans, the exercise of any delegated or transferred functions, powers or duties, and compliance with resource consent conditions.

In a further initiative MfE have established an environmental performance indicators programme. A first framework document on national indicators was published in 1996, followed in 1997 by proposals for air, freshwater and lands. However, as of mid-2002 there were no agreed indicators for these critical issues under the RMA. The marine environment, solid waste, hazardous wastes and contaminated sites alone have confirmed standard indicators. MfE has begun working with regional councils on a 'partnership approach' to sharing environmental information and implementing a national environmental monitoring system. This approach is to be applauded. However, one is left wondering why it has taken a full decade since implementation of the RMA to initiate such a programme.

## Local political economy

There is one further issue at the local planning level that should not be overlooked.

> Business has a generally privileged place in politics ... [and] is most privileged at the local level. Local politics tend to revolve around matters of land use and economic development, dominated by informal networks of local builders, developers, bankers, lawyers, retail merchants, and politicians. To the extent that environmental values can be made congruent with these vested interests, they will flourish; to the extent that they can be painlessly afforded, they will be tolerated and indulged. But to the extent that they challenge local development and economic growth, the power of the vested interest will swing against them in most places.[94]

This reminds us of the pragmatic political economy that is the basis of local body politics and that there are powerful proximate forces acting in local planning arenas outside of the heady concerns of sustainability and integrated environmental management. Such considerations also provide a primary explanation for the lack of progress on implementation of sustainable management in rural areas, noted by Salmon,[95] despite a high level of official awareness of the severity of the problems caused by rural land use. In rural regional and district authorities many of the elected councillors not only represent farmers politically but are also rural landholders themselves.

The provisions in the RMA for notification of resource consent applications have been criticized as allowing councils too much discretion, providing a loophole to avoid scrutiny of proposals. If consent applications are publicly notified they are then open to submissions, objections and a formal hearing. And to have standing to appeal a decision to the Environment Court a party must have been a submitter to the original consideration of the consent. Hence the discretion that councils have to not notify applications is a significant power. Avoiding notification becomes the main game for developers wanting fast results, and the discretion is a means for developer friendly councils to fast-track consent processes.[96] The Ministry reports that a steady average of around 5 per cent of consent applications are notified, and this falls to 3 per cent for TLAs only.[97] This issue requires further scrutiny to establish the cause of such a seemingly low rate of felt need for public involvement in the consent process. The problem is not necessarily that too few applications are being notified, but it is certainly the case that more information is required.

**The Role of the Environment Court**

The Environment Court hears appeals by resource consent applicants or other parties to consent procedures who are unhappy with the decisions of the decision-making authority, and matters concerning the contents of policy statements and plans.

The crucial weaknesses and uncertainties in the institutional food-chain highlighted in this case study tend to accumulate to the extent that, in many cases, dispute over regulatory outcomes is inevitable. From enactment there has been a high level of demand on the Environment Court, exacerbated by a history of significant underresourcing of the Court,[98] with accompanying costly delays in settlement of resource consents and changes to plans and policies of up to three years.[99] From the start the Court has expressed frustration at the lack of specific rules in the legislation. The failure of the Government to promulgate NPS to clarify and develop the principles of the Act and NES to set environmental standards has led to inconsistency across regional policy statements and plans in the way the Act is applied and to the litigation of these issues on a case-by-case basis.

There has been some expectation that the Court would, early in the implementation, deal with a few fundamental issues in precedent-setting cases,[100] such as the meaning of Section 5 and the other issues set out in Part II of the Act. A 1997 review of case law found an inconsistent approach taken by the Court, sometimes supporting a balancing view and sometimes the environmental bottom line.

> The dominant feature of the cases considering s5 is the inconsistency of reasoning. The non-specific language of s5 provides an opportunity for flexibility in decision making, but the danger is that the complexity of the language will result in inconsistent and uncertain decisions. The evidence to date suggests this is occurring.[101]

Despite consistent political rhetoric on the intent of the Parliament in respect of Section 5, both in the final reading speech and in subsequent speeches and published legal papers by the Minister responsible at the time of enactment, the courts seem to prefer to interpret inconsistently than to take such advice. It seems the only cure for this, as it would be for many other ills of the regime, is to develop the purpose and principles of the Act through national policy statements. The National Party led Government of the 1990s stubbornly refused to initiate this process until their eleventh hour, but it seems the current Labour Government (at 2002) is at least prepared now to proceed with the mechanism.

Clearly the Environment Court has been put in a difficult position by the combination of the Act as it is and the lack of policy action by central government. The higher up the chain issues are dealt with, the more certainty is created at the lower levels. The system is designed to deal with complex systems and issues that are strongly dependent on context, with decisions being made at the most decentralized level appropriate – the subsidiarity principle. The Environment Court catches the issues left unresolved by the hierarchy, but where high order rules are missing it ends up with a large caseload and having to consider fundamental issues. Had the Ministry for the Environment been resourced to continue to work on policy development and extension at the rate they did in the RMLR period, and a few NPS boards of inquiry been established early in the piece, many of the issues frustrating the Court would have been dealt with by now. The costs of delay and litigation incurred through neglect have certainly been greater than would have been the costs of policy development.

But there is another important aspect of policy for sustainability that is reflected in the cases heard by the Environment Court; that is, risk and uncertainty. Risk and uncertainty are inherent in sustainability policy issues and are in fact defining characteristics. The hierarchy of rules provided for by the Act should progressively reduce uncertainty for local decision makers in the realm of collective values and objectives while coordinated information systems do the same in the realm of scientific knowledge. These systems help in risk assessment but cannot eliminate the uncertainty inherent in complex social, economic, institutional and environmental systems. Where the subsidiarity principle is applied to decision making, responsibility for risk and uncertainty associated with decisions is thereby borne at appropriate political level. Leaving such decisions to the courts is inappropriate in unfairly passing political responsibility for decisions involving inherent scientific uncertainty over outcomes, to the judiciary.

A statistical study of Environment Court records, reported in 2000, revealed evidence highlighting the problem of dealing with disputes over issues involving scientific uncertainty. The Court, it appears, relies heavily on the testimony of expert witnesses in such cases. Where potential environmental effects are contested the study found that the outcome of cases is significantly predicted by the presence and ratio of the number of expert witnesses testifying for each side. Hence to have a reasonable chance of carrying the Court an NGO, for example challenging a major development, must be able to at least match the number of expert witnesses testifying for the vested interests involved.[102]

In a recent paper on dealing with risk and uncertainty under the RMA, Somerville comments:

> To try and depoliticise environmental policy-making by expecting a court to develop strong precautionary environmental risk management policies to be included in policy and planning instruments in resource consent and designation conditions is unrealistic because a court is not in a position to undertake robust policy creation.
>
> ... The Environment Court operates more effectively when it addresses evidence against pre-established central and local government environmental policies and standards and is not required to speculate in their absence where risk–benefit evidence may be uncertain. The role of the Environment Court is not to be a national environmental regulator.
>
> ... Formulating national policy statements under the RMA by using an independent board of inquiry depoliticises a regulatory response as much as possible. The courts can also become involved if these instruments are ultra vires the purpose of the RMA.
>
> ... When national policy statements which incorporate the precautionary principle are in place, the specialist environment court can develop legal principles to guide primary decision-makers as they determine what an acceptable level of environmental risk is.[103]

One last issue in relation to court proceedings is the funding of litigants bringing cases of public interest. The original draft RM Bill introduced by the Labour Government in 1989 included provisions to establish a fund for this purpose. This was disposed of in the review carried out on the change of government in 1990. Labour returned to power in 1999 and within a year had established this mechanism at a cost of around $1M per year. Again, this points to ideological differences in the oversight of the RMA as being not only operative but also, considering the relative costs of various facets of the workings of the Act, often of greater significance than the financial costs of initiatives.

## LEARNING FROM THE NEW ZEALAND EXPERIENCE

The RMA is an example of institutional reform that lies toward the rational-comprehensive end of a continuum intergrading this extreme with the incremental approach to policy and institutional change. It represents a phase shift not only in its coverage and integration of sustainability issues under a single legislative framework but also in the value set enunciated by the law and in the resulting general framing of policy for resource management (social policy learning). In turn this has redefined the role of local government, their rationale, responsibilities, functions and duties. This is social policy learning as defined in Chapter 1, but the normative change was by no means general in the community. The new set of values resulted from a convergence of influences competing in an open (pluralistic) political process. However, the dominant discourse – in the sense that it is expressed most strongly in the legislation – derives from the international sustainable development debate. To the extent that the operation of the RMA is now promoting a general change in social attitudes towards sustainability, this approach to the sustainability transition can be characterized as 'normative push'.

The RMLR was 'an enormous and impassioned effort' and despite the tinkering, both before the Bill was passed and through subsequent amendment, the RMA remains a substantial achievement in the statutory expression of the spirit and substance of the sustainability idea. The detail of legislative drafting can always be contested, and has been in this case due to substantive divisions on what the Act should be doing, but at some stage, to paraphrase a key influence on the genesis of the Act, we must stop tinkering with it and get on with walking the walk.[104]

The need to reform both the administration of resource management and local government structures, and their convenient combination, created the platform for a broader vision of sustainable development. The advent of the Brundtland Report at the time of the RMLR supplied, readily available, a politically viable synthesis of the issues. The reforms brought together the range of resource management functions and to some extent integrated them, and linked them into a broad system of environmental policy, management and administration. It was not totally comprehensive and integrated but it represented a huge leap forward for New Zealand and an outstanding attempt by international standards.

A full-blown attempt to legislate for sustainable development was resisted as evidenced by the choice of 'sustainable management of natural and physical resources' as the central purpose of the RMA. However, the objectives and principles of sustainability had their impact on the drafting in the critical definitions of 'environment' and 'sustainable management', and in numerous other sections of the Act. The structure of the hierarchy of policy, rules and plans provides for the integration of national (and international), regional and local concerns. Instruments are available at each level to define and protect environmental values with the force of law. Ecological sustainability is given precedence over socioeconomic concerns, but group values are given weight where social externalities result from private actions. The 'environmental bottom line' is to be protected but social and economic values are recognized as an integral part of resource use decision making.

Perhaps we can theorize that it was the animating idea of sustainability – and a determination that this unique opportunity for institutional reform should not be used to bolster the modernist project but to intervene somehow in the stream of its cultural development – that produced an Act that is so provocative. It seems to embody the spirit of sustainability in many ways – not as a perfectly designed legal construction and yet well enough to accommodate Somerville's 'New Public Law' analysis. Law for sustainability cannot be deterministic in a policy sense, because policy for sustainability must be adaptive in the face of uncertainty and variation in context. Therefore law must allow policy to adjust to circumstance and changing knowledge. Indeed, the courts participate in the formulation of policy by making judgements about whether particular policy interpretations are in compliance with both the letter and spirit of the Act. That a new kind of law and judicial practice is required for sustainability should not come as a great surprise given the unique character of the problem set.[105] In the end, everything flows back to the purpose of the Act, the abode of what is undoubtedly a somewhat mystical vision of a sustainable future. The RMA itself has bequeathed to future generations the responsibility for working out how they will refine and achieve the vision.

The RMA and the wider New Zealand environmental and local government reforms demonstrate that large-scale coordinated structural change to promote sustainability (government learning) is possible. In attempting to integrate across policy fields as well as spatial and administrative scales the reforms have created a complex dynamic system for the production of law, policy, management rules and information. Drawing on systems theory, the problems associated with the system in practice to some extent reflect a lack of built-in redundancy. However, the key operational failure is clearly identified in this study as lack of active participation and support by executive central government and the key ministry following passing of the legislation. There is not much chance of building provisions into legislation for bypassing Cabinet when they choose not to act.

But perhaps there is a lesson here in identifying a need to insulate sustainability capability from short-term political change. This might be achieved through long-term commitments of funding through trusts or reserve funds that are allocated to sustainability initiatives through mechanisms independent of political control. Producing realistic estimates of the budget requirements for implementation before legislation is passed is no doubt possible, although not common, and is less likely where support for particular initiatives is already weak. Another option is the inclusion of provisions at constitutional level to obligate governments to provide adequate resources for the pursuit of sustainability, but this is not likely before a more generous broad acceptance of the concept as a fundamental principle of governance. More realistically, lessons from the case study of the European Union environment policy (Chapter 3) indicate possible structural features that can isolate sustainability policy subsystems from political change. Reiterative mechanisms in particular have served the EU system well and are missing from the New Zealand framework. A regular periodic policy cycle to revisit government commitments to principles – and thereby require the development of their meaning and implications in the intervening years – and review practice could assist.

Hence attempts at ambitious reform should be encouraged, but proposals need to be realistic about the degree of political commitment and leadership required in such a complex and uncertain area. Sustainability requires a high social investment – like education, health, welfare – because it is an investment in the future well-being of the entire population and society as a whole. As with these other areas, we neglect sustainability policy at our peril. 'Future generations' can seem rather distant, but we know it does not take that long for lack of investment in these other areas to show up in social outcomes. Despite the inevitability of making mistakes, lack of action on sustainability is not a long-term option.

What should not be forgotten when considering the costs of reform of institutional systems for sustainability, amongst the heat and dust and effort to build cost-effective administrations for efficient allocation, is that sustainability substantially raises the bar for institutional achievement. The long-term costs of unsustainability are, by definition, high if not infinite. It is not against the inefficiencies of current administration of natural resource management that we should measure the costs of sustainable institutions but against the future costs of lack of early action.

Another issue highlighted in this case study is the distribution of complexity and uncertainty in an institutional system dealing with sustainability issues. Conceptual complexity is high at the level of the values, principles and overall institutional design. Complex and extensive consultation and policy development processes are invoked in the development of NPS and other national-level instruments. At the regional authority level complexity is manifest in catchment-wide biophysical processes, and in territorial local authorities the definition and integration of specific social and environmental values with economic development and infrastructure planning comprise a complex and detailed task. Each level in the schema has its own set of complex problems to deal with. It is just as much of a mistake to assume that functions at the local government level are simple and straightforward as to think that changing rules is all that central government needs to do.

In dealing with complex environmental, economic, social and institutional systems some uncertainty is irreducible. To the extent that uncertainties are reducible, this is promoted by information flow. The inaction of central government in generating and distributing information throughout the system is a key cause of the problems experienced in implementation of the RMA. The production of an information hierarchy or network is an essential aspect of the framework. Information of general applicability produced higher up the chain prevents costly duplication at the lower levels. Where this fails and each lower level unit must produce the same information separately, not only does this produce variation in a range of functions where coordination is desirable but also this activity displaces effort that should be applied to the actual functional responsibilities of the administrative level. The RMA case suggests that, at the end of the line, it is generation of information on the biophysical environment – data gathering, assessment and monitoring – that suffers the most. In the final analysis, if we do not know much about the state of the environment, clever policy is unlikely to save us.

In the case of the RMA there has been an, albeit belated, recognition of the need to generate information, but the approach until very recently has been somewhat ad hoc, providing contestable funds, and not directed policy effort. Hence large numbers of reports have been generated from generally useful work; but have they got out there where they could be used, and have they covered the urgent priorities? Evidence such as is available would suggest not, or at least not yet. The same amount of funding for the development of policy, directed research and training, consensus processes such as NPSs, and coordination of information, applied from day one, may well have been much more effective. The hands-off approach to implementation taken by the National Party-led governments during the 1990s seems to reflect ideology and policy fashion, whereas the RMA itself provides for structure and process that together could represent government learning in the sense explored in this study. The ongoing implementation experience of the RMA may well learn much from the somewhat confused early years, but this is by no means assured. The Labour-led coalition re-elected in 2002 has plans for RMA changes, and this could be a critical juncture in the history of the Act.[106]

Perhaps many of the issues of neglect in implementation can be understood a little better in the context of the historical development of ideas and ideology. The neo-liberalism that rose to political prominence in the last quarter of the twentieth century has its blind spots. One of these is due to the neo-classical economic blind spot with regard to institutions and transactions costs. In short, the approach taken to the implementation of the RMA seems to assume transactions costs and, in particular, information costs are insignificant. A delayed realization of the need to purposively generate information produced schemes such as the SMF – outsourced, leaving much of the generation of ideas about needs to the market. This can work to some extent but is limited. Many needs go unidentified and, as with many markets, these tend to be associated with the most needy. Once the information has been generated there is still the danger of assuming that it will distribute itself to those who could benefit from it. The experience of the RMA implementation suggests that this is a very long way around the block. Sustainability is not particularly anti-market, but it does tend to contradict the maxim of consumer sovereignty and asserts the need for a more deliberate cooperative learning approach to dealing with our common future.

There has clearly been a failure at the centre of the system, a failure to articulate values, a failure to clarify meanings, responsibilities and boundaries, a failure to communicate, support and encourage the practitioners of sustainable management. This is a failure of understanding, vision and leadership. In short, it is a failure of commitment by central government to support its own legislation. Absent such an ongoing core dynamic, the framework has become rather lifeless and the legislation a target of the inevitable frustration and resentment generated by a dysfunctional system. The system is put at further risk because of the lack of flow of good news stories. This study found little analysis highlighting the positive functionality of the system. This needs to be part of a moral support function of central agencies, as a by-product of monitoring the functionality of the system, to spread the positive lessons of best practice.

Out in the regions and districts there is great variability in understanding and performance but it is mostly lacklustre. There have been notable successes of the regime, for example in halting any further examples of substandard landfills or new discharges of raw or crudely treated sewage or leachate into water and coastal systems.[107] And there seems to be some optimism that the second generation of policy statements and plans now in preparation will be a marked improvement on the first. There is now also a seemingly cautious change in strategy at the centre by the current Labour Government. For most of their first term they were embroiled in a controversy over genetically modified organisms, driven by the Green Party, on whom the government coalition was dependent for its survival. To some extent this has displaced other environment issues, including the RMA, from the political agenda, although some movement is perceptible.

A new amendment Bill for the RMA was introduced to Parliament in March 2003 proposing incremental changes to the mechanisms of the Act and no major changes to the essence of the system. The first NPS since the Coastal Policy Statement – on biodiversity – has been slated for notification (the first public stage in its development) during 2003, and one other has been hinted at by the Minister for the Environment. Perhaps a positive experience with the process will embolden the Government to invest in some of the other issues requiring clarification and policy development. For some issues it will be too late – the work has been done multiple times at other levels and a national process may do more harm than good. But it is not too late to act. Policy leadership and credible commitment from Government can still contribute to the sustainability of the RMA.

The approach taken in New Zealand with the RMA and associated reforms was bold, with broad-ranging restructuring of the institutional arrangements creating a new framework with new potential and dynamics. However, the case study indicates that, given a reasonable framework, even if implementation went well, transition to a state where the new framework is performing well could take decades rather than months or years. There is plenty of tension in the system created by the RMA: between legislative prescription, subordinate instruments and the role of the courts; between emphasis on process and the need for robust policy and issue analysis; between private rights and public good; and more. Such tensions are inevitable and we should not shy away from them. Arguably they keep the process of the social construction of a sustainable future vital.

Sustainability is a big and complex problem set and meta-problem. An adequate long-term response requires a complex institutional system and sophisticated ideas, understanding and analysis. No perfect set of rules and institutional arrangements can be created for achieving sustainability. However, attempts must be made and adaptation anticipated. At some level and to some extent such systems will need to run on faith and commitment to sustainability as a principle of governance – that to strive for sustainability is right – whether we can precisely articulate that in legislation or not.

## NOTES

1. Consistent with obligations under Chapter 8, Agenda 21.
2. WCED (1987).
3. National Development Act 1979.
4. Memon and Perkins (2000).
5. In fact many staff transferred from the old to the new agencies, including senior management. This legacy was to remain a source of internal conflict and confusion for many years, particularly within the Department of Conservation.
6. Young (2001), pp.19–20.
7. Frieder (1997).
8. Young (2001), p. 34.
9. Ibid, p. 32.
10. Memon and Perkins (2000).
11. Young (2001), pp. 89–90.
12. RMA Section 5.
13. RMA Section 2 – Interpretation.
14. RMA Section 3.
15. These matters are set out in RMA Sections 6, 7 and 8 respectively.
16. *Wahi tapu* translates as 'sacred places', and *taonga* often as 'treasures'. *Taonga* represents a totality of objects, tangible and intangible, considered of sufficient significance to be protected, managed and controlled. Cases before the Waitangi Tribunal have included land, forests, fisheries, the Maori language and literature – all regarded as taonga. See http://www.kaitiaki.org.nz/virgule/article/2.html

17. *Tangata whenua* means 'people of the land', and *tikanga* Maori is the Maori culture or custom.
18. The Treaty has had a chequered history since its signing in 1840. In 1877 it was declared by one judge to be a legal nullity, and was treated as such for a century despite consistent Maori protest. In 1975 the Labour Government passed the Treaty of Waitangi Act which established the Waitangi Tribunal to hear Maori grievance relating to the Treaty. The scope of the Tribunal was further expanded in 1985, and by the time of the drafting of the RMA the Treaty had increased greatly in legal stature.
19. Note that the Act does not set out the Treaty Principles. The following interpretation is provided in MfE (1999).
20. Buhrs and Bartlett (1993).
21. Young (2001), p. 12.
22. The Act requires the Minister, on proposing an NPS, to appoint a board of inquiry of 3–5 members to investigate the issue and take submissions from the public, hold hearings and so on, before making recommendations back to the Minister, who has the final say on the content of the statement.
23. Section 30 RMA.
24. MfE (1999).
25. RMA Section 79.
26. Taylor (1995).
27. See Palmer (1999).
28. Commissioners are drawn from a range of roles in the community but often have experience on consent authority planning committees, in mediation roles or as environmental specialists.
29. http://www.courts.govt.nz/environment_court/environment.html
30. For example, see Kerr (2002).
31. See, for example, Salmon (1998); McNeil (1998); Young (2001).
32. This view of the intent of the RMA risks being seen as idealistic, and as we shall see these intentions have not been broadly achieved as yet. Nevertheless this is one vision of the functioning of the RMA that can be read from Part II.
33. Buhrs and Bartlett (1993).
34. Young (2001). The Ministry for the Environment (MfE) was only created the year before in the first round of reforms of environmental administration.
35. WCED (1987).
36. RMLR (1989).
37. Upton (1995).
38. RMLR (1989) quoted in Upton (1995).
39. Quoted in Upton (1995).
40. Upton (1991); Young (2001), p. 32, quoting interview with G. Salmon.
41. Upton (1995).
42. For more on the work of the Review Group, see Randerson (2001); Salmon (1998); Upton (1995); Young (2001).
43. Upton (1991).
44. Upton (1995).
45. Ibid.
46. For example, see McShane (1998).
47. Grundy (1995).
48. Dixon (2002); Perkins and Thorns (2001).
49. Grundy and Gleeson (1996).
50. Young (2001), p. 33, quoting interview with G. Salmon.
51. McShane (1998), p. 5.
52. Bachurst (2002); Dixon (2002).
53. Nixon (1998), p. 21.
54. Somerville (2002).
55. Williams (2000).

56. A new amendment Bill was introduced on 20 March 2003, at the time of writing, that promises to improve Maori consultation, simplify the NPS process, broaden NES coverage and make simplifying changes to planning procedures. The major reforms of previous bills have been rejected.
57. For example, see Williams (2000); Somerville (2002); Ericksen et al. (2001); Randerson (2001); various commentators in Young (2001).
58. Buhrs and Bartlett (1993), p. 132.
59. Bollard (1995).
60. Somerville (2002).
61. Young (2001), p. 59.
62. Williams (2000).
63. Ericksen et al. (2001), p. 32.
64. Young (2001), pp. 31, 39.
65. Buhrs and Bartlett (1993), p. 130.
66. Young (2001), p. 31.
67. Ibid., p. 36, quoting interview with John Hutchings.
68. Buhrs and Bartlett (1993), p. 130.
69. Young (2001), p. 37.
70. RMA Sections 45–52.
71. Williams (2000).
72. The Government intends notifying the Biodiversity NPS during 2003, but seems to have taken a very long time for this initial (pre-public consultation) stage of policy development. The Minister has indicated that possibly one other NPS might be developed by the current Government (Hon. Marian Hobbs, first reading speech for Resource Management Amendment Bill (No. 2) 2003, 20 March 2003); not a very ambitious agenda.
73. Young (2001), p. 36, quoting interviews with C. Wallace and C. Lawson.
74. MfE (1999).
75. Young (2001), p. 85.
76. http://www.smf.govt.nz
77. RMA Sections 30, 31.
78. Frieder (1997).
79. Ibid.
80. Ericksen et al. (2001). This report was produced as part of a long-term study: Planning Under a Cooperative Mandate (PUCM).
81. See, for example, MfE (2001).
82. Perkins and Thorns (2001).
83. Ibid.
84. Frieder (1997).
85. Bachurst et al. (2002).
86. McShane (1998).
87. Nixon (1998).
88. Ericksen et al. (2001).
89. Bachurst et al. (2002).
90. Ibid.
91. Ericksen et al. (2001), pp. 14–16.
92. Frieder (1997).
93. MfE (2001).
94. Buhrs and Bartlett (1993) p. 129.
95. Salmon (1998); Young (2001), pp. 65–6.
96. Palmer (1999).
97. MfE (2001).
98. Randerson (2001).
99. Young (2001), p. 72.
100. Williams (2000), quoting G. Palmer, 'The Making of the Resource Management Act', *Environment – the International Challenge* (1995), pp. 145, 169.
101. Smith (1997).

102. Ong Su-Wuen, MPP Masters thesis, VUW, cited in Young (2001), p. 77.
103. Somerville (2002).
104. Interview with Denise Church, quoted in Young (2001).
105. See Chapter 2, this volume.
106. See note 56.
107. Gow (1997).

# 5.  National councils for sustainable development: Experiments in national policy development and integration

## BACKGROUND

Since the United Nations Conference on Environment and Development (UNCED) in 1992 many countries have established some form of inclusive body dealing with sustainable development policy at the national scale. These are generally termed national councils for sustainable development (NCSDs), although precise titles, roles, functions and status vary. The general intent of NCSDs is to continue, at the nation state scale, the widely shared policy discourse that occurred around UNCED and similarly shared discourses around national sustainable development policy that occurred in many countries in the years after UNCED. In short, the principle of partnership common to most discussions of sustainability policy is manifested at a national scale in something like an NCSD. As well as continuing dialogue and communicating the logic of sustainability NCSDs are intended to further the implementation of Agenda 21, the core policy outcome of UNCED, through national level sustainable development policy.

Agenda 21 and numerous other statements argue that furthering the sustainable development agenda will require ongoing, purposeful collaboration between (loosely) governments, the private sector and community organizations (civil society) in development and implementation of national policy that integrates ecological, social and economic dimensions over the long term.[1] In NCSD quarters this is referred to as a multi-stakeholder approach. Although not specified as an institutional response at UNCED, NCSDs have been promoted in many quarters as one core element of such an approach for particular purposes and at a particular scale. That is, NCSDs are necessary but not sufficient and would complement other policy and institutional responses at sub-national scales, in the community sector or with respect to subsidiary issues. None the less, as the primary extant model for establishing inclusive policy dialogue at high levels within the institutional system, NCSDs warrant close attention even at this early and formative stage in their development. The endorsement of the NCSD model at the 2002 World

Summit on Sustainable Development reinforces the imperative for critical analysis.

Given their formative stage of evolution and the lack of extant analysis of NCSDs, here we begin with the a characterization of what NCSDs have been envisaged as possibly being, and weigh extant examples against that. The features of an 'ideal' NCSD, as perceived by their proponents and many of their members, include:[2]

- A focus on the broader field of sustainable development (that is, long-term and integrative of ecological, social and economic dimensions) rather than shorter-term or on subsidiary issues, resource sectors or portfolio areas.
- Membership representative of different levels of government, major non-government stakeholders (including the private sector and community groups) and relevant academic, scientific and professional communities. This gives the actions and opinions of the body a prominence only possible through broad consensus amongst key groups.[3]
- Sufficient status and mandate within the institutional system to have an impact on policy and institutional change. This may be conferred by the nature of the membership, the status of leadership within that membership, legal mandate and/or the perceived value of roles filled and tasks undertaken.
- The capacity to engage in ongoing discussion, enquiry and development of policy options (if not recommendations), recognizing the long-term and difficult nature of policy and institutional development for sustainability whether such likely or guaranteed longevity is conferred by a statutory basis, by evolving linkages and interdependencies within the institutional system and/or by other means.
- Clear roles related to sustainability that are recognized and perceived as useful throughout the broader policy community, for the value of these roles in themselves, to validate the effort of members and contributors and to avoid any tendency to descend into the status of a 'talking shop'.
- Structural and functional linkages, through membership, roles and information transfers, to other relevant institutions and organizations relevant to sustainability (given the nature of sustainability problems, this casts a broad definition of 'relevant').

As we shall see, beneath the positive rhetoric and actual development of NCSDs around the world few current arrangements do especially well against the ideal, although some do better than others at least on a prima facie basis. However, analysing NCSDs for the purposes of a study such as this faces serious barriers. The wide variation in form and function of NCSDs reflects particular national contexts, influenced by legal, political and cultural traditions as well as the substantive issues deemed most significant. Also, most NCSDs are recent phenomena, and so their success at this stage is difficult to evaluate. In addition there is little independent, critical literature evaluating the impact of NCSDs – and even little consistent basic description – and so the following portrayal and analysis is of necessity limited by information scarcity and the impossibility of undertaking the necessary primary research into a sufficient number of individual NCSDs.

None the less the ideal and the many manifestations of it are highly relevant to institutional change for sustainable development and thus relevant to the intent of this study. The recent development of NCSDs and the fact that these bodies have only been created in some countries also suggest wide relevance. Although 'partnership' approaches have not been uncommon in the past in environmental policy, they are mostly utilized at more specific scales (e.g. regions, catchments) or with respect to specific issues. Moreover, the lack of standardized information on NCSDs makes the extent and efficacy of the model difficult to assess. For example, Australia has no such body, but in 2002, in the NCSD Network's database of NCSDs around the world, Australia does in fact have an entry, the Intergovernmental Committee on ESD, a very limited version and one which became defunct in 1997. This confirms that care should be taken with the apparent status and role of any country's arrangements as these are reported in the limited literature that is available.

## FEATURES OF NCSDs

The precise number and nature of NCSDs around the world is difficult to ascertain due to incomplete databases and some vagueness in defining what constitutes such a body. The core database on NCSDs is serviced by an NGO, the Earth Council, via the NCSD Network.[4] The Earth Council provides a coordination service and various forms of support for NCSDs particularly for developing countries. At end 2002, the Network listed over one hundred and thirty countries as having a central coordinating agency or body for sustainable development while the UN lists some one hundred and fifty countries with a coordinating mechanism for sustainable development.[5] However, many of these are units within government, and it is generally stated that in the order of seventy countries have an inclusive body that reflects, at least in intent, the ideal above. Of these NCSDs or equivalents there is considerable variation in form and function, and in this study it has not been possible to investigate the detail of each or even a significant sample, involving as that would primary research in the absence of sufficient descriptive or analytical literature. Communication with the Earth Council confirms 'a dearth of critical analysis and evaluation of NCSDs', although such evaluations are currently being initiated.[6] However, some of the main commonalities and variations can be noted and general observations made on effectiveness and constraints before profiling a few councils to illustrate these points further.[7]

In terms of geographic spread, NCSDs and their equivalents are located evenly across regions and amongst developed, developing and transitional economies. Titles of the bodies combine environment, sustainable development, Agenda 21, development, advisory, council and commission. The enabling instrument for different bodies is a mix of statutory instrument, head of state decree, policy decision and non-government action. Administrative locations vary also, from highly unclear, through advisory to first minister or head of state or environment or development minister, to largely non-government status. Membership varies, as already noted, from wholly government to largely non-government. The most common pattern of more inclusive membership is a combination of business, environment and scientific representatives, with development, consumer, economic and health interests often drawn in as well. In some cases membership quota are pre-determined by interest sectors (e.g. business, environment NGOs, labour movement) even where individual appointments are political. Expertise-based membership is common, either defined primarily by that criterion or where an individual is drawn from a stakeholder category. Leadership within that membership varies, for example ministers of state, heads of state or prominent individuals from business, science or environmental groups.

Roles vary widely, but commonly include (whether by the council's own decisions or by government commission): maintenance of policy discourse; public education; advice to government; review of environmental and related policy experiences; consideration of international dimensions; and research and development. Many councils use working groups and external advice to undertake specific tasks. Few councils enjoy a continuity of resources, either human or financial.

**Effectiveness**

A World Resources Institute review drawing on eight brief case studies of NCSDs recorded a trend to include more non-government representative members in NCSDs, following early tendencies in many countries to either exclude such groups or to dominate councils with government members.[8] This study confirmed the emerging consensus among NCSDs that their effectiveness was determined by: the maintenance of ongoing dialogue; use of consensus processes; ability to integrate social, environmental and economic policy; and a focus on complementing and extending rather than supplanting government decision making. Variation was noted in the appropriateness in a given national context of engaging with a broad or visionary agenda as opposed to concentrating on a fewer, more specific tasks. A further positive trend recorded with some NCSDs was the development of unlikely coalitions of interest between sectors or stakeholder groups that had little contact prior to engaging through a council. The review noted the following key issues determining the (provisional) success of councils:

- The importance of continued political support, with interest fading after the immediate post-UNCED years or as the task is perceived to have been completed. Changes of government are often particularly influential as weakening events.
- The lack of a clear institutional mandate and roles in the policy system has retarded the effectiveness of councils, and definition of the actual role has absorbed significant resources and energy. (It may be that this tendency reflects national governments' lack of a clear construction of the responsibilities for implementing sustainable development policy, therefore finding it convenient to pass this undefined 'problem' on to an NCSD in the hope that it will either diminish or become clarified).
- Councils commonly suffer a lack of financial and human resources, especially in developing nations. In developed nations, erratic budgetary support and lack of dedicated staff are noted as common problems.
- The importance of engagement with civil society and a broad range of stakeholder groups, either through membership or communication, to increase both the effectiveness of council actions and the political support for its existence.

Finally the review emphasized the repeatedly noted deficiency that, although often supported by international agencies and their submissions and actions accepted, NCSDs do not have formal recognition or status within the UN system or in its processes dealing with sustainable development. Such formal recognition – such as recommending that national government consult their NCSD if one exists – might sharpen the profile and in all likelihood the performance of councils, collectively in the international domain as well as within countries. However, the review noted that various UN agencies have begun in the last few years to include NCSDs in meetings and ongoing processes.

Significantly the World Summit on Sustainable Development in September 2002 called for further establishment and enhancement of multi-stakeholder NCSDs and similar bodies to provide a high level focus on sustainable development policies.[9]

The most comprehensive analysis of NCSDs was undertaken by the Earth Council for the period 1999–2000.[10] This contains summary reports from 27 countries, commentary on specific roles and issues, and a review of positive and negative experiences across the range of councils. The latter review is the most pertinent here and included the following issues:

- Positively, Councils were beginning to evidence their role and value as 'outreaches' of the UN Commission on Sustainable Development at the national scale, and a further potential role exists in enabling regional dialogue amongst countries on specific issues as well as broader dimensions of sustainable development.
- NCSDs were showing an ability to advance the core task of policy integration (ecological, social and economic) and for integration of the various parts of environmental policy (e.g. water, biodiversity, forests and so on). This occurs even where the structure of government and other institutional settings do not encourage such cross-sectoral linking and may serve to 'mainstream' sustainable development by bringing in economic and other government agencies to the policy debate.
- Against this, however, there is the observation that sustainable development is still viewed too often as an 'environmental' matter, to be handled by the environment agency or minister.
- A key challenge, for NCSDs and more generally, is the integration of information, dialogue and policy across spatial and administrative scales.
- An emerging focus on the potential roles of NCSDs following the 2002 World Summit on Sustainable Development, on the assumption that a revival of interest and urgency in the sustainable development policy agenda will arise out of that meeting and last for some time.

On this last point, 28 Councils are listed by the NCSD Knowledge Network database as having prepared WSSD (Rio +10) Assessment Reports for their country in 2002, recognized by national governments as either the official national report to the Summit or part of the official preparatory process. This implies either acceptance by governments of NSCDs as legitimate parts of the policy system or that such modes of reporting were easier or more convenient than reporting by government. A further dozen NCSDs (or equivalents) have prepared alternative reports. Interestingly, both sets of Councils are almost entirely middle- and especially lower-income countries, with developed countries with NCSDs either relying on a formal government-only response to the international process or not reporting NCSD input. Many of the NCSDs who prepared such reports followed a standard format which serves to force a broad (that is, inclusive of social, equity and cultural dimensions) view of sustainability in keeping with Agenda 21.

In a report on the outcomes of an international forum on NCSDs held in 2000 the UN Department of Economic and Social Affairs and the Earth Council emphasized three constraints and tensions.[11] The first is obvious but an important reality to recognize and manage – the presence of competing priorities for the attention and resources of both government and non-government participants. Second was a lack of expertise on multiple dimensions of sustainable development. Again this is obvious but should be explicitly recognized as inevitable given the nature of the task lest the enterprise of sustainable development policy be perceived as amateurish by more mature, established policy sectors. Third was the importance and difficulty of integrating across spatial and administrative scales (local, regional, national, international). This issue emphasizes the importance of council membership and communication pathways opened through that membership as well as again emphasizing the complexity of sustainability policy.

## SPECIFIC NCSDs AS EXAMPLES

This section profiles several selected NCSDs to illustrate elements of the review above. The focus is on councils in high- or at least middle-income countries for greater comparability with the largely developed world context established through the focus on the EU and New Zealand in the previous two chapters. It may be noted at this point, though, that NCSDs in the developing world are in many instances serving to create more than complementary basic institutional capacity and operate under particular resource constraints. The lack of English language sources for many (especially in Continental European and the Central and Southern Americas) examples limited their accessibility for this analysis. The choice of examples below is informed by availability of information as well as a range that illustrates variations in genesis, membership and roles.

### Belgian Federal Council for Sustainable Development

This particular NCSD is of interest due to its membership arrangements, clear focus on the whole sustainable development field and range of activities.[12] Known by the dual Dutch–French acronym FRDO–CFDD, the Council was established under law in 1997 to replace the previous National Council for Sustainable Development that had operated since 1993 in response to UNCED. The enabling law deals with the coordination of federal policy on sustainable development, and the central tasks of the Council are to:

- advise federal authorities on sustainable development, either at the request of the government and parliament or from its own initiative
- operate as a forum to encourage debate on sustainable development through organizing meetings and so on
- sensitize organizations and individuals on the subject of sustainable development.

Activities of the Council are undertaken by formal working groups in areas including genetic modification, scientific research, international relations, socioeconomic dimensions, biodiversity, and energy and climate.

The prescribed membership of the Council is of particular interest, with representatives of federal and regional governments and their agencies having only advisory roles, with private-sector, non-government and expertise-based members having voting rights. This 'domination' by civil society is rare and deemed progressive. The voting membership of the Council is as follows:

- four presidents and four vice-presidents
- six representatives from environmental and six from development NGOs, and two from consumer protection NGOs
- six representatives each from labour and employer organizations
- two representatives from the energy production sector
- six scientific experts.

Together with non-voting participants and advisors seconded for particular purposes, the Council involves and draws on a substantive representative and expertise base, supported by a dedicated secretariat. A flavour of the main products of the Council – which translate as 'advices' or submissions – can be gained from some of the topics of the following recent advices:

- in 2001, to the EU on Green and White Papers on a strategy for sustainable development, integrated product policy and chemicals policy
- in 2000, to the Belgian Government on wind energy, the EU's sixth environmental action plan, and the federal sustainable development plan for 2000–03
- in 1999, to the Belgian Government on taxation instruments and climate change and the implementation of the Convention for Biological Diversity.

In 2002, the Council prepared a detailed document to the Belgian Government regarding the forthcoming World Summit on Sustainable Development (WSSD). As a statement of priorities authored by a broadly representative body, intended for its national government to carry to the international level, the strength of the document and its construction of a systemic sustainability policy agenda are notable. Among the ten priorities proposed for the federal government to champion and implement are: integration of ecological, social and economic policy (including in integrated product policy); utilizing sustainable development as an overarching whole-of-government framework; indicators and targets for sustainability policy; transport and energy as crucial sector where policy needs to drive change in current unsustainable trends; democratisation of global (especially financial) institutions; and development aid issues. This equals a policy and institutional approach to sustainability stronger and more progressive than that mounted by any national government.

**Canada: National Round Table on the Environment and the Economy**

Canada's National Round Table on the Environment and the Economy (NRTEE) is one of the longest-standing NCSD equivalents and one which has changed its focus and mode of operation over a relatively long period. In 1986, prompted by the remaining impetus of the World Conservation Strategy and the visit to Canada in that year of the World Commission on Environment and Development, the Canadian Council of Resource and Environment Ministers established a National Task Force on Environment and Economy.[13] The Task Force recommended establishment, at national and provincial levels, of round tables on environment and economy, as multi-stakeholder, consensus-driven advisory bodies. These were established between 1988 and 1991, becoming Canada's principal institutional response to sustainable development – notably, pre-UNCED in 1992. Here we only focus (and then only briefly) on the national body, while noting that the coordinated development of the Canadian round tables is an interesting aspect.

The current NRTEE arrangement was confirmed in legislation in 1994. An independent advisory body, its members are high-profile individuals appointed by the Governor-in-Council, at the nomination of the Prime Minister to whom NRTEE reports. It is tasked with identifying issues with both environmental and economic implications and actions that will balance economic prosperity with environmental preservation. Members come from federal and provincial government, business, NGOs, academia and First Nations, and are supported by a secretariat of more than twenty staff. Normally the full NRTEE meets quarterly and oversees all programmes that are undertaken by a task force including Round Table members as well as others from government and non-government bodies.

Over more than a decade NRTEE has amassed a sizeable literature of reports and has convened countless meetings and processes of dialogue. The emphasis in terms of issues has shifted over time, as projects are completed and as the understanding of and approach to them has evolved. Recent and past programme areas illustrate the range and both continuities and change.

Past programmes are

- sustainable development issues in the new millennium
- health, environment and the economy
- Aboriginal communities and non-renewable resources development
- brownfields and contaminated sites
- climate change
- sustainable cities
- greenhouse gas emission trading.

Current programmes (at 2002) are

- environment and sustainable development indicators
- eco-efficiency
- ecological fiscal reform
- domestic emissions trading
- conservation of natural heritage
- urban sustainability
- national brownfield redevelopment strategy.

A constant work area is the preparation of an annual budget submission, recommending new or refocused expenditure. In 2000 it is claimed that half of an increase of C$700 million federal environment spending reflected NRTEE budget proposals.[14]

One particular programme area illustrates the sophistication of approach to sustainable development the NRTEE is capable of and the evolution over time that has led to this situation. Ecological fiscal reform (EFR) is a recent work programme that comes under a more generic heading of economic instruments and budget.[15] While economic policy instruments and recommendations for federal budget spending have featured on the NRTEE's agenda for some time, this was (as is usually the case elsewhere) limited in scope to specific sectoral issues or single annual budget cycles. The EFR programme seeks to establish the potential for a more integrated approach to utilizing the market, via reform of fiscal policy in the broadest sense, through generating awareness and options via a consultative research process. This process has thus far reviewed theory and international experience, explored three case study sectors (agricultural landscapes, cleaner transportation, substances of concern) and recommended further processes and research. As well as the Round Table's own economic instruments committee the process has involved, through an expert advisory group and a process of consultation, over fifty additional experts, government representatives and stakeholders. Whether or not the programme impacts on policy settings remains to be seen, but the topic and the process illustrate the role the Round Table plays in maintaining and invigorating a progressive sustainable development policy discourse, at least within the immediate policy community.

As the oldest NCSD-like arrangement, the Canadian experience begs more detailed exploration than that undertaken here. As with any (in institutional terms) recent development, it is difficult to ascertain the translation of research, process and discourse into positive change in the environment or human interactions with it. Also, the NRTEE is an advisory body, albeit a vigorous one, and it is not the NRTEE but rather policy makers and private decision makers who affect that translation. Given the emphasis on the 'eminent' status of the members – as opposed to explicitly representative, such as in Belgium (above) or Ireland (below) – some expectation of policy impact must exist. However, it is apparent that the NRTEE is embedded well in the political and policy system, that it maintains a progressive and broad construction of sustainable development and that it is productive. This favourable position, relative to many other NCSDs, is due to sufficient human and information resources (the latter being often self-generated), political and stakeholder support, and the momentum that comes from a degree of longevity. That longevity itself is notable, arising from national policy discussions driven by government prior to UNCED and even before the appearance of Our Common Future (WCED 1987), and linking the 1980 World Conservation Strategy with the then unfolding and broader sustainability debate.

### Comhar: Ireland's National Sustainable Development Partnership

Ireland's National Sustainable Development Partnership, known as Comhar, is instructed in its Terms of Reference to 'advance the national agenda for sustainable development, to evaluate progress in this regard, to assist in devising suitable mechanisms and advising on their implementation, and to contribute to the formation of a national consensus in these regards'.[16]

More specifically the Commission, through its members and small secretariat, acts to consider policy proposals for government, undertake research and communication activities, review implementation of international treaties and contribute to reports to the UNCSD, and consider policy integration strategies. It may consider issues by reference from a government minister or on its own initiative.

Comhar develops and implements work programmes over a three-year cycle, and is instructed to take account of the role and functions of other bodies in so doing. Its terms of reference allow for it to be designated as representing the Irish Government at international meetings and for the Partnership to invite submissions and comment on issues from government and member bodies. All annual and other reports are submitted to the Minister for the Environment and Local Government.

The membership of Comhar is by quota of members from each of five 'pillars' or areas, with a number of designated organizations within each of those areas nominating two candidates and the Government appointing no less than four members for each area, with members serving a three-year term. Currently there are five members for each, with a total membership of 25. The five pillars are: state and public sector; economic sectors; environmental NGOs; social and community NGOs; and professions and academia. The public sector members include local government while the economic members come from employer, labour, farming and industry groups. The professional and academic members represent environmental science, planning, education and architecture.

Comhar's (2001) assessment of Ireland's implementation of Agenda 21 evidences the particular national context and priority areas. The review was developed as an input to the WSSD as part of broader NCSD network approach but also to the Irish Government. Particular emphases in the review, which amounts to a consensus view by major stakeholder groups of sustainable development policy and prospects, include the following:

- a theme of assessing the implementation and effectiveness of the 1997 'Sustainable development: a strategy for Ireland', with a focus on problems of consistency between this strategy and the National Development Plan 2000–06
- a strong emphasis on social development and equity issues, and on the implications of rapid economic change and industrialization in Ireland in recent years, for example, for transformations in rural and semi-natural landscapes and emerging pollution issues
- clear connections between sustainability and spatial planning and urban and regional planning.[17]

As well as these particular emphases the membership structure of Comhar is noteworthy, as is the explicit mandate to investigate and report on issues on its own initiative.

**United Kingdom: From Round Table to Commission**

The UK's Sustainable Development Commission was established in 2000, consolidating and entrenching the approach taken with the previous participatory UK Round Table on Sustainable Development (largely non-government, established 1994) and British Government Panel on Sustainable Development. In keeping with the recent and ongoing devolutionary trend in the UK, the Commission has been established jointly with the Scottish Executive, Welsh Assembly and Northern Ireland Executive.[18] It is sponsored within the UK Government by the Cabinet Office and reports to the Prime Minister and first ministers/secretaries in Scotland, Wales and Northern Ireland. In this mode, although within an admittedly rapidly devolving unitary political system, the Commission has features of a body operating in a federal system. The basic roles of the Commission are to:

- review progress towards sustainable development, and identify policies and processes operating to retard progress
- identify unsustainable trends requiring new policy action to reverse
- further develop understanding of sustainable development and required responses
- encourage and stimulate good practice.

The membership of the Commission totals 22 and includes prominent figures from regional and local government, environmental, health, consumer and development NGOs, business and farming representatives, and academics. It was chaired in 2002 by high-profile environmentalist Jonathon Porritt. A secretariat of nine supports the Commission. The 2001–02 work programme provides a summary of the target policy areas identified by the Commission. This is organized into five project areas and four sectors with which the Commission will target its work and communication. Project areas are:

- 'Productivity Plus' – examining the reconciliation of economic growth, social progress and environmental protection
- 'Climate Change' – judged the single most important issue
- 'Food and Farming' – with an emphasis on the total production system
- 'Regeneration' – focusing on policy integration in community and economic regeneration programmes
- 'Communicating Sustainable Development'.

Sectors are:
- business, covering sectoral strategies and business leadership
- central and local government

- English regions
- devolved areas.

Although very recent, the UK Commission has attributes worthy of emphasis. First, the shift from a Round Table with poorly defined roles and separate government panel to integrated and more substantial Commission with clearly defined membership and functions suggests an evolving appreciation of the potential for an NCSD approach. Second, the membership reflects a broad construction of sustainability, including development, health and consumer interests as well as resource and environment. Third, the focus of regions and devolved authorities evidences the co-evolution of sustainability concerns with broader political change and institutional shifts in a specific national context (cf. the subsidiarity principle in Europe).

## US Presidential Council on Sustainable Development (Defunct)

The US Presidential Council on Sustainable Development (PCSD) was established by Executive Order by President Clinton in 1993 in the wake of UNCED, with a limited lifespan of two years. Amendments to the executive order extended the Council's life through until 1999 when it was not renewed and it subsequently became defunct. An advisory body it originally had 25 members although this grew to 35 by 1999, with members drawn from government, NGOs and industry. The Council was charged with three broad tasks addressed through task forces:

- advising the President on sustainable development issues
- producing a national strategy on sustainable development
- educating the public.

One analyst identified three phases during the life of the PCSD and labelled these as great expectations, a rocky road and a balancing act.[19] In the immediate post-UNCED years, building towards a national strategy, expectations of policy development and support for that were high. But traditional divisions and tense politics post 1995 Congressional elections prompted the Council to focus on longer-term visions rather than specific current problems, and in 1996 it presented its strategy, snappily titled 'Sustainable America: a new consensus for prosperity, opportunity and a healthy environment for the future'. The Council then sought to 'sell' the strategy in the public, private and community domains, with only partial success, culminating in a 1997 assessment of implementation of the strategy delivered to the President. Following that experience the Council entered its third phase and focused on building consensus on one key, contentious issue

– climate change – perceiving that painting the broadest canvas was less valuable use of its potential than focusing on balancing interests in one strategic area. However, in 1999 the Council was not renewed and has not been resurrected by the Bush administration which came to power in 2000.

It is considered that the Council made advances in proving the potential of the multi-stakeholder approach in articulating a national direction and highlighting a range of encouraging local and regional developments. However, in comparison to many other NCSDs, it struggled to establish itself and, most tellingly, no longer exists. Why? The short-term life of the Council, with a number of short extensions, would not have served to encourage a longer-term view of its functions and potential. Arguably the outcomes and agenda generated at UNCED were less prominent in the USA than elsewhere, and indeed the Council had less of an international focus than most other NCSDs. It may be also that the NCSD model was unsuited to the US political system, with its distance between the executive and legislature, or simply that the changing political climate over the 1990s did not suit the consensus/multi-stakeholder approach. In particular, although the President and Vice-President supported the Council, especially in the early years, Congress was after 1995 dominated by the other political party who were less impressed by the sustainable development agenda or even by narrower environmental issues. Most important of all, though, was that, apart from the near term task of producing a strategy, the PCSD was given no focused tasks and strong linkages were not developed with other parts of the policy system.

**NCSDs and International Agreements**

Although the vignettes above concentrate largely on developed nations comparable to the EU and New Zealand analysis thus far in this book, additional perspectives can be drawn from NCSDs in developing nations. A review of the role of six developing country councils in localizing the implementation of global environmental conventions (GECs) drew broad conclusions about the efficacy of NCSDs in assisting in this role.[20] (Note that this role is also performed by some developed nation councils, e.g. in Belgium, but no comparative analysis is available.) It may be generally assumed that implementation of GECs in nations such as, say, the USA or Australia is well embedded in the institutional system; however this is not necessarily the case. For example, community and stakeholder understanding of the 35 multilateral and regional environmental conventions to which Australia is a signatory is patchy, as are the degrees and styles of implementation. Virtually no legal or policy analysis has engaged with this topic in the broad, as opposed to piecemeal examination of a few, specific treaties.

The overall lessons drawn from the six case studies of NCSDs included:

- the importance of multi-stakeholder mechanisms, sufficient legal and policy frameworks, education and capacity building, and the monitoring of and learning from regional and local projects
- there was little attention paid and resources designated to realizing synergies that can occur between GECs in their implementation, that is, similar demands arise from different GECs in terms of policy development, information and capacity building but these tend not to be connected fruitfully; efficiency and effectiveness can be enhanced by recognizing and acting upon such commonalities
- that the presence of a functioning NCSD had a demonstrably positive effect on understanding, communication, implementation of, and the recognition of synergies across, conventions through their ability to enhance communication across jursidictions, policy sectors, profes-sional domains and interest groups.

In that sustainability is a global scientific and policy agenda to which nations respond, the issue of implementation and adaptation of general principles into national contexts is a significant one. It appears to also be one where an NCSD may play a significant role.

## LESSON DRAWING

Consistent with the style of this study the lesson drawing from NCSDs around the world focuses on broader themes of policy and institutional change rather than drawing on specific models for prescription.

NCSDs are for the most part recent and experimental, and it is as yet difficult to find clear evidence of their impact. However, the more impressive of them do evidence strong potential to add value to the more standard administrative and policy arrangements in the near term and even to drive longer-term change. The best of the NCSDs do evidence 'credible commitment'. Furthermore, reviews of NCSDs to date report positive impacts. Most interesting are cases where the NCSD arrangements have been strengthened after an earlier, less permanent model, creating 'second generation' NCSDs that are stronger than the earlier form (Belgium, UK, Canada). That further embedding of the NCSD model suits the sustainability problem as it has been constructed and pursued in this study – a multi-faceted task that must be pursued and implemented through complex, adaptive institutional systems. NCSDs may be contingent organizations, springing up to address an emerging task, but it could be expected that the need for such a mechanism, whether known or constructed as an NCSD in the current sense or not, will remain for decades rather than years. Engendering a culture of policy discourse and learning around sustainability, and even more so driving institutional change, are long, slow undertakings.

Only one-third of nations have established an NCSD or equivalent, and both these and those that have not span the diversity of nation states. Considering as examples two rich, liberal democracies that are well-developed institutionally, the USA and Australia, there are some rather obvious lessons that emerge should an NCSD-equivalent body or process be entertained. First is the need. Sufficient comparable countries have established such a body, and sufficient positive experiences exist to suggest that it can be a very useful addition – and in some ways an integrative mechanism – to the institutional response to sustainability. Second is the issue of form and functions. Sufficient variation exists to suggest that the NCSD should fit the national context, and that there are multiple and equally valid structures. Central elements of form are wide membership, adequate status within government, strategic links to other key nodes in the system, a resilient mandate whether legal or not, and sufficient human and financial resources. There is also strong evidence that clear responsibilities and roles need to be allocated, with close reference to gaps and under-attended policy tasks within the existing policy system. While such gaps would vary between jurisdictions and sectors they could include R&D directions, cross-sectoral policy dialogue, long-term strategic consideration of policy options, and information and communication flow.

Some emerging dangers are also forewarned from international experience. Chief amongst these is a new body being set up for failure through inadequate resources and unclear mandates and functions. Isolation and irrelevance through lack of connection with other agencies is a danger, emphasizing the need to conceptualize and design such a response with a broad understanding of the need for a nested hierarchy of policy and institutional responses to sustainability. Also there is the prospect of displacement of responsibility from government agencies: 'passing the sustainability buck' without the wherewithal to acquit the tasks mandated.

The connection between NCSD and government and the wider public is a critical issue. Again, a contrast with the Australian situation can illustrate. The widespread practice (although not in developed countries) of utilizing an NCSD for reporting to the 2002 WSSD makes an interesting contrast to the Australian experience in this regard. Stakeholder interest in the government-run Australian preparations during 2002 was difficult to engender, evidenced through low attendance at public meetings and small number of submissions. It could be assumed that the existence of an NCSD, through membership of key non-government group representatives, would have sensitized the policy community in the lead up to the Summit and made such preparatory discussions more inclusive. The likelihood of greater interest by the general community – a basic principle of sustainability policy since UNCED – would have probably been increased. Whether the effect of such inclusion on subsequent policy development would be notable is another matter.

One further observation is on the tendency for NCSDs to pursue a more comprehensive and less compartmentalized conception of sustainablity policy than many government-led processes. This applies to cultural, equity, human development and global dimensions of sustainability as well as the economic and environmental ones. This is very apparent, understandably, in developing country NCSDs but also in the developed countries of Northern Europe. In view of the limiting of the sustainable development idea in some countries – again, the USA and Australia can serve as examples – equating it mostly with separate domestic environmental, economic and to a lesser extent social issues, the possibility that an NCSD would change the terms of such policy debates warrants consideration.

It is often the case that an inclusive body or process dominated by representatives from the private, community and academic sectors will propose, through consensus, policy and institutional options more bold than would government. At least, such a body may spur consideration of stronger or more systemic policy concepts and institutional possibilities than might be expected to emerge from government. The Belgian and Canadian NCSD experiences support this, for example the former's advices to government and the latter's creation of a discussion of ecological fiscal reform. On the one hand this is understandable in political terms, given that the art of political leadership and government in modern liberal democracies often involves a wariness of championing bold and risky initiatives that have not been already discussed amongst key stakeholders. On the other hand it may be viewed as counter-intuitive, especially when 'environmental' issues are too often crudely characterized as conflicts between conservation and development interests.

For example, in Australia this potential was evident with the Ecologically Sustainable Development working groups 1990–92, where analysts and participants noted the muting, even regressive, effect of representatives of key government departments against stronger policy proposals developed by industry and green groups.[21] Part reason for this is that private sector representatives involved in such processes are likely to be involved in companies or sectors where economic benefit and environmental performance are either more demonstrably mutually possible (e.g. tourism, biotechnology, IT, sustainable agriculture) or at least not as obviously exclusive as in traditional extractive industries. While that may mean that other business interests will not support such policy proposals – and, indeed, other environment interests may view them as insufficient compromises and continue lobbying for other outcomes – at the very least the policy discourse is made more proactive. Whether such forward agenda setting potential enabled via engagement of non-government groups in ongoing policy discourse is viewed positively or negatively would vary according to perspective, involving as it does some degree of shift in control of the policy agenda away from government and towards civil society.

Overall, the limits of an NCSD should be appreciated. NCSDs are not major institutional reforms or for that matter even institutional measures in the strict sense of that term. They are, rather, organizational and communicative interventions in the institutional system that may produce institutional transformations over time. Of relevance to the themes of this study, they represent quite explicit recognition of the need to enhance policy learning opportunities across different parts of the policy community and potentially the broader public.

## CONCLUDING COMMENT

Overall this case study leads to two conclusions that sit a little uneasily together. First, the strong rationale for such a body and the positive features of at least some international examples suggest that an NCSD or equivalent could fill an important gap in the policy and institutional system of a country without one. Second, though, the lack of longevity among, consistency across and critical analysis or even basic description of the NCSD phenomenon means that prescribing the features of an NCSD for a country without one, on the basis of international experience, is difficult.

However, it is apparent that the large variations in NCSD form and function is consistent with the need for institutional responses to obey broad principles while fitting within specific contexts. Sensitivity to the particular national context would be important. Given the variation in form of extant NCSDs in different countries and that they are by definition experimental and evolving, the precise form may not matter as much as simply establishing such a body in line with the generalized ideal and proceeding with the stated intent of reviewing and evolving the approach over time. Yet, of course, the willingness or capability of a specific country to establishing even a loosely defined experimental body will vary. In considering why relatively few NCSDs exist in Asia compared to other continents, Boyer discusses traditional patterns of state–civil society relationship that may or may not be conducive to establishment of such a deliberative, multi-stakeholder forum as part of the policy system in a particular nation.[22] That is, these patterns in Asia may be less conducive to the establishment and operation of NCSD-like bodies than in, say, Europe or Africa.

Creation and maintenance of shared discourse is one reason for considering an NCSD. Another is that there is widespread acceptance that integration of ecological, social and economic imperatives, understanding and policy – especially if this process is construed as demanding both governmental and non-governmental action – is a venture barely begun. So is the establishment of effective connection across policy sectors and jurisdictions. The question is whether an inclusive NCSD would be, in the context of countries currently without one, a major contributor to such tasks or whether other mechanisms recommend themselves more.

National Councils for Sustainable Development, including equivalent bodies and those at present far from the ideal, can best be seen as experimental organizational responses to key elements of the sustainability agenda aimed at driving more profound institutional change in the longer term. Most of the constraints on their establishment and effective functioning flow logically from this – NCSDs sit uneasily in their operating environment and if they did not their rationale would not exist. 'Goodness of fit' is a principle for institutional survival, but it is of course recognized that some well-fitted institutions may be undesirable and that, for emerging societal goals, institutional change that is ill-fitting is necessary.[23] Sustainability is an unsettling challenge in policy and institutional systems. In large part it is Councils' relationships within the existing (and by definition inadequate for sustainability) institutional system that at once define their reason for being and their operational difficulties. NCSDs should be seen as a contingent strategy, meant to drive change in the institutional system and moreover to keep changing themselves in pace with that. Acceptance of that balance and tension between goodness of fit within and disturbance of the institutional system is important to both conceptualizing the nature of NCSDs and establishing and maintaining them. The most significant international experience with NCSDs to date is that at least three 'second generation' models exists, and in each case they still serve to constructively unsettle while having been embedded more deeply in the institutional system.

## NOTES

1.  See United Nations (1992), for example chapters 8, 27, 30.
2.  See, for example, d'Evie and Beeler (2002); d'Evie et al. (2000).
3.  In that such membership will draw on major non-government groups rather than the broader community, it resembles a form of 'corporatism' that may be viewed suspiciously by many smaller community-based groups, small business interests and advocates of participatory rather than representative democracy. However, it is stressed that an NCSD in its ideal form operates as one part of a nested hierarchy of institutional and organizational responses to sustainability, some which would be largely within government, some largely community driven, at various spatial and administrative scales.
4.  www.ncsdnetwork.org
5.  Boyer (2000).

6. Personal communication, Dr Fayen d'Evie, Earth Council (2002).
7. For basic descriptive material, see d'Evie et al. (2000); d'Evie and Beeler (2002).
8. Maurer (1999).
9. WSSD Plan of Implementation, advance unedited text, 4 September 2002 (www.johannesburgsummit.org).
10. d'Evie et al. (2000).
11. See Annex 3 in d'Evie et al. (2000).
12. Basic information and a range of the Council's submissions to governments are available in English via www.belspo.be/frdocfdd
13. Doering (1993).
14. NRTEE (2001).
15. See NRTEE (2002).
16. See Comhar (2001) and www.comhar-nsdp.ie
17. Closer connection (relative to, say, Australia or the US) between traditional spatial planning and sustainable development is evident in most Northern European countries.
18. Information on the Commission can be found at www.sd-commission.gov.uk
19. Maurer (1999).
20. D'Evie and Beeler (2002). The six case studies were Burkina Faso, Costa Rica, Dominican Republic, Mexico, Philippines and Uganda. In addition the review focused on the uptake and use of multi-stakeholder integrated sustainability planning (MISP), a broad framework methodology.
21. See, for example, various contributions in Hamilton and Throsby (1998); Dovers (2003).
22. Boyer (2000).
23. Goodin (1996).

# 6. Strategic environmental assessment: Policy integration as practice or possibility?

## INTRODUCTION

Core to the idea of sustainability is that of policy integration, with the aim that environmental, social and economic policies are not treated in isolation but together, and where environmental dimensions achieve parity in the policy process where previously they did not. This may occur either through systematically inserting environmental considerations into existing structures and processes for the formulation of social and economic policy or through a more complete form of integration outside of those processes. The broad instruction for policy integration exists in the Rio Declaration and Agenda 21, in EU environmental policy and in all policy and statutory expressions of sustainability in many countries. However, it is, as we have already noted, proving particularly hard to implement.

Strategic environmental assessment (SEA) is the most well described and long-standing proposal, and in some places actual process, for attempting such integration. The core logic of SEA stems from perceived inadequacies of project-based environmental impact assessment (EIA), a mainstay of environmental management for the last three decades.[1] EIA reviews and proposes changes in the light of the environmental impacts of specific developments, and does not have purchase on cumulative impacts over space or time or the more strategic environmental issues associated with classes of development, plans or broader policy decisions. Further, project-based EIA, in the view of many commentators, does not consider the 'no' option sufficiently; that is, it may ameliorate impacts of predetermined developments rather than seek alternatives.

While such larger-than-project considerations may be attended through sectoral or regional policy and planning, it is widely considered that such attention is inadequate and that systematic SEA of policies, plans and programmes (PPPs), as opposed to projects, is necessary. A core rationale for SEA, or some equivalent, is that environment or sustainability impacts should be considered at higher levels of the policy and institutional hierarchy than that of direct, obviously project-related environmental impacts. This defines two related but distinct areas for policy assessment: likely direct impacts arising from a class of development (e.g. transport infrastructure, copper mines) or in specific regions or sectors that are cumulative in space and time; and indirect impacts that none the less have important environmental or sustainability implications through shaping production, consumption or settlement patterns (e.g. tax, industry, energy policy). The first form of policy assessment is an important elevation of the EIA idea; the second is a better approximation of policy integration in the sustainability sense.

SEA has been advocated for several decades; indeed the idea and even some legislative provision predate the creation of the sustainability agenda by the WCED-UNCED. But current provision for SEA in policy and law is far from widespread, and even that provision well exceeds its application in practice. However, in the past decade advocacy of SEA and to an extent implementation of it has increased, especially in Europe. This is largely tied to the issue of policy and institutional reform for sustainable development, the subject of this study, and considerable effort has gone into rethinking SEA in the light of the altered policy agenda post-Rio.

This chapter examines SEA in that light – as a mechanism for policy integration for sustainability, in theory and in (limited) practice in parts of the world. The following offers a summary history of SEA, describes the basic elements of SEA, reviews its status in selected countries and regions, and identifies apparent barriers to implementation. The level of detail is kept to the minimum required for the purpose: more detailed sources are available and cited. As will become clear, SEA as a general term at once includes and is sometimes differentiated from other environmental assessment (EA) procedures or proposals. These include cumulative assessment, plan-SEA and legislative EA. The detailed differences amongst this at times confusing array are not dealt with here. The issue of proposed, more sustainability-specific forms of assessment, such as sustainability and integrated assessment (SA and IA), specifically targeting the integration of environmental, social and economic policy is discussed towards the end of the chapter.

## THE ROOTS OF STRATEGIC APPROACHES TO POLICY ASSESSMENT

An important contextual and historical question underlies the situation with SEA: why has it been long proposed, even formally provided for, but so rarely implemented? The Australian situation – crucially influenced by then recent events in the USA – can illustrate.[2] In the late 1960s Australia and other countries considered how to incorporate growing environmental concern into government decision-making processes, especially regarding environmental protection and development control. There was strong promotion of a refocused planning system, with coordination at the national level, to insert environmental considerations into policy in an integrated fashion through longer-term forward planning, consistent with the British–Australian planning tradition. However, a stronger, more convenient and instantly appealing influence outweighed that tradition. Project-based EIA was a cornerstone of the USA's *National Environmental Policy Act 1969* and that international benchmark piece of legislation was looked to in the early 1970s when the Australian Government was considering the need for overarching environmental legislation. The convenience and simplicity of a project-based approach proved more attractive and formed the central plank of the *Environment Protection (Impact of Proposals) Act 1974* (EPIP). In related moves across the states and territories in the 1970s EIA became core to environmental management, and even where other approaches – such as regional planning or even SEA – were catered for, project-based EIA dominated.

This emphasis was a key determinant of the style of environmental policy over the ensuing three decades – reactive rather than proactive. Specifically this reinforced a focus on direct and discrete causes of environmental degradation ('end-of-pipe') rather than indirect and long-term causes, with subsequent lack of emphasis on consideration of the environment early in the decision-making process (that is before specific project proposals are put forward). It also created an unfortunate distance between longer-term planning and environmental policy, in contrast to some other parts of the developed world, such as Europe, where sectoral, regional, social and economic planning were more closely linked to environmental policy (Chapter 3), or New Zealand, where planning law was the central mechanism used to express sustainability (Chapter 4). Harshly the reductionism inherent in a reliance of project-based EIA could be portrayed as anti-sustainability.

Although the EPIP Act contained discretionary provisions for SEA, as does the *Environment Protection and Biodiversity Conservation Act 1999* which has replaced it, these were never utilized. And the same discretionary provision and lack of implementation is the case with the 1969 US legislation. Until recently the few examples of SEA in policy and law elsewhere in the world were also discretionary. The irony in this history is that despite having available, in national and some sub-national legislation, a recognized approach to policy integration, this potential has been ignored even as the need for it has become more sharply apparent. Policy integration has been an accepted need for some time, and that acceptance has sharpened, especially since Rio, and various mechanisms are possible: sectoral policy, regional planning, resource allocation processes, enquiries, and so on. Yet none of these has lasted or achieved much impact on the broader policy system. However, the policy integration task remains.

SEA is not the only approach to policy integration and is nowhere proposed as sufficient in itself. Rather it is one of the 'family' of environmental assessment approaches and tools which in turn is one part of the larger, evolving toolkit of policy support options. However, that it has been available for some time but little used even though increasingly suited to the logic of sustainability, and that alternatives to it have been only sporadically utilized, sets the context for this case study. Currently, the issue of policy integration is being debated and some possible approaches being proposed and/or implemented, yet SEA is often strangely overlooked. Henceforth not only are the arguments for and status of SEA reviewed here, but attention is paid as well to alternatives to SEA that serve at least some of the same ends and to apparent barriers to the implementation of SEA.

## THE ESSENTIALS OF SEA

The US National Environmental Policy Act 1969, which in many senses gave birth to project-based EIA, stated in Section 102 a need to 'include in every recommendation or report on proposals for legislation ... a detailed statement on ... the environmental impact of the proposed action'. That loosely defined one form of SEA (legislative SEA) and began a longer and inconclusive debate. Other key dates in the history of SEA include:[3]

- 1978 – US Council for Environmental Quality regulation for National Environmental Protection Agency and USAID regarding programmatic environmental assessments
- 1989 – World Bank internal directive on sectoral and regional assessment
- 1990 – first EU proposal for an SEA directive
- 1991 – OECD adopts principles for environmental assessment of programme assistance; Espoo Convention (EIA in a Transboundary Context) promotes environmental assessment of PPPs
- 1992 – EU Habitats Directive includes a (contested) instruction regarding SEA of plans affecting special protection areas; UNDP introduces environmental overview as planning tool
- 1994 – UN Convention on Biological Diversity at Article 4.1 calls for 'appropriate arrangements to ensure that the environmental consequences of programmes and policies likely to have adverse effects on biodiversity are duly taken into account'
- 1997 – EC issues proposal for SEA Directive

- 2001 – the European SEA Directive comes into force (Directive 2001/42, Assessment of the Effects of Certain Plans and Programmes on the Environment)
- 2003 – adoption of the SEA Protocol to the Espoo Convention.

Although understanding and, to a lesser extent, implementation of SEA have advanced, the past three decades have not seen a clear direction emerge for SEA. Note that the EU SEA Directive, the most significant advance in SEA implementation to date, took ten years from proposal to coming into force, and now awaits implementation.

The following two, standard definitions capture the core idea of SEA as it is presently understood, as well as its still inherent vagueness and variability:

> the formalised, systematic and comprehensive process of evaluating the environmental impacts of a policy, plan or programme and its alternatives, including the preparation of a written report on the findings of the evaluation, and using the findings in publicly accountable decision-making.[4]

> SEA is a systematic process for evaluating the environmental consequences of proposed policy, plan or programme initiatives in order to ensure they are fully included and appropriately addressed at the earliest possible stage of decision-making on par with economic and social considerations.[5]

Key elements in these definitions are worth emphasizing. The targets of policy, plan and programme, along with the instructions that SEA be applied early in the process and that alternatives be considered, suggest a longer time-horizon and separate it clearly from project assessment. SEA is meant to be systematic, applied through a transparent and publicly accountable procedure rather than in an ad hoc or opaque fashion. Finally, the aim of environment gaining parity with economic and social consideration places SEA firmly as an instrument of policy integration.

A central issue, but one little discussed in an explicit manner, is what elements of SEA serve to make it 'strategic', although the converse issue of what makes EIA not strategic is more often discussed. In general terms, to be strategic implies a long-term view (thinking ahead), a broader rather than specific focus, and the consideration of means towards chosen ends relative to the chosen ends of others. Strategy suggests a strong purpose, in this case the elevation of environmental considerations in the policy process, and more recently that of sustainability. While implicit in the idea of SEA and the definitions above, this is worth emphasizing.[6] The consideration of environment early in the policy formulation process is one strategic element, as is the consideration of alternatives. This is especially the case if these two features of SEA lead to, as they inevitably must, more open deliberation of the ends and means of policy rather than only considering the amelioration of impacts caused by a means already selected. That is, SEA may lead to the selection of alternative policy pathways or instruments to achieve the same social or political goal. Further, the aim to create parity with social and economic considerations is, in environmental terms, strategic, and from a sustainability perspective an expression of the idea of policy integration.

Policies, plans and programmes (PPPs) generally define the targets of SEA; that is, those things that should be subject to assessment. Some practitioners and analysts sub-divide SEA in separate forms, such as a plan-SEA. These terms stem particularly from the European context where SEA has been most fully conceptualized and implemented, reflecting the EU-level policies and plans, and national plans and programmes. Outside of that context the terms require clarification in particular settings. Figure 1 illustrates the idea of the hierarchy of the policy and planning, noting subsidiary forms of SEA.[7] Further sub-categories often referred to are: plan-SEA, specific to that level; legislative EA, of proposals for new or amended statute law; and cumulative assessment (CA), applicable specifically to attending that deficiency of project-EIA.[8]

The notion of 'tiering' is commonly used to both reflect this hierarchical construction of the policy- and decision-making process and to instruct the way in which SEA should be applied. However, there is a recognized danger that the rationalistic and strictly hierarchical view of policy making inherent in the tiered approach may not ring true in practice or in different jurisdictions and sectors.[9] This is often the case in, for example, federal systems, given multiple loci of decision-making power and less consistent structures and hierarchies of policy making than, say, in a unitary system. Even in the EU, where the PPP terminology originates, reality is messier than the strict implied hierarchy. Standard models of public policy making, stressing sub-systems, non-linear and/or cyclic progression and incrementalism, offer sufficient warning against overly rational conceptions of policy processes.

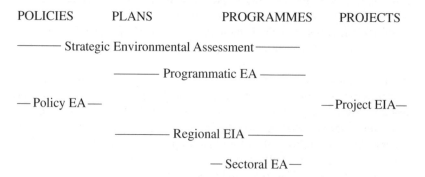

POLICIES          PLANS                    PROGRAMMES          PROJECTS

———— Strategic Environmental Assessment ————

———— Programmatic EA ————

— Policy EA —                                    — Project EIA—

———— Regional EIA ————

— Sectoral EA —

*Figure 6.1    Strategic environmental assessment and related assessment tools*

**Targets and Triggers**

Beyond the general notion of PPPs there is less consensus in theory or practice about what might constitute the more precise targets of SEA and even less over the triggers of magnitude or significance that would require an assessment within a particular category of PPPs, assuming that not every plan or policy could or should be subject to detailed assessment.

The following sample of SEAs undertaken to date and reported in the literature is indicative of targets rather than exhaustive: some seventy transport and land use plans in Europe; the Irish National Development Plan 2000–06; regional planning for sustainability in the UK; and national automobile industry policy and coastal zone policy in China.[10]

Given the scarcity of SEA applications outside Europe there has been more work on the prospective targets of SEA, producing a wide and often quite profound set of suggestions, such as in the following list of potential targets:[11]

- international agreements on trade, finance or defence
- development assistance programmes
- privatization of public functions
- interstate agreements in a federation
- foreign ownership approval processes
- government budgets
- sectoral policies, plans and programmes (e.g. energy, water, transport)
- structural adjustment programmes
- tax systems.

This casts the net much wider than the targets of SEA to date, and raises the issue of thresholds and triggers for assessment within these categories. This remains a problematic area, with terms such as 'serious', 'significant' and 'irreversible' being used to indicate when an assessment would be required. Although these terms would be considered qualitative and subject to contestation, it should be noted that such concepts are common, and commonly dealt with, in law, suggesting that, while a scientific or administrative rationality may find them problematically vague, other rationalities – legal certainly, perhaps communicative or discursive possibly – would not.

The differentiation between kinds of targets within the general PPP set and degree of potential environmental impacts that would trigger an assessment has not been well explored. The following general triggers have been proposed for SEA applying to policy or legislative proposals or institutional changes:[12]

- with apparent and significant potential to impact on the environment
- with cross-sectoral impact; that is, affecting policy and management practice across a range of policy sectors, portfolios and substantive issues
- of a whole-of-government nature; that is, affecting most or all portfolio areas and agencies
- likely to result in significantly altered public expenditure
- determining patterns of research and development investment
- involving major restructuring or changed capacity of relevant public institutions with responsibilities for resources or environment, or with significant relevance to resources and environment (e.g. mining, transport, planning, land management, statistical agencies)
- involving significant changes to land tenure or resource rights and allocation
- likely to substantially affect the rights of communities and stakeholders to participate in environmental decisions, or the ability of the public to gain access to information about the state of the environment or about environmental law, policy and management.

Such triggers are rarely quantifiable in that they rely on terms such as 'significant', except in the case where the scale of the proposal can be measured in expenditure terms. A measure of discretion and qualitative judgement is inevitable in triggering an SEA, which suggests that independence and transparency of the triggering process would be essential for consistency and public trust in the process.

A set of principles for SEA has been promulgated and has received wide support in the literature, and summarizes the consensus among academic and professional proponents of SEA of the basic features of a SEA system.[13] These principles can be summarized as:

- The agency initiating a policy, plan or programme proposal is responsible for the assessment.
- Assessments should take place as early as possible during the formulation of a proposal.
- The terms of reference and objectives of an assessment should be clearly defined.
- The scope of the assessment should be commensurate with the scale of the proposal and its environmental consequences.
- Public participation in the process should occur, consistent with the significance of the potential environmental consequences.
- Alternatives to the proposal should be considered as well as its potential environmental impacts.

- Consideration of the significance and acceptability of environmental impacts should be undertaken with reference to a policy framework of environmental objectives and standards.
- Public reporting of assessments and decisions based on them should occur.
- Assessment processes should result in the further incorporation of environmental factors in policy making.
- Assessments should be tiered to other assessments, to project EIA and to ongoing monitoring.

These principles provide an ideal – a set of criteria against which proposed or existing SEA arrangements can be critically evaluated – and apply across the various subsidiary forms identified above. If the logic of SEA or other policy integration mechanisms is accepted, the principles are also unexceptional in that they reflect sound policy practice rather than radical notions.

One argument for SEA is that it can create efficiencies in project-EIA, in that broader assessment at the sectoral or regional level or of classes or developments may establish general criteria and guidance. This would, in turn, allow more certainty that a proposed development will be acceptable (although not unchallengeable) and allow for less exhaustive EIAs. This has been an attractive prospect for business, although balanced by a fear that SEA will be simply another layer of scrutiny and delay. Environmental interests have often been suspicious that SEA in this manner may lead to less critical examination of individual projects.

**Subsidiary Methods**

By now it should be clear that SEA is not a method, even in the more prescriptive constructions of it, but rather a policy strategy and general procedural requirement. In terms of implementing an SEA a variety of techniques and methods have been and might be used depending on topic, jurisdiction and the layer of the policy system in which the application occurs.[14] Here we can simply note this diversity, as the current analysis is more about the general nature of SEA than its specific undertaking. Methods and techniques of potential use in SEA include: scenario modelling; multi-criteria analysis; simulation analysis; expert workshops; extended cost–benefit analysis; cross-sectoral policy analysis; impact matrices and geographical information systems (GIS) and other dynamic mapping techniques.

It should be noted that the kind of methods appropriate varies significantly with the level of abstraction of the application. SEA of broad policy will tend to utilize less quantified methods (expert judgement, policy analysis, workshops and so on) than at finer resolutions for example with more targeted and tightly defined programmes. Also, the kind and degree of uncertainty will also change. If SEA merges with sustainability assessment (SA) or integrated assessment (IA), a wider toolkit becomes necessary for purchase on, and integration of, social and economic data and techniques. For example, tools such as social impact assessment, multi-criteria analysis (including more heuristic modes) and non-market valuation would be expected to feature.

## THE STATUS OF SEA

Currently, recognizable provisions for SEA are found largely in the developed world. Jurisdictions reported at 2000 either with or actively developing legislative or policy provisions for SEA include Australia, the UK, Canada, Denmark, Finland, France, Hong Kong, Japan, Norway, The Netherlands and South Africa.[15] The specific features of these provisions, and especially the extent to which they are actually implemented, vary greatly, and to describe this detail is beyond both the scope of this book as well as unnecessary to its purpose. At the international level the World Bank and other international agencies are beginning to implement forms of strategic assessment of development programmes in varying ways.

One key variation is the source of mandate or requirement for SEA. Jurisdictions with some legislative source of mandate – whether this is sufficient or even implemented – include The Netherlands, New Zealand and Australia. Strong policy directives for SEA are found in other countries such as Denmark and Canada. Most often the policy directive is from the Cabinet Office or similar central agency. That implies a degree of force of requirement across government. Elsewhere SEA is simply recommended in non-binding policy. However, provision in legislation does not correlate to application of SEA, as already noted. The strength of that provision (discretionary or mandatory), the adequacy of the procedure, if any, set out and the institutional capacity to implement SEA are the crucial variables. The institutional location of SEA varies, with planning ministries being the most common in Europe and environment agencies or environmental ministerial councils in most other countries.

The capacity to implement SEA as a new and poorly understood approach is widely recognized as problematic. However, there is a chicken-and-egg situation – without widespread and mandatory application, SEA will remain an unpractised tool. Even so, as well as the research and policy literature cited here, a growing set of countries has produced guidelines for implementation of SEA whether the practice is mandatory or not.[16]

The prospects for SEA are at present unclear. Despite three decades of acceptance of the need for SEA or equivalent measures, strong advocacy and considerable analysis, implementation is patchy, thin and recent. Against this, it is widely expected that the EU's 2001 SEA directive will spur considerable further implementation in Europe, as will the SEA protocol to the Espoo Convention on transboundary EIA.

The detail of history and provision for SEA (or lack thereof) varies significantly country to country, and discussion of that detail is not possible here. The Australian case – including possible alternative or default mechanisms for strategic assessment and policy integration – can serve to illustrate such contextual variation. In Australia, policy and legislative provision for SEA is reasonably strong in comparison to other countries outside of Europe but implementation has been minimal.[17] As already noted the 1974 EPIP Act contained rudimentary SEA provisions, but these were not activated. In 1994 a report subsequent to a 1991 intergovernmental review of EIA considered Commonwealth EIA arrangements and the issue of cumulative and strategic environment assessment. The report recommended legislation in the form of an 'ecologically sustainable development' (ESD) Act with clear provision for SEA.[18] This recommended that all legislative proposals as well as policy programmes of designated kinds or expenditure levels be subjected to an SEA informed by ESD principles and in a publicly accountable fashion. These recommendations were not acted upon. However, discretionary SEA provisions of a general kind are contained in s146 of the *Environment Protection and Biodiversity Conservation Act 1999* (EPBC), which supplanted the EPIP Act.[19] More specifically, SEA of Commonwealth-managed fisheries are required under ss147–54 of that Act, and these provisions, although yet to be implemented sufficiently for detailed analysis, are considered to be reasonably consistent with the principles of SEA and much more so than the general provision at s146.[20] It may be the case that such a sectorally specific application of SEA is a useful first step toward wider SEA, proving the concept and building capability. Impact statements are required for National Environmental Protection Measures (NEPMs) under the *National Environmental Protection Measures (Implementation) Act 1998*. In the states and territories the situation varies. The most advanced case is Western Australia, where promising but underutilized SEA provisions of the *Environmental Protection Act 1986* are currently undergoing change to allow SEA, informed by ESD, of policy proposals across a variety of sectors.[21]

However, except in the case of fisheries SEA under the EPBC Act, what provisions there are for SEA in Australia are discretionary and the process for undertaking SEAs not clearly formulated – just as in the bulk of countries with SEA provision. Some Australian jurisdictions require legislative impact considerations in the Cabinet process. For example, the federal cabinet handbook requires ESD considerations be taken into account, but this is a lesser requirement than the focus on economic considerations via a financial impact statement. Overall, consistent procedures for assessing the environmental implications of non-environmental PPPs and legislation such as economic development, trade, transport and so on are largely lacking – again, a common situation in other countries.

Other mechanisms and processes that may be seen as fulfilling the purpose of SEA have been provided for and utilized often enough. For example, the inquiries by the Resource Assessment Commission from 1989–93 before it was disestablished have been judged as equivalent to strategic sectoral assessments. The Regional Forest Agreements process beginning in the late 1990s has been also proposed as a partial equivalent to SEA.[22] But sectoral policy in the resource management arena (forests, water and so on) should, of course, by definition, consider environmental, and possibly sustainability, issues. However, this is far less often the case for other sectors, which is the rationale for SEA. The 1990–92 ESD process whereby Australia developed a national sustainability strategy – although to a lesser extent the subsequent implementation of that strategy – had elements of a strategic assessment. State and territory planning processes, particularly at regional or sectoral scale, may serve to fulfil some of the goals of SEA, such as state environmental policies (e.g. under the NSW Environmental Planning and Assessment Act 1979). However, the situation is variable and often characterized by a lack of statutory status and impact of such plans.

Against the ideal described by the principles stated earlier, it appears to be the case that no existing SEA process, or provisions for a process, in Australia or elsewhere, meets the ideal fully and in fact most are deficient in various ways. This arises from the discretionary nature of most processes, the related ad hoc implementation of SEA, and the fact that few processes have been in place for more than a few years.

## CRITIQUE OF SEA: BARRIERS AND WEAKNESSES

### Key Issues with SEA

Given the uneven provision for, and scarce implementation and procedural details of, SEA internationally, despite the long time since its first appearance, clearly there are unresolved issues. The following identifies key issues congruent with the themes of this study.

If the importance of environmental issues and of sustainability are accepted, including the imperative of policy intergration, then there is an irresistable logic to the essential aim of SEA or some equivalent. This is reflected not only in advocacy of SEA but also is endorsed in major international and national policies. However, there is still only an emerging consensus, in theory and practice, of the essential features and requirements of SEA. This can be interpreted as being a result of the appearance of the sustainability agenda driving a more focused reappraisal of environmental policy, and especially the sustainability-inspired imperative of mainstreaming environmental considerations. That this mainstreaming has been most evident in Europe is unsurprising given the much longer evolution of the sustainability idea and related policy change there (see Chapter 4). Nevertheless, it is only since the early to mid-1990s that widespread research on and implementation of SEA has occurred.

In addition the inherent slowness of deeper institutional and policy change should be taken into account. A full and proper implementation of SEA would impact across the policy system and not be marginalized, as is the case with most environmental policy, into one or two relatively junior portfolios. As an invasive, transformative and relatively new, poorly understood policy approach with relatively few consistent applications to provide empirical testing, policy learning has been slow and uneven.

There is little agreement beyond generalities on targets for SEA. Obvious targets, with well-recognized and direct environmental impacts such as transport plans, are much more commonly discussed than indirect drivers of production and consumption such as, say, tax systems or non-environmental international agreements. To an extent this will be always decided in specific jurisdictional contexts. However, there is a perceived need for at least some consistency in expectations.

This relates to the existence of two distinct although not mutually exclusive approaches to SEA, referred to generally as top-down (or trickle-down) and bottom-up.[23] One simply extends the EIA tradition and environmental concerns 'further up the chain' of decision making towards programmes and plans arising and dealt with in existing policy agencies and processes, and, although the simpler of the two, this has proved difficult enough to implement. The other takes a more radical and systemic approach, stemming from a deeper dissatisfaction with the broader policy system and seeing SEA as a mechanism for mainstreaming environment and sustainability across the higher levels of policy making, and is closely related to more integrated forms such as IA and SA. The top-down approach suggests inadequacies of existing policy processes and thus a more substantial degree of organization and institutional reform to accommodate than the bottom-up approach. For understanding the potential for environmental assessment generally and for policy integration specifically, the existence of two differing strategies and their rationales is arguably healthy as long as the implications and limitations of each are explicit.

The definition of triggers for SEA (also known as 'screening') is also contested, given that it is generally accepted that not all PPPs should be subjected to full assessments and that the matter of choice of those that should be is thus crucial. Given the danger that making this discretionary would invite opaque processes without clear justification for referrals, further discussion of transparent, consistent two-stage triggering processes seems desirable.

There is continuing argument for more rigid and universal procedures for SEA on the one hand and for more flexible forms adapted to particular contexts on the other, and considerable lack of clarity of the implications of these choices. Clearly transfer of rigid models into unsuitable legal, social or organizational settings is not desirable. Recent literature and experience has emphasized a lack of understanding on the part of SEA advocates of the immensely variable policy systems in which SEA must fit and the need to pay far more attention to this.[24] An attractive position emerging is that a cogent and widely accepted set of guiding principles can emerge, providing for consistency matched with flexibility.[25] The flexibility issue also concerns the status of alternatives and subsidiary constructions of SEA, such as plan-SEA, legislative EA, and so on.

If it is true that a poor or at least variable understanding of the policy process underlies some of the confusion and lack of implementation of SEA, then this raises the issue of policy learning. At present the SEA literature, advocacy of SEA and thus understanding of its nature and potential is limited within a small professional community. Discussions of SEA are mostly contained within the environmental assessment literature and community, and moreover within a subset of that professional community. In fact, the SEA literature is mostly limited to a few specialist journals, books and conferences. The broader policy community of sustainability and natural resource management are not greatly concerned with EIA or with debates within that topic area and thus have little exposure to arguments for or against SEA. Yet that broader policy community is often intensely interested in the issue of policy integration.

Another issue is often underemphasized but critical to considering prospects for SEA in a political context. An important and distinguishing feature of SEA as opposed to EIA is that there is a much stronger focus on intervention in government policy processes as opposed to the discrete projects most often (although not only) proposed by the private sector. Even where projects are proposed by the public sector and subjected to scrutiny through EIA that scrutiny rarely touches the policy process that gives rise to them. However, acceptance that broader government policies, programmes, budget allocations and legislation are strong influences on patterns of production and consumption, and thus must be closely considered for their environmental (if not sustainability) implications, reflects the sustainability idea that indirect as well as direct causes of unsustainable behaviours must be dealt with. This moves government from the position of regulator or enabler of the activities of individuals, households and firms to a subject of scrutiny in its own right. That shift raises issues of the independence and transparency of an SEA process, and it may be that resistance to SEA stems from parts of the public policy system who view unfavourably the prospect of a focus being turned upon their own processes.

There is a dearth of evidence and analysis of the actual impact of SEAs that have been applied in terms of environmental impacts identified and avoided, remedied or mitigated. This is understandable given the recent and sparse applications of SEA and the difficulty in establishing a control scenario (i.e. what would have happened in the absence of an SEA). Such a situation is common enough in the sustainability field given the diverse range of policy options and the similarly recent and sparse applications of them. Nevertheless this issue is a researchable one, preferably in a comparative manner across a diversity of situations.

Finally there is the issue of burdens of proof applicable in SEA, both in terms of choosing PPPs for assessment and of justifying changes once environmental impacts are established. Given the inherent uncertainty of prospective impacts, and in methods applicable especially at higher order policy levels, this issue requires further attention. It also begs closer connection with discussions of the precautionary principle as the core sustainability principle instructing policy making under conditions of uncertainty.[26]

Taken together, unresolved issues such as those above serve to explain the SEA implementation deficit. However, at a deeper level this deficit is entirely understandable given that SEA or equivalents, if taken seriously, represent a rather serious policy change. SEA raises political issues of territoriality within the public policy system, it seeks (or threatens) to make the currently minor policy concern of environment more mainstream, lacks an agreed home in the institutional landscape, and is a new and relatively untested approach. Whether it is a policy change that particularly suits sustainability is considered next.

## SEA and Sustainability

The purchase of SEA on the different agenda of sustainability remains unclear. The traditional notion of SEA as applying EA above the project level is certainly relevant. However, the question of its ability to drive policy integration is less clear despite considerable attention to this issue in more recent years.[27] It is arguably the case that bottom-up constructions of SEA, rooted in EIA traditions, are less suitable for sustainability but more practical to implement. More sustainability-relevant approaches to SEA, located firmly in higher levels and a greater range of portfolios in the policy system run into the confusion of more explicitly integrative approaches such as integrated assessment and sustainability assessment.[28] In that IA and SA are even less manifest in operational terms than SEA the question of whether they are better is a theoretical or conceptual rather than empirical one. At the least, explicit recognition of the differences and clarification of whether they are semantic or substantial is necessary to any consideration of creating or strengthening an SEA regime in any jurisdiction. One question to be considered is whether SEA, through its explicit championing of the environment, may offer a more effective political strategy than IA or SA, when the latter may serve to submerge environmental (and perhaps social) considerations within a process dominated by more powerful economic ones.

To some extent the lack of consensus and clarity is predictable, given the novelty of the approach and the more general state of policy development for sustainability. However, a more problematic issue is that SEA has not been prominent as a policy option in the broader sustainability policy debate but rather has remained contained mostly within the EIA community. That may be because the sustainability policy community has not heard much of SEA, or has but the idea has not appealed, or it may be that the 'sustainability policy community' does not yet exist in a coherent form, inclusive of all relevant subsets of interests.

That constrained debate perhaps accounts for a crucial aspect not well covered in the recent literature: the institutional home and role of SEA, a matter of close relevance to this study. Although there are numerous variations in SEA provisions (whether these provisions are acted upon or not) there is little current literature that undertakes comparative analysis of institutional dimensions. While such analysis is beyond the scope here, some comments can be made. Policy integration, and serious forms of SEA that target PPPs with potential indirect (that is, more subtle but systemic) as well as direct (that is, obvious) environmental implications, is a quintessentially whole-of-government issue. Therefore the question of where to locate the mandate for and carriage of SEA is important. Environment departments are generally regarded as sub-optimal for placement of sustainability options given their typically junior status and the likelihood of territoriality problems when a line agency is given whole-of-government functions. Central responsibility (e.g. a first minister's department) or suitably empowered independent agency are more attractive options.

Finally, and returning to an opening theme of this chapter, it is pertinent to ask whether SEA would be necessary given good strategic, regional planning and sectoral policy processes. The answer is probably no, but that begs the question of the adequacy of planning and sectoral policy to advance sustainability, and this is widely viewed as insufficient. Also there is some incompatibility of centralized planning or vigorous sectoral industry policy with modern political trends that emphasize neo-liberal ideas and a reduced public sector. The most viable standpoint on this issue is that SEA can be best construed as a means of driving good planning and sectoral policy, not as a sufficient alternative.

## LESSON DRAWING

Despite an SEA implementation deficit and remaining questions over particulars there is sufficient theoretical basis and practical experience for it to be a leading policy option for sustainability. A substantial literature exists, and interest, advocacy and implementation have increased markedly since the mid-1990s, especially in Europe with the appearance of the EU SEA Directive. The need for SEA or equivalents is clearly stated in policy and, if SEA is understood as a category containing variations and alternatives such as SA and IA, then no clear alternative options have emerged to answer the need for policy integration. The emerging principles for SEA provide a central rationale, while sufficient diversity exists in proposed and actual arrangements to allow flexibility in specific contexts. Remaining issues, such as institutional location and issues of targets and triggers, can be evolved and defined at the level of the implementing jurisdiction. Whether SEA is a policy option suited to strong implementation in any particular jurisdictional context is another issue. To illustrate again, Australian possibilities are discussed briefly in closing.[29]

Policy integration is one of the major ideas in sustainability, but as yet no well-accepted approach or mix of approaches has emerged to operationalize it, in Australia or elsewhere. We are still very much in an experimental stage. The idea is clearly expressed in Australian rhetorical commitments to ecologically sustainable development (ESD), but actual mechanisms are largely lacking. SEA has existed in legislative and policy commitment in some Australian jurisdictions for many years, and it might have been expected that this policy option would have been implemented in response to the ESD policy integration commitment. That it has not allows two judgements on Australian prospects to be entertained: that SEA is a tool whose time has come and gone and alternatives should be pursued; or that, given recent development of SEA theory and practice, the time is now ripe.

While SEA is as yet doubtless imperfect as a response to sustainability, and not well understood or implemented, that is a criticism even more true of alternative measures to address policy integration. Implementation of SEA would seek to advance policy integration but can also be understood as involving, in the terms this study, a strong element of policy learning. Moreover, that learning is potentially widespread across the compartments of government, in industry and in the non-government policy community. Simply, if we do not understand how to achieve policy integration, implementation of a strategic policy assessment process should increase that understanding significantly – 'learning by doing'. A barrier to viewing SEA in those terms is the poorly distributed understanding of SEA in the policy community.

The lack of interest in SEA outside the environmental assessment community could suggest that it is seen as an idea insufficient for sustainability, perceived as merely an extension of traditional project-EIA rather than a proper policy integration mechanism suited to sustainability. That is, SEA's time has come and gone. Yet SEA or equivalents clearly can be policy integration mechanisms, depending on targets and triggers. A lack of shared understanding of that potential may therefore be the major obstacle. On the other hand, the lack of support from governments – or, rather, unimplemented commitments – arguably stems from the (potentially) radical and disruptive prospect of systematic scrutiny being applied to public policy-making processes. If that is the case, that resistance could be assumed to apply to any other mechanism that sought to firmly embed either policy integration or environmental assessment of social and especially economic policy.

The second perspective follows from this. It may be that the case for SEA could not be made before the policy integration element of sustainability had been stated, pursued, and its complexity and difficulty more widely understood; that is, very recently. Policy integration, if attempted seriously, needs a prior problem reframing phase that has so far not been widespread within policy communities. It took over a decade for SEA to move from proposition to directive in the EU, with the directive coming into force only in 2001. The EU case is pertinent to Australia and other federal systems, indicating the complexity of negotiating SEA in an intergovernmental setting. Within individual jurisdictions most other significant cases of SEA implementation are also very recent, so Australia is not far behind in that sense. The lesson here is that evolution of policy responses to sustainability is more often a tortuous process leading, after time, to significant but incremental advances, especially where intergovernmental agreement is required. While that takes time, it increases the chances of embedding a new policy style within the policy and institutional system.

Should Australia, or any other country, move towards implementation of SEA as a major policy response to sustainability, there are four critical issues that deserve wide airing and debate before principles and procedures are set out suited to the existing institutional and policy system. While there are many other issues of design and implementation, these four are less operational and more conceptual, with decisions made on them (whether wittingly or not) determining the trajectory and purpose of an SEA process. These other issues are not unimportant (for example, the relationship of SEA to other processes, definition of triggers, organizational form and so on), but they are subsidiary to the following considerations of the deeper intent of SEA.

The first issue relates to more generic questions over the best pathway toward policy integration: forcing environmental considerations into economic and social policy making in their existing locations, or seeking a more complete integration involving new organizational and institutional forms. There is no clear answer to this, whether it is sought in theory or limited practice. The former option is arguably more achievable in existing institutional systems that are not integrated, with poor whole-of-government structures, strong delineation of portfolios and policy sectors, and generally weak environmental agencies. The latter fits less well into existing institutional systems but reflects rhetorical policy commitments on sustainability and policy integration far better. Whichever is chosen – or even the more likely and preferable mixed and experimental strategy – the danger of double dilution of environmental considerations should be recognized. This phenomenon sees environmental, social and economic imperatives traded off within an environmental or resource management agency or process and then traded off a second time, with environmental concerns diluted, when policy consideration subsequently occurs in core economic agencies or in Cabinet.[30]

The other issues follow. The second is whether the primary focus is on cumulative, direct environmental impacts, or on indirect, systemic and arguably more significant determinants of unsustainable behaviours. The latter focus is more consistent with the modern agenda of sustainability, but by definition much more difficult as it is genuinely and disruptively whole-of-government and cross-sectoral in nature. The third issue is the institutional location and source of mandate for assessment, accepting the politically sensitive nature of this if a stronger style of SEA is proposed. The fourth issue is the burdens of proof both for triggering an assessment and for justifying amendments to policy and legislative proposals when deleterious sustainability impacts are identified.

Is SEA an option for Australia and other jurisdictions where it either languishes unimplemented or where there is no provision? That question has two elements: practical feasibility and political likelihood. SEA is as operational as any other pathway towards policy integration, if not more so, and can be complementary to other strategies (e.g. an inclusive national discourse and learning body such as a national council or commission – see Chapter 5). Basic principles exist, and provisions in some Australian and many other jurisdictions provide a platform for implementation and evolution. Whether the political environment is suitable for comprehensive debate of the issues above, and for subsequent implementation SEA, is another matter. A scenario can reinforce the two elements in the question.[31] In Australia, as elsewhere, neo-liberal political and neo-classical economic thought have been pervasive in recent years. A major Australian policy manifestation of that, National Competition Policy (NCP), has created vigorous and effective assessment procedures that insert the meta-policy idea of competitiveness across all policy sectors, with ESD a subsidiary component of the NCP public interest test. A legislative review – of nearly two thousand statutes for 'anti-competitive elements' – shows that a major, determined, cross-sectoral policy and/or legislative assessment process is entirely feasible within the normal parameters of governance, given political support and adequate resources. If a comprehensive and strong SEA mechanism had been in place in the early 1990s NCP itself would have been an obvious and important target for proactive assessment for consistency with another meta-policy idea: sustainability. Certainly that would be feasible, whether or not it would be possible politically. That question of political likelihood is, in all probability, the crucial determinant of not only SEA's future but also of the idea of policy integration for sustainability in a broader sense.

## NOTES

1. For a review of EIA, see Petts (1999).
2. This historical note is informed by Patrick Troy, personal communication. For a current review, see Marsden and Dovers (2002).
3. Partidario (2000); Marsden (2002).
4. Therivel et al. (1992), pp. 19–20.
5. Sadler and Verheem (1996), p. 27.
6. See Noble (2000).
7. This draws on Partidario (2000); Fischer (2002a).
8. Piper (2002).
9. For example, Nilsson and Dalkmann (2001); Noble (2002); Fischer (2002a).
10. Department of the Environment, Transport and the Regions (1999); James and Donaldson (2001); Zagorianakos (2001); Fisher (2002b); Che et al. (2002).
11. Drawn from Buckley (1998); Goodland (1998).
12. Dovers (2002a).
13. Sadler and Verheem (1996).
14. For example, Fischer (2002b).
15. Partidario (2000).
16. For example, Department of Environmental Affairs and Tourism (2000); Ministry of the Environment (2000); Canadian Environmental Assessment Agency (1997); Department of Environment, Transport and the Regions (1999).
17. For a review, see Marsden and Dovers (2002).
18. Court and Guthrie (1994).
19. The inclusion of SEA to apply to legislative proposals was proposed in Senate committee discussions; however, this proposal was not supported.
20. Marsden (2002).
21. Malcolm (2002).
22. Ashe (2002).
23. For example, Partidario (2000).
24. Nitz and Brown (2001).
25. Brown and Therivel (2000).

26. For an initial discussion, see Dovers (2002a).
27. For example, Stinchcombe and Gibson (2001); Dovers (2002b).
28. For example, Nooteboom and Wieringa (1999); Ravetz (2000); Abaza and Hamwey (2001); Bond et al. (2001).
29. For more detailed discussion, see Marsden and Dovers (2002). For a discussion of SEA in the New Zealand RMA (see also Chapter 4) context, see Dixon (2002).
30. For a legal and Australian perspective on this phenomenon, see Bates (2003).
31. The ESD-NCP comparison is pursued further in Curran and Hollander (2002); Dovers (2002a, 2002b).

# 7. Property rights instruments: Transformative policy options

## INTRODUCTION

Over the past two decades, coincident with the rise of the sustainability discourse, the application of property rights instruments (PRIs) to natural resource management has been advocated as a means to efficiently allocate scarce resources. PRIs here refer to entitlements to resource use that have been endowed with characteristics of property interests, such as the ability to trade them in a market and capture changes in their value. Often these are quantified entitlements. Such instruments have been implemented for the control of sulphur emissions from fossil fuel burning power stations, in controlling discharges into rivers affecting water quality, for the allocation of water abstraction, and most notably in marine fisheries management. Such policy instruments have been proposed in other areas, including carbon emissions and sequestration, and biodiversity conservation. Although often characterized as just another tool in the policy toolbox, this chapter argues that, in many cases, PRIs involve a fundamental change in distributional logic and in the culture of resource use.

Property rights are a fundamental component of a society's institutional systems. They arise and are conditioned by rules in constitutional documents, statute law and the doctrines and precedence of Common Law. Informal rules – social norms – also sanction property rights. Property rights provide the backbone of incentive structures that reduce uncertainty about the behaviour of others and make higher levels of coordination and social organization possible. Property rights are so basic to natural resource use as to be inherent where they are not specified, in the sense that the lack of property rights is a recognizable regime, that is, open access.[1] Hence the introduction of PRIs in a given resource use situation is not so much the de novo introduction of property rights but represents a change to the existing property rights regime.

Changes in property rights, in turn, change incentives for individual behaviour and the logic of collective action. In the transition from one property rights regime to another, a transformation takes place in the nature of relations between individuals and resource use, and in the modes of work and social relations of individuals. Depending on the context of each situation this transformation may be more or less profound, personally, socially or economically. Depending on the processes through which change is introduced, it may be disruptive of, or contribute to, social cohesion, which may be more or less important to stakeholders than the economic changes involved. Finally, these management policy processes will have profound impacts on how changes are accepted by stakeholders and on the costs of implementation, monitoring and enforcement.

Above all a change in the property rights regime changes the logic of access to resources and how that access is distributed and redistributed. In so doing it drives a transformation in the social construction of fairness or equity. Under PRIs ecological integrity and economic efficiency achieve parity with, and may altogether trump, equity as the traditional first priority in distributional logic of resource access. Although economic efficiency is central to the dynamic logic and history of PRIs, in the sustainability era it is generally ecological integrity that is put first, not least due to uncertainty about interactions, irreversibility and long-term impacts.

Thus the equity notion must itself adapt to the new constraints of sustainability in order that the world should seem fair. In this new situation under a new set of rights and incentives, what comprises fairness in terms of a set of conditioning rules, and in terms of resultant distributions of costs and benefits, is up for negotiation. With precaution applied to the environment, concessions to existing constructions of equity are generally at the expense of potential efficiency gains. Such a trade-off in the name of sustainability is more likely to be accepted and adopted by stakeholders and community when an informed discursive management policy process has occurred to arrive at an agreed regime change.

This chapter explores these issues in an effort to bring to attention the broader complexity of property rights change. Policy advocates favouring market instruments take for granted that efficiency is the first priority social goal and therefore, to them, such proposals represent an evolution of means to achieve what we all want – increases in net social benefits. Implicit is the assumption that other, subsidiary, goals will be better able to take care of themselves if we get the economics right. The portrayal of PRIs as policy instruments with universal application and predetermined natural characteristics tends to set them apart from the normative discussion. By not being included in the sustainability discourse, where expectations over value preferences can be aligned, their application to resource and environmental management, and consequent transformative impacts, can be, or at least can be perceived as, hostile to sustainability principles.

The chapter proceeds in several parts. The first section briefly introduces a framework for understanding property rights regimes in relation to the use of

*Case studies in institutional change*

common pool natural resources. The second part describes the historical origin of cap-and-trade property rights instruments in applied economics and explains the linkage with the concerns of sustainable development. This section goes on to discuss the use of PRIs to establish an environmental bottom line and the problems with the 'leave it to the market' approach. In the third section we turn to the social construction of equity and links to culture in natural resource use. Here frontier culture is contrasted with that of the commons to establish a continuum on which a new culture might be constructed for sustainable resource use, with the transformation being assisted by a property rights regime change. In this context the importance of process and path dependence is briefly discussed. Next a simple addition is made to the conceptual model built thus far in including the prior longevity of an established property rights framework as a negative correlate of the adaptability of equity notions to regime change. In the final section the conditions for success in using PRIs are traversed in drawing lessons from the case study.

## PROPERTY RIGHTS AND COMMON POOL RESOURCES

Confusion in concepts and terminology is endemic in the discussion of property rights and natural resource use. Contemporary discussions of market-based instruments (MBI) (economic instruments, price mechanisms) for natural resource management include environmental labelling, taxes, levies, philanthropic purchase of land for conservation, pollution credit systems and cap-and-trade resource rights regimes. There are enormous differences between these initiative types (some not policy instruments at all) in terms of their intent, design and implementation requirements and in the degree to which their implementation equals a potentially transformative intervention in the institutional system. We argue here that property rights instruments (such as cap-and-trade permit or quota schemes) are different in kind, due to the required change to a deeply socially embedded set of institutional relations. Too broad a grouping of initiative types can only serve to further obscure important differences between policy options. With such potential confusion at hand an explication of the nature of property rights instruments in natural resource management seems desirable.

The term 'common property resource' has been used erroneously from the earliest modern analysis.[2] In fact the expression is analytically meaningless as it conflates the nature of the resource with the property regime prevailing. To assist in clarification of these issues the term common pool resource has been specifically coined[3] and is used extensively in the informed literature, although some authors persist with the old terminology.

A common pool resource is a valued natural or human made resource or facility that is available to more than one person and subject to degradation as a result of overuse. Common pool resources are ones for which exclusion from the resource is costly and one person's use subtracts from what is available to others.[4]

The nature of common pool resources (CPRs) is distinguished from two other classes of economic goods, private goods and public goods, as indicated in Table 7.1. Common pool resources generally comprise a resource complex such as a fishery or forest that often has multiple uses and multiple products. Often, although exclusion is not theoretically impossible, the costs of ensuring exclusivity are so high as for it to be both uneconomic and impractical. Subtractable resource units are appropriated from the resource complex by individuals and thus become unavailable to other appropriators. This relationship is often referred to in the economic literature as rivalry in consumption.

*Table 7.1   Relation of common pool resources to other classes of economic good*

|  | Excludable | Subtractable |
| --- | --- | --- |
| Private goods | Yes | Yes |
| Common pool resources | No | Yes |
| Public goods | No | No |

Common pool resources can be managed under a range of different property rights regimes. These fall on a continuum but may be classified under four headings: private property; common property; state property; and open access (non-property). Table 7.2 sets out the basic characteristics of these regimes. The costs of exclusion from extensive resource complexes has made private ownership of many CPRs rare, although forests are one resource regularly held under all four types of property regime. Although often hailed as 'private property rights', or 'privatization of public resources', PRIs such as tradable permits or quotas do not fit neatly into the above schema. They generally comprise a socially constructed right to a benefit stream from the resource and hence are a species of property right or property interest. However, in relation to a CPR in its entirety, PRIs relate to only one stick in a bundle of rights pertaining to an ownership and management regime of one of the types set out in Table 7.2. A general characterization of the rights involved in CPR ownership is provided in Table 7.3. The operational level rights of access and withdrawal may be allocated to individuals and hence made subject to a system of PRIs. So, while sitting in the broad institutional setting

*Table 7.2   Four property regime types*

| | |
|---|---|
| Open access | Absence of well-defined property rights, often unregulated and free to everyone |
| Common property[a] | Resource held by community of users, excluding outsiders, may self-regulate, appropriate uses may still be defined by larger society or external power |
| State property | Resource rights held by government that may regulate access and exploitation, may grant free public access and use force to enforce rules |
| Private property | Individual has right to specified uses of the resource and to exclude others from those uses, and to sell or rent the property to others |

*Note*:   [a] Referred to by the original authors, Burger et al. (2001), as 'communal property'.

*Source*:   Burger et al. (2001).

characterized in the schemata above, PRIs specify a socially sanctioned exclusive right to the described benefit stream associated with withdrawal of resource units from the resource complex. The holder of the alienation right owns the resource itself. In the case of a privately owned forest or irrigation scheme, alienation may be viable. However, for fisheries, aquifers and surface water the ownership right generally is ultimately attenuated by some sort of constitutional rule. For example, the public trust doctrine as developed in the USA holds the state as the trustee of such resources on behalf of the citizenry and thus is unable to alienate the resource.

*Table 7.3 · Property rights to common pool resources*

| | |
|---|---|
| Access | The right to enter a defined physical area and enjoy non-subtractive benefits (e.g. hike, canoe, scuba dive and so on) |
| Withdrawal | The right to obtain the resource units or products of a resource (e.g. catch fish, take water and so on) |
| Management | The right to regulate internal use patterns and transform the resource by making improvements |
| Exclusion | The right to determine who will have an access right and how that right may be transferred |
| Alienation | The right to sell or lease either or both of the above collective choice rights |

*Source*:   Ostrom and Schlager (1996).

For small community-owned resource complexes a socially and culturally bound understanding often pertains that recognizes the ultimate survival and meaning of the group is dependent on retaining resource ownership.

Between ownership rights and use rights lie the 'collective choice' rights of management and exclusion. These rights may be exercised by the owner or delegated to an individual or group. For example, they may be held by a government agency, a council of community members or of resource users, or perhaps by a single senior resource user such as a master fisherman. These rights are very powerful as they affect the conditions under which the operational rights may be exercised.[5] For example, holders of these rights may control at what time of the year and with what technology the resource may be harvested, how much may be taken and who may be allowed to be an operational level right holder. The management right is perhaps the most important stick of the rights bundle to think about when considering a change to the property rights regime for natural resources. Whether PRIs are used or not at the operational level, who gets to participate in the management decision making, what processes are used and the transparency and accountability of these are crucial to the welfare of all parties and the sustainability of resource use.

Finally, having located PRIs in a broad framework for considering property rights for natural resources, we might consider the qualities of such a quantified withdrawal right. The basic requirements of a meaningful property right are that they be well defined, secure, divisible and transferable. Defining a withdrawal interest in a CPR can be as easy as stating a fixed number of resource units may be extracted in a given time (e.g. per year) as long as the definition of the unit is uncontestable. Measuring the valued dimensions of some resources can be difficult – for example, soil fertility. In practice, PRIs are often effectively specified as a share of a variable available harvest. In most cases the total availability is estimated before start of the harvest season, and shareholders then know the actual quantity they may take through the year.

Security is a key issue in establishing incentives through property rights instruments. If the right is able and likely to be revoked at any time it is of little value in structuring incentives for sustainable behaviour; likewise if its exclusivity is not enforced against others without rights. Divisibility in relation to CPR entitlements refers to the ability to divide up the rights to harvest a quantity or share of resource units, and sell or lease any amount. This provides the ability to adjust holdings of rights to intended harvest levels so as better to match other production inputs. And transferability allows resources to flow to their highest valued use. Sale of rights allows those wishing to exit from resource use to take with them the capital stake implied by the expected income stream from harvesting, encouraging less efficient resource users to leave and be replaced by the more efficient.

## PROPERTY RIGHTS INSTRUMENTS: ORIGINS AND OBJECTIVES

Historically the development of the sustainability idea can be viewed as a convergence of three largely separate spheres of concern with respect to the use of common pool (CP) resources: ecological integrity, economic efficiency and social justice (equity). The nexus of these concerns formed, with the realization of their inextricable interdependence, in the emergence of the sustainable development concept in the 1970s and 1980s. The development of property rights instruments predated the Brundtland Report[6] but, by the same token that that report can be judged a fountainhead for ideas that had been incubating within global civic society for several decades, PRIs had been one of the interim responses to a subset of the same issues.

Sustainability itself is a holistic concept that by definition integrates the three component concerns. This integration takes place at a conceptual level but, for sustainability to be implemented, more detailed and contextualized articulation of values, problem definitions and policies needs to be worked out. Part of the policy process involves the selection of appropriate instruments to effect policy objectives, supporting the agreed set of value priorities. In the context of the original development of PRIs as a policy instrument the holistic conception had not yet occurred. However, a partial synthesis has occurred, involving economic and ecological (or, at least, biological) concerns in natural resource management, just as similar joint concerns have long been active for the interaction of social and economic values. The environmental justice concern is the third partial synthesis.

A key early bio-economic analytical integration on the road to the sustainability concept was that of the economist H. Scott Gordon[7] in the 1950s. Gordon drew together a biological model of logistic growth for a single-species fish-stock biomass and the impacts of fishing mortality with an economic analysis of costs and benefits of fishing. It is the interaction of the economic incentives controlling fisher behaviour, and thereby harvesting effort, with the model of stock response to fishing mortality that produces the so-called 'bio-economic equilibrium'. This analysis assumed that there were no institutional impediments to fishing effort – that is, no rules or property rights exist. This is the open access condition. This bio-economic analysis made it clear that, without rules, and under increasing scarcity (that is higher demand and prices for product), exploitation of biologically renewable resources was capable of both depleting resource productivity and being economically wasteful.

In a further relevant theoretical development, Ronald Coase[8] highlighted the notion of 'negative externalities' in resource use in relation to the definition of property rights. The problem of the inequality of private and social cost brought economic attention to such environmental issues as air and water pollution. Again, these issues were recognized as joint and inseparable problems for economy and environment, with an underlying factor being the lack of institutional rules defining property rights.

Economists' engagement with the pollution problem in particular led quite quickly to the development of ideas for PRIs. Having realized that the uncontrolled dumping of industrial wastes into common waterways and the atmosphere – long recognized as a danger to public health – actually comprised an economic cost to society, but that there were also benefits derived from the production processes involved, economists sought means by which these costs and benefits might be balanced so that the net benefits to society would be maximized. Thus the idea of optimal pollution levels was conceived. This notion, a difficult one for many to accept, posits that the socially optimal level of pollution occurs when the production of one more unit of goods yields a social benefit equal to the additional social costs imposed by the polluting production process.[9] This is optimal in the sense that, at any other level of pollution, greater or lesser, society would be less well off in total. This proposition is underpinned by the standard economic assumptions that, with increasing quantity, marginal costs increase and marginal benefits reduce. However, while the external costs remain so, more production and more pollution than the optimal level will occur. The policy implication is that, in order to achieve such an optimal equilibrium, a mechanism is required to bring the full social costs of production to bear on the producer. Such policies are said, in the jargon, to 'internalize the externalities'.

The seemingly most obvious way to achieve this internalization is for the direct charging of the external costs to the producer by way of a tax on production. This mechanism is known to economists as a Pigovian charge, proposed first by A.C. Pigou[10] as a general mechanism for equating private and social cost.[11] By adding to the costs the producer faces such charges cause a reduction in the polluting activity. The problem is to accurately estimate the external costs in order to set the charges appropriately. A moment of reflection on environmental pollution issues provides its own explanation. Not only would calculation of direct financial losses from pollution be difficult to estimate and would be very context specific, requiring a great deal of data collection and analysis, but non-use values need to be counted as well. We must then add some allowance for uncertainties of ecological interactions and threshold effects and so on. There turn out to be a range of technical difficulties with this approach apart from estimation of the damage function, and it seems the potential for estimating the correct level of charges (getting the prices right) for social optimality is unlikely to be realized.

Once we turn away from optimal charges, having raised the issue of the uncertainty of ecological interactions and long-term outcomes, these considerations tend to take over from the issues of immediate social cost, and a logical approach seems to be to set a quantitative limit on resource use. For pollution this may be represented by a minimum standard of air or water quality but, given more than one polluter, the aggregate outcome is out of the individual polluter's control and is subject to great variability in time and space. A charging system can be applied together with a standard. Here adjustments would be made to charges until the desired standard is attained, but the resulting uncertainty about the eventual costs of production will distort investment and upset stakeholders. The political risks associated with frequent changes in resource use charges to industry may mean that once the initial (usually soft) implementation is in place further adjustments may be avoided, with little net effect of the policy.

An alternative to charges is to set a total limit to resource use and allocate fractions of that allowable limit to individual users as a quantified use entitlement. For pollution this means a total amount of particular pollutants is specified as allowed for each emitter. This introduces significant costs of monitoring and enforcement, and hence is suitable for such large point-source emitters as power generation utilities but not so for, say, small industrial or agricultural producers. Once individual entitlements are established, if, as is usual, reductions in total emissions are desired, making the entitlement tradable allows such reductions to be made at least cost.

In the case of pollution, if it is assumed that different firms will have different costs of abatement, then the social cost of reducing pollution by a certain amount is minimized if those with lower costs reduce pollution first. If pollution quotas are all cut proportionately when the cap is lowered, to be able to keep producing at the same level as before each firm must either reduce pollution technically or obtain more permits from others. If information about costs flows freely among the participants in the market for permits, those with the lowest costs of abatement will reduce pollution and sell excess permits to those for whom abatement is more expensive. Some may choose to close down production altogether and sell their quota to others, but it is possible that the incentives introduced will stimulate innovative technologies that can clean up production at a low cost. Then production can continue with reduced pollution levels.

Finally, the opportunity costs of holding permits with an asset value will be reflected in output prices (that is, prices of goods and services will rise) and this is likely to reduce demand for the 'dirty goods'. Consumers will tend to switch to alternative goods (substitutes) based on the price signal about the social costs of production. The widespread adoption of such price signals based on the environmental costs of production has the potential to shift general production and consumption patterns on to a more sustainable path.

## AN ENVIRONMENTAL BOTTOM LINE

Limits to resource exploitation or pollution in cap-and-trade type permit or quota systems such as this tend to be set on the basis of concerns for whether they are environmentally sustainable first, before the maximization of benefits is considered. In most cases this a complex enough problem without taking on the problem of a social optimum within that primary constraint. This can be characterised as an environmental bottom-line approach: set the maximum quantum of resource use acceptable on environmental grounds and then try to maximize the value of resource use within that constraint. For pollution that involves estimating assimilative capacity and encouraging least cost abatement. For renewable resources such as fisheries, or ground and surface water abstraction, environmental bottom lines are at least as contestable, if not more so, than for pollution. At whatever level exploitation takes place the ecological systems involved are disturbed, with – for all practicable purposes – unknowable ultimate consequences. Each resource type has its own distinctive characteristics and complexities.

In fisheries, for example, according to generally used concepts and models of fish population dynamics, fish stocks initially respond to fishing mortality by increasing their biomass growth rate as the reduced population level releases niche space.[12] As the stock is reduced the growth rate increases further until a maximum is reached, commonly when stocks are about one-third of their original biomass. At this point the annual increase in biomass of the population is higher than at any other population level, and this annual growth, it is assumed, can be harvested sustainably (the so-called maximum sustainable yield) while maintaining the population at a steady level. This is the standard model used in estimating suitable catch levels in commercial fisheries. It does not take account of interspecies interactions and ecosystem dynamics but treats the subject species in isolation. This approach is both oversimplified and somewhat contradictory, given that the growth logistic is based on assumptions about resource niche constraints, but the impact of reducing the population by two-thirds on competitors for these resources is ignored. However, the information required for just basic stock biomass estimates is, on its own, difficult and costly to assemble. In general, data for estimating stock condition is derived from catch and effort time series data supplied to management agencies by commercial fishers, from which an index is compiled. Unless validated by fishery independent sample survey techniques and other methods, catch per unit effort analysis is problematic, as the measured parameters of effort are generally very crude and do not account for technological change, a factor that has been conspicuous in increasing fishing power in recent decades.

Even if we assume that enough information is available to accurately estimate the sustained yield curve for a fishery or other resource, and assuming this is stable or predictable over time, this does not in general solve the problem of selecting a point on that curve as a management goal. In fisheries this is a point of stable biomass with a (theoretically) stable annual surplus production available for harvest. For a river this is the equivalent of maintaining a particular flow level, or flow regime, with required minimum and peak levels and associated frequencies of extreme events, so as to maintain particular ecological processes. Again, with water resources, there are many linkages with the wider hydro-geological and ecological systems that may be more or less important in particular circumstances to the health and integrity of the greater system. But, as with fisheries, even a first cut estimate of sustainable water yields is difficult, costly and inherently uncertain. Hence, in effect, the environmental bottom-line approach becomes a matter of strategic risk management that attempts to minimize the risk of irreversible environmental change while encouraging economic activities to shift away from damaging practice and over-exploitation.

For all the economic and scientific theory and data collection and analysis, in all these common pool resource issues there remain some basic management problems. By the time that particular circumstances draw serious policy and management attention there is generally a problem evident as resource depletion or conflict among resource users. Baseline data may not be available and ecological change is likely to have occurred. In this type of situation a realistic management goal is to try to get things moving in the right direction rather than attempting to estimate some ecological goal state or an economic optimum. However, the basic messages of the original economic analysis need to be kept in mind, in particular that economic waste is generally occurring where resource use is free. The consequent external costs imposed on others are then not being counted as production costs, and hence more production occurs and more external costs are generated than would be the case if these costs were internalized. Thus policy instruments that adjust the rules and incentives so as to bring at least some of these costs into the producers accounting framework may offer a way forward. Despite the problems with quantification of the resources and choice of a management goal in terms of a quantified environmental bottom line, cap-and-trade property right instruments can, if well designed, provide these incentives and thus jointly address economic and ecological concerns.

## LEAVING IT TO THE MARKET

Before moving on we comment on the often-heard approach to property rights instruments that extols the virtues of the market in establishing suitable goal states. This 'leave it to the market' argument approaches the externality problem as evidence of incomplete property rights. This is based on the work of Coase[13] mentioned earlier. It argues that if property rights were completely specified – that is, if all resources, including water in rivers, air, and fish in situ in the oceans, were privately owned – any externality issues would be taken up by the owners offended against. For example, if a factory owner discharges waste into a river he or she does not own, the river owner would sue for damages. In anticipation of such action the factory owner would engage in prior negotiation with the river owner and offer to compensate them for the costs imposed if they grant permission for the discharge to go ahead. Likewise any downstream impacts on other property owners would be negotiated between the river owner and affected parties until all social costs are incorporated and sheeted back to the polluter. Given such complete specification of property rights and costless negotiation, contracting and enforcement (that is, no transactions costs), such a scheme could attain the goal of a socially optimal level of pollution we discussed earlier.

However, there are at least three major problems with this approach. First, there are problems with specification of property rights; second, transactions costs are significant; and third, markets have shown themselves to be unable to cope well with long-run time horizons. The specification problem is intuitively obvious to many. The large number of attributes of common pool natural resource complexes such as rivers and other ecosystems, and even the atmosphere, many unknown in character and unpredictable in interaction with other natural and human induced factors, make full specification of a rights system a practical impossibility. Transactions costs, only focused on by economists relatively recently, have been estimated to comprise over 40 per cent of the economy of the United States.[14] In fact, analysis of common pool resource management problems, using the same economic principles and arguments that give rise to the complete property rights position, show that property rights systems have not developed, primarily because of high transactions costs. However, the social capital of our complex society can be brought to bear on such situations to reduce transactions costs and organize a rights system if required, and new valuations of the risks associated with not controlling excessive resource exploitation can justify such a social expenditure. And this brings us around to the third problem, that of market myopia. Perhaps the market ideal is best exemplified in the real world in the global financial markets. Price signals are clear, huge amounts of information are readily available, transactions are cheap, formalized and generally legally fire-proof, and hedging instruments are widely used to insure against unpredicted variability. These markets have become very much more sophisticated and stable since the Great Depression, and yet speculative bubbles, crashes and instability in these markets send shudders through the global economy on a daily basis. So, even if a reasonable level of rights specification were possible, leaving sustainability entirely to the market could only ever be equivalent to an act of religious faith.

However, as discussed above, the environmental bottom line approach to PRIs in the form of cap-and-trade instruments offers a means to act in a precautionary manner in accordance with available knowledge of the environment while gaining some traction on the problem of economic waste associated with unpriced resource use. In general, given reasonable availability of information, these PRIs will tend to allow access to resources to flow to its highest valued use. Even with very limited anecdotal information on sale prices, such markets have been shown to operate to redistribute access to increase gains from limited resources available under the cap.[15] The value of the access rights provides a set of incentives for resource users to increase the value of each unit used as much as possible or minimize resource use per value unit of output. Hence incentives are produced for irrigators to apply water in a manner that is most effective per litre and to drive the development of cheaper and more efficient irrigation technology. A price for water encourages a re-examination of the economics of one crop or mode of production against another, with those using less water per unit of final revenue gaining an advantage, and so on.

These incentive effects have been discussed at length elsewhere[16] and it is not our purpose to explicate these arguments in detail but merely to examine how the operation of cap-and-trade PRIs addresses the concerns of sustainability. As we have shown, these instruments can usefully tackle the joint problems of ecological overexploitation and economic waste. However, in doing so the incentives established change the dynamics of resource allocation and open up new potential for social structural change. This in turn creates uncertainty for communities and individuals in terms of economic viability of traditional resource uses and thus for established patterns of use, social opportunity, cultural norms and life patterns. Particularly when under economic stress already, such uncertainty can unsettle resource users to increase their resistance to the introduction of PRIs even when potential economic gains overall are evident.

# EQUITY CONCERNS

Wherever groups of people have jointly utilized common pool resources the first issue in any concern for coordination of use is that of resource sharing, based on some notion of fairness – that is, a concern for equity. Some examples of rules or norms that might be applied to sharing include 'first in best dressed', 'might is right', a hierarchy of priority access based on hereditary social status or historical use, equal access for all members of a defined group – possibly constrained by season or area closures, and so on. Such formal or informal rules of fairness are linked strongly to local culture and can in turn have a strong effect on social structure. For example, in animistic cultures, hereditary social status and power relations may be based on strong links between ancestors and totemic animals, landscape features, natural resources or their spirit guardians. Status positions in the social group may carry responsibility for resource management and authority for imposing restrictions on harvest. In fishing towns on the coast of the US State of Maine patterns of work and social interaction, social and local government structure are all directly related to exploitation of the lobster resource.[17] A good lobsterman gains the respect of his peers, but history of family fishing practice and community membership as well as professional prowess all help to determine precedence in allocations of access to resources.

Although aware that using a model idealized community of small producers, tightly integrated and co-dependent, is not very realistic in large, complex contemporary economies and has its dangers, we believe using such a model to think through some of the issues of PRIs can be helpful. Similarly the issue of dispossession of indigenous peoples of their land and resources by colonial power and the often-seen result of social and cultural collapse can help us understand fear and resistance to profound contemporary changes to natural resource allocation patterns and the logic behind them. Any insights from such conceptual exploration need to be tempered with the realities of context, and context is a key issue with PRIs. We assert that both the usefulness and success of the application of PRIs depends just as much on context and process as it does on the incentives created by the re-specification of the social goals of management.

It is the logic of allocation patterns and the social meaning associated with them that are the nub of the matter. When instruments such as PRIs are applied they have the potential to change both the social goal and the associated social logic of allocation and resource use behaviour. The socially constructed equity norm, located in a specific time and place with an inheritance of historically grounded meaning, is likely to be profoundly contradicted. Depending of the context this may threaten social cohesion, and, even where resource users are relatively independent of community, it may undermine individual self-image and self-respect by rendering less valuable the knowledge and skill sets developed in a life's work.

People with any social interdependence sense a danger to the cohesion of their group under these circumstances. The logic of PRIs is fundamentally modernist. It creates a relation, an exclusive property right, that privileges and focuses economic self-interest on the individual with respect to resource use. This relation is one sanctioned by the state in an effective contract with each right holder. Other individuals are excluded, and the community and its needs are bypassed. Potential is created for individuals to sell out part of what has historically bound the community together, and possibly to powerful outside interests that could further threaten established ways. The primary policy objective is generally articulated as economic efficiency through allocation of resources to their highest valued use, but as discussed here, PRIs are able to jointly address the ecological-economic concern.

However, arguments made from an economic perspective maintain that PRIs are also particularly good for addressing equity concerns. Where equity is viewed simply as a matter of the redistribution of wealth according to some given, politically derived formula, the creation and allocation of PRIs is an opportunity to address equity concerns, although not often enough used.[18] One case where this has been used for the dramatic settlement of long-standing equity grievance is in the New Zealand fisheries, where the indigenous Maori people have acquired large amounts of fish quota from the Government in recognition of historical dispossession. Much of this was bought back from the existing fishing industry by the Government so as not to create further inequity.[19]

Most applications of PRIs have allocated quotas or permits such that the existing distribution of rights is altered as little as possible, through so-called 'grandfathering'. Grandfathering consists of the allocation of resource use rights free of charge to existing users in the same quantity as their historical use, or at least the same proportional share of an adjusted total. This too can be viewed as equitable, as any change in distribution of access is voluntary, by way of stakeholders selling their shares either to each other or to new entrants. Such a one-dimensional view of the notion of equity indicates a limitation of the assumptions of a purely economic rationality. Equity involves more than the distribution of wealth, because it is constructed from a base of values and beliefs about who we are and what we are here for. Hence equity is context bound, and different for each context. Significant change in the basic logic and goals of life and work, especially in the incentive structures for economic behaviour, is likely to clash with existing notions of what is fair and equitable. However, where established patterns of allocation and use of resources have brought about the situation where institutional change has been initiated because of threats to resource sustainability, change of some sort is inevitable.

Instrumentalities that do not change allocation patterns and logic may not threaten social cohesion or cultural norms as much as PRIs but they may not be very effective either. This has been demonstrated time and again in fisheries around the world. Regulatory controls on fishing effort, so-called input controls, have been used as standard management instruments for decades. These attempt to put the brakes on to existing methods of exploitation without actually changing the incentive structure or behaviour patterns. They merely restrict behaviour for which incentives are active and hence serve to frustrate the energies of resource users. Typically controls are applied to a single parameter of the mode of exploitation at a time and another added when this proves ineffective. The existing incentives for each individual to try to capture a greater share of available fish drives the displacement of effort around the large range of effort parameters available. Hence if boat days are restricted, boats work longer hours per day; if gear size is restricted, effort may be directed to new net design; if hull size is restricted, engine power may be increased; and so on. The best that can be said in most cases where technological change is active is that input controls can slow the rate of increase in resource exploitation. In the process they tend to exacerbate economic waste because their logic is to make fishing less technically efficient.

Thus it could be argued that a contributing cause to sustainability problems has been an absolute priority for maintaining existing constructions of equity as a social goal in regulating resource use, and thereby both ecological and economic concerns have been underemphasized. Property rights instruments turn the tables on this priority, and the application and enforcement of precautionary hard limits on resource use can assert an environmental bottom line as the primary concern.

An additional normative force at play is integral to the sustainability debate. That is the internationalised norms of human rights and social justice that combine with environmental and resource access issues in the environmental justice partial synthesis of sustainability concerns. Thus inequity in resource distribution and control may occur under current property rights regimes, viewed through this normative lens. This clash of equity cultures is yet another example of the normative change demanded by sustainability principles. Recognized dangers of the introduction of PRIs include the concentration of ownership of access rights, and this may also lead to marginalization of vulnerable groups. Because both property rights regimes and equity norms are socially constructed the characteristics of each may be adjusted so as to produce a fit with the social consensus. Property rights are always conditioned by rules, and PRIs in practice often involve extensive rule sets to protect social and cultural values. Again this makes them less transformative. Highly constrained PRI regimes, that may be gradually relaxed over time as normative change occurs, are being implemented in fisheries management.[20]

## FRONTIERS AND COMMONS

Another characterization of the economic, cultural and institutional aspects of resource use and the sustainability transition is made by Hanna.[21] This establishes two modes of resource exploitation as extremes on a resource management spectrum, the frontier and the commons. She uses the concepts of resource stocks and flows, and of three types of capital: natural, physical and institutional capital.

> Frontiers are developed by extracting natural capital's surplus flows to the extent of eroding its stock. Physical capital is expanded, while institutional capital is left undeveloped or developed only at rudimentary levels. Commons use the three types of capital differently; natural capital's flow services are used in ways designed to leave stock values unimpaired. Levels of physical capital are stabilised, and the institutional capital underlying the rules of resource use is developed to a sophisticated level.[22]

Hanna describes the culture of pioneers in terms of the ideals of discovery, conquest, invention, individualism, competition and change.

> Frontiers provide undeveloped and unbounded resources ... [p]roperty rights to the resource are attained at the point of capture, [and] ownership is created through possession ... The end of the frontier is marked by the emergence of spillover effects between various resource uses as the lack of new resources keeps pioneers from moving on.

Although Hanna writes in the context of the challenge to develop new institutions for governance of American fisheries, this characterization has potential value elsewhere, including in land, water and waste management, in understanding how attitudes to change are grounded. The construction of equity norms in pioneer societies is linked firmly to these individualistic ideals and property relations. That is, these factors provide the logic of values and fairness. Abundance of resources provides great freedom of action and inventiveness, and rewards in wealth and prestige. The minerals exploration industry, for example, maintains the ethos of the frontier in full swing. However, other cases, such as the continuance of extensive land clearance in the face of alarming increases in salinity-affected land in Australia – the former is a cause of the latter – highlight contradictions between the historically developed culture of the frontier and the realities of spillover effects unmediated by the development of adequate institutional capital.

Where pioneers at the frontier expand, innovate and profit amid abundant resources the culture of the commons resides at the opposite end of the spectrum. Here, cooperative shareholders in common pool resources must coordinate to maintain long-term productivity of the resource complex. They must diversify activities to cope with variation in resource availability and learn to negotiate and manage risk in their stewardship role.

*Table 7.4    Comparison of traits of resource users*

|                          | Pioneer                   | Shareholder          |
| ------------------------ | ------------------------- | -------------------- |
| Expectation of tenure    | Variable                  | Long-term            |
| Risk attitude            | Risk taker                | Risk averter         |
| Work style               | Independent               | Cooperative          |
| Behaviour                | Innovator                 | Maintainer           |
| Decision making          | Individual                | Collective           |
| Role                     | Developer                 | Steward              |
| Strategy                 | Specialist                | Generalist           |
| Response to variability  | Substitution              | Diversification      |
| Skills                   | Exploration, entrepreneur | Negotiation, manager |

*Source*:   Hanna (1997a).

Attempts to develop aspects of a commons culture are being made in many areas of natural resource management through various more participatory and cross-tenure initiatives. There are many positions that may be legitimately occupied on the spectrum between these two ideal types, but where a pioneer culture still predominates in situations where resources are under stress from overexploitation and spillover effects are apparent, conflict and difficulty in adjustment can be expected. Institutional systems need to be built that not only address the resource issues but also adequately cope with these cultural issues. New institutional arrangements for decision making need to focus as much on accommodating and shifting attitudes and understandings as in developing new rules and rights, for without change in culture and values rules tuned to a commons sensibility will make no sense to pioneers. Nor will they appear as fair. A sense of fairness is a judgement about the congruence of actions, events or rules with cultural norms. Incentives established by rules should reward valued attributes, but those attributes of pioneers and shareholders are qualitative opposites. Hence to pioneers the incentives established by institutions to encourage commons values will seem illogical and unfair, and vice versa.

These attitudes about how the world should work can be viewed as part of an individual's ideology, and are changed and shaped by experience, new information and new understanding. This is normative change. As value is attached to ideology, individuals are prepared to forgo benefits to adhere to their belief about what is right. This is the cost of one's convictions.[23] Hence if normative change can be achieved to align the ideology of resource users with more sustainable institutional arrangements potential conflict is reduced and such change becomes possible. Such alignment will also mean reduced cheating (opportunism) where enforcement is less than perfect, as it must be, and will reduce the costs of maintaining the regime.

## PROCESS AND PATH DEPENDENCE

The need to attempt to pre-align values and expectations of stakeholders when considering policy change indicates the importance of process and of an adequate time frame to develop management policies. In a further paper, Hanna demonstrates, through a series of case studies, the importance of constituency building for natural resource policy change and its dependence on three important factors. These are the initial conditions at the point of programme development, the attributes of managers and user groups, and attributes of the process used to develop the management programme.[24]

The stage of the exploitation of the resource – whether it is still abundant, has peaked and starting to decline or has already become scarce – and the associated profitability and costs of information, monitoring and enforcement determine the initial conditions for developing a new management regime. The second, transitional stage is arguably the most tractable in which to begin negotiating change. Here resource users are aware of the declining conditions but are generally still able to profit by resource use. They perceive the threat to their livelihoods as external to the resource user group, and the focus becomes protecting the resource from outsiders. If action is delayed until both the resource condition and appropriator economics are in deep decline the group is likely to become focused on internal wrangling over allocation.[25]

The skills, knowledge and relationships among the management policy community and their history of interaction are important attributes that affect outcomes. Continuity of interaction promotes credible commitment between participants that allows exchange and reciprocity. Without this credible commitment time is spent monitoring the validity of others' statements and positions. The ability to craft mutual interdependencies and expectations creates assurance and minimizes conflict. All this relies on a group size small enough to allow information transmission and collective action.[26] Fisheries examples have shown that more ad hoc and less representative processes with short time-frames are less likely to succeed in developing credible commitment, good information and mutual assurance.

The attributes of the process of programme development are important to the legitimacy of the rules among resource users and therefore to their effective implementation. Legitimacy can hinge on the problem definition or framing, and whether this is shared by a consensual majority. Where problems are framed by special interest groups that want to change the rules to benefit themselves, conflict is more likely. To gain consensus the process of change needs to begin with a wide representation of interests that works toward an informed problem definition. This again highlights the need for adequate time-frame for the development of the programme to allow for social learning to occur among stakeholders. Lastly the organization of the process affects the costs involved and their distribution, and this is important to maintaining representative involvement and legitimacy.[27]

In Hanna's example of the introduction of PRIs into a North American fishery, the process failed in part due to a failure to recognize differing views of the problem held by large- and small-scale users. Both required more flexibility than the existing regime offered, but for different reasons. The short process time-frame driven by one problem framing did not allow for learning to occur about the needs of all stakeholders.

The introduction of PRIs as individual transferable quota (ITQ) into fisheries management in New Zealand represents a policy programme development task of much greater scope. The declaration of the 200 mile Exclusive Economic Zone in 1978 set in train a decade long policy process culminating in the introduction of ITQ for the large majority of commercial fisheries. The process of engagement between the fishing industry and government agencies built up through this period, as did the organization of the industry itself. Most interests were included and extensive consultation processes were carried out, led jointly by industry and government, both in defining the problem before policy direction was set and in working out how implementation was to proceed.

Allocation processes took more than a year due to processes that accepted objections at an administrative level before the scheme became operational. Appeals against final allocations went to a quasi-judicial tribunal involving industry members in judgements. This took almost a decade to resolve on a case-by-case basis, but this did not hold up the operation of the programme. The stakeholder group that went unrecognized by the process was Maori, New Zealand's indigenous population. A year after the ITQ policy became operational the High Court ordered a halt to further implementation of it because Maori claims to a resource share had not been heard. This issue, further development of the scheme, and the many operational issues that have since arisen have kept the stakeholders in constant dialogue with the regulating agency and government, and this ensures that adjustments to the rules and implementation occur regularly. In fact the demanding nature of regime, in terms of information demand and flow, has created and sustained a vital and innovative policy culture amongst all stakeholders.

## ADAPTABILITY OF CULTURES OF RESOURCE USE

There is not space here to gather or deal with large quantities of data from the extensive literature on correlates of adaptability of societies and cultures to change. However, the following assertion may be defensible from the anthropological literature and seems reasonable on evidence from analyses of the management of fisheries.[28] It seems that cultures of resource use that are more longstanding are less easily able to adapt to changed property rights regimes. This may be a result of the deep implication of the property rights regime in structuring social identity and relationships and cultural meaning.

By way of example we use recent attempts to change property rights regimes in fisheries around the world through the application of PRIs in the way of individual transferable quota (ITQ). A recent survey of empirical studies of the social impacts of ITQ implementations covered fisheries from Norway, Denmark, The Netherlands, Iceland, Canada, USA, Australia and New Zealand.[29] Arranged in this order these countries cover a range in the time of origin of their contemporary resource exploiting cultures from prehistoric times to about 1800. Table 7.5 sets down some general observations on the difficulties experienced in regime change.

*Table 7.5   Evidence for trend in cultural fixity with time*

| Country | Origin date | Difficulties with regime change in fisheries |
| --- | --- | --- |
| Norway | Prehistoric | Major ongoing social and political issue |
| Iceland | AD 1000 | Constitutional crisis |
| Canada | AD 1500 | Great hardship and difficulty – gradual steps and experiments |
| USA | AD 1600 | Stalled – issues around decision process, written constitution and revolutionary origins of the state |
| Australia | AD 1780 | Fractured but progressing |
| New Zealand | AD 1800 | Relatively easy and complete – progressive |

A seemingly plausible argument can be made that the longer a culture continues in a particular stable tradition, the more completely the practising culture, including belief system and values, is based on that context. One effect of culture is to scope our expectations of the possible. For example, for recent settler cultures such as New Zealand and Australia the radical change in location, lifestyle and livelihood undertaken by recent antecedents is an intrinsic part of contemporary culture and therefore possible again. At the same time many Anglo-Celtic and other European cultural traditions run through these settler cultures that do not derive from current relationships with place and resource use. This independence of at least part of cultural practice from the current physical context could imply greater adaptability to further change because cultural portability has also been shown by experience to be possible.

Contrast this with the fate of longstanding indigenous cultures such as the Australian Aborigines following disruption of their relationships with place and natural resource use. The traditions involved are so longstanding as to have no beginning except in creation myth tied explicitly to a specific landscape and natural resource context. The New Zealand Maori, although profoundly culturally undermined by dispossession, have proved more resilient. Their traditions embrace a history of the Polynesian radiation and settlement of the new lands as well as a culture of warfare and conquest.[30]

A great many other factors impinge on the process of attempted property rights regime change, and some of them are also related to the tenure of the general culture. For example, there seems to be a tendency for the Old World countries to use more conservative administrative process and be less flexible and adaptive in the way they deal with policy development. Related problems also exist in the US where the checks and balances of governance produce so many veto players that any potentially controversial issue can relatively easily be blocked by vested interests. The US also has a problem with the interpretation of property rights, with the 'takings' clause of the Constitution and with aspects of the common law such as the public trust doctrine. This case demonstrates how complex institutional systems tend to stability, a desirable characteristic, but also how experiences and rules made in earlier centuries do not necessarily embody the imperatives of sustainability, making the transition long and fraught.

Much of Iceland and Newfoundland in Canada have a great deal in common in comprising isolated coastal communities with egalitarian traditions, almost entirely economically reliant on small boat fishing for Atlantic cod. The Canadians have not brought in ITQs for the small boat fleet, although they have in the offshore trawler fishery. Social resistance to such change is very high as PRIs are a contradiction of the five-hundred-year-old egalitarian culture. However, due to failure of the overstressed fishery many have been without work for a decade. Icelandic fishing communities have worked off the same beach catching the same fish from the same boats for a thousand years; fishing being the primary reason for settlement by their Norwegian antecedents. The implementation of ITQs without a widely consultative process that accommodated the concerns of small boat fishers and their communities has led to rising social rejection of the regime and continuing challenges to its constitutional legitimacy a decade after the change.

By contrast Australia and New Zealand have had an easier run. Implementation in the Australian South East Fishery suffered through some unfortunate process issues including concurrent organizational restructuring, key species in rapid decline and a rushed and non-consultative development of the allocation formula. However, following a process to redress the consequent grievances the fishery has adjusted reasonably well to the new rights regime.[31] New Zealand has become the international exemplar for ITQs due to the comprehensiveness of the regime and the success achieved in acceptance of change. In eight years property rights in fisheries were transformed from completely open access to an ITQ regime that covered some 83 per cent of the total commercial finfish catch.[32] The transition occurred during the first and second stages in Hanna's framework (see section on path dependence). The offshore fishery was still in the expansionist phase and the inshore had recently peaked but had not gone into serious decline. The policy development process was inclusive and the implementation accommodated concerns for both administrative errors and injustice in the allocation. Resource users embraced the new property rights framework and adjusted their behaviour rapidly to the new incentives. One year after the new regime was implemented a survey found that 40 per cent of fishers in the Auckland region were changing methods of catching and handling fish to increase the value of their quota limited catch.[33] Behaviour was adapting to the new incentive structures intended in policy design.

## CONCLUSION

The implications of this case study of the nature of the impact of property rights regime change are not so much profound as subtly informing. They bear on the place of property rights in the institutional system and how the application of a seemingly simple policy tool can have profound impacts on economy and society.

Property rights are fundamental components of the institutional system and changes have implications for social and cultural change as well as for ecological and economic factors in the use of resources. Hence the adoption of PRIs should not be taken lightly. Individual circumstances need to be analysed carefully to anticipate the degree of difficulty and anticipated costs and benefits of achieving regime change, including a realistic time-frame and the extent of process issues. Time is required for learning to take place among the stakeholders about the imperatives for change, the nature of policy proposals and the implications of change for individual and overall group circumstances. Policy makers also need to be open to learning about the circumstances of resource use culture and to be prepared to accommodate transitional or long-term modifications to preferred policy models to enable more gradual change. Trade-offs of potential economic efficiency gains to ease equity concerns of stakeholders may well be more efficient in the long run.

As powerful institutional settings, changes in property rights regimes for the management of natural resources can have transformative impacts on the culture and value of resource use. Regime changes involve shifts in opportunity sets and expectations that can provoke major changes in investment patterns and resource allocation. These are generally intended consequences but are only likely and positive in the long term if there is credible commitment to maintaining and supporting the new regime. Property rights change needs to be understood by policy and decision makers and by the wider stakeholder group before being applied.

If the power inherent in regime change can be brought to bear in a satisfactory manner, PRIs can contribute substantially towards achieving sustainability goals. Resource use behaviour can be changed to positively support these goals through altering property rights regimes to produce incentives compatible with social goals. PRIs can jointly address an ecological bottom line and produce greater benefits from the use of scarce resources. The fact that both distribution and the logic of distribution of resource use will change should not be a surprise. This tends to challenge prior constructions and meanings of social equity, but these constructions can adapt and change and arguably must change in some circumstances in order to advance sustainable development.

PRIs could be helpful in moving from pioneer culture towards a more commons oriented culture consistent with ecological constraints. The incentives inherent in individual use rights can change behaviour without requiring group cooperative management. However, PRIs also clearly identify a group of which each individual is a part – authorized users. This in turn can lead to a new dynamic in management and an evolution of attitudes towards viewing involvement in cooperative management, monitoring and enforcement as being in the interest of the individual. This is now occurring in advanced implementations such as in New Zealand fisheries. In part it has been triggered by the application of fiscal policy by government to recover management costs from the identified users with quantified interests. Here, quota owners are forming associations, building legitimacy among their constituents and with the government resource owners and managers, acquiring skills and knowledge and preparing to take on management responsibilities. These developments are not without dangers, including moral hazard, but these are well recognized, and open policy processes can help to avoid potential pitfalls. Stakeholders readily admit that when the ITQ system was introduced they would not have given any credibility to the suggestion of accepting such responsibilities in cooperative management. However, within a decade this became thinkable, and after 15 years is now beginning to take place.

## CLOSING COMMENT

While this discussion has been more conceptual than prescriptive or even suggestive it raises important considerations of practical significance that can be reiterated. These considerations should be a necessary input into discussions of economic- or market-based policy instruments generally, and especially when property rights-based policy options are proposed or analysed.

An overall message is that the broad class of policy instruments, known variously as economic-, price- or market-based, in fact contains a number of distinct options with different intents, design requirements, and social and ecological implications. Following from that, as proposed at the start of this discussion, PRIs are not 'just another tool in the policy toolbox', but have deeper implications. The impact of PRIs on the balance between environment, social and economic goals is complex and may be profound. The fact that PRIs are transformative interventions – and to some degree irreversible ones – invites a long term view of implementation and of the maintenance and evolution of the policy regime.

The complexity of concerns associated with PRIs in a practical policy-making context implies difficulties in coming to a fully integrated policy perspective, and conflict is often encountered. Where cultures and economies are most exclusively dependent on resource use relations there are no easy routes to change. A wide variety of perspectives is required to inform discussions about change, policy design and implementation: not just economic, but ecological, legal, sociological, administrative and, not least of all, the perspectives of affected stakeholders. This is already widely appreciated. However, this chapter points to a need to understand the nature of property rights regimes more broadly, and within the context of the wider institutional system, before changes are made to existing rights. This institutionally informing view is often missing from policy debates.

Finally the lack of empirical analyses of existing PRI systems in some topical resource management sectors (e.g. water, salinity, biodiversity) invites lesson drawing from arenas where these approaches have been in place for some time and have been analysed more extensively (e.g. fisheries). However, while there are valuable lessons to be learned across sectors, any policy intervention, and especially transformative policy interventions, must be considered within specific contexts. The conceptual analysis presented here establishes a framework by which lessons drawn from specific experience can be understood in generic terms before being applied to a new context. This process avoids the risk of mimicry and provides a model for instrumental policy learning.

## NOTES

1. Feeny et al. (1990); Ostrom (1990); Baland and Platteau (1996).
2. For example, see Gordon (1954); Scott (1955).
3. See Ostrom (1990), although the term originated with this author in earlier publications.
4. Dietz et al. (2002).
5. This discussion based on Schlager and Ostrom (1992); Ostrom and Schlager (1996).
6. WCED (1987).
7. Gordon (1954).
8. Coase (1960).
9. Social costs and benefits include both the financial costs and benefits to the producer together with all other external costs and benefits to society (externalities), with pollution being an external cost, known as a negative externality.
10. Pigou (1946).
11. Pearce and Turner (1990).
12. The assumptions of climax equilibrium ecological theory are used in the model, and it is thereby taken that an undisturbed (by fishing) population will be in equilibrium with its habitat, having expanded to the maximum level supportable by available space, food supply and/or other constraining parameters. Releasing niche space here refers to the effects of reducing the population on these constraining parameters. Fishing also changes the age structure of the population, lowering the average age, so that a greater percentage of the biomass comprises younger, faster-growing fish.
13. Coase 1960.
14. North and Wallis (1986).
15. Connor and Alden (2001).
16. See, for example, Young et al. (1996).
17. Acheson (1988).
18. Tietenberg (2002).
19. Connor (1997, 2001a).
20. For examples, see case studies in National Research Council (1999).
21. Hanna (1997a).
22. Ibid., p. 225.
23. North (1987).
24. Hanna (1997b).
25. Ibid.
26. This paragraph is adapted from a passage in Hanna (1997b) p. 141 that in turn draws on a range of sources, particulary Williamson (1985); Schelling (1960); Runge (1984); Olson (1965).
27. Hanna (1997b).
28. Aslin et al. (2001).

29.  Ibid.
30.  These examples are not intended to reiterate, contest or establish anthropological theory. They are put forward merely as provocative correlations to stimulate thinking about the links between changes in property rights regimes and social and cultural impacts which may bear on the appropriateness of particular policies and processes.
31.  Connor and Alden (2001).
32.  Connor (2001b).
33.  Boyd and Dewees (1992).

# PART III

# Conclusions

# 8. Principles and elements of institutional change for sustainable development

## INTRODUCTION

Notwithstanding its deep and diverse historical roots the issue of the long-run ecological sustainability of human society has only been clearly articulated for 15 years and only stated as an international and national policy agenda for a decade.[1] In institutional terms that is a short time. In its broadest manifestation this policy agenda, generally known as sustainable development, is arguably the most profound intellectual and political agenda facing human society today.[2] Sustainable development is about far more than 'the environment'. It presents a suite of interrelated and significant challenges: protecting ecological life-support systems; reconciling ecological, social and economic imperatives in the long term; correcting grossly inequitable levels of human development; developing precautionary approaches to interventions in natural systems; creating participatory modes of policy and management; and using innovative policy tools.[3]

If past patterns of production and consumption, settlement and governance have been unsustainable and have evolved to be so over a long period of time, it follows that the problems are structural rather than superficial and not amenable to marginal organizational or policy change. That is, there is a prima facie case that the deeper institutional system of modern society is not suited to the different and difficult social goal of sustainable development.

There is a strong consensus in the theoretical and empirical literature, and even in official policy, that sustainable development requires significant institutional change. After more than a decade of debate these calls for institutional change are not only still occurring but have intensified. This indicates that there has been insufficient institutional change for sustainable development and that what institutional change has taken place has either proved inadequate or is too recent and piecemeal for clear ideas to emerge as to what kinds of institutional reforms will work. Ten years after Rio, in the lead-up to the 2002 World Summit on Sustainable Development, discussions at that event and statements of intent thereafter, we can witness the deepening realization that responses to sustainability have been insufficient in both intent and effect.

This book aims to inform discussions about policy and institutional responses to sustainable development. As the case studies in preceding chapters and much other evidence show, these discussions and resulting policy change in specific jurisdictions vary greatly. They do so both in terms of the current state of play and in the way in which these responses have evolved – indeed, strengthened or weakened – over time. For example, the New Zealand RMA was an early and significant system-wide response, but since then the totality of the sustainability agenda has been less than well attended (see Chapter 4). In the EU, even earlier responses to environmental issues have been steadily developed to embrace the broader sustainability idea, whether adequately or not, and beneath that level specific jurisdictions have proceeded at varying pace (Chapter 3). In the USA the sustainability idea has struggled to take root at national level. Australia was a reasonably vigorous player in the initial period of the sustainable development debate, quick to engage stakeholders and construct a national strategy, and closely involved in negotiation of international agreements. It has a long history of environmental policy and is well known for specific environmental and resource management approaches, such as Landcare, integrated catchment management, cooperative protected area management, and so on. However, the overall Australian response to sustainable development has not involved significant institutional reform, with a preference being shown for targeted participatory programmes, limited organizational change and non-binding policy frameworks.[4]

To assess any national response and further prospects against the backdrop of realized inadequacy of institutional change it is necessary first know something of what is happening elsewhere and second to process that information within a conceptual framework which throws light on the nature of institutions and institutional change. So the question for this chapter is, given that institutional change for sustainable development is necessary but poorly progressed, understood or even described, what is it about institutional change that we need to better understand in order to consider options for reform? Given the broad scope of the topic and the endless and crucial variations in detailed context in any jurisdiction, the aim now is to identify generic principles rather than specific recommendations for institutional reform, even though some of the following discussion will indicate our considered opinion on the evident and general value of particular policy and institutional options. On the basis of the conceptual framework established in Part I, and utilizing lessons from the case studies presented in Part II, the next and major section of this chapter develops overall principles and positive elements of institutional and policy change for sustainable development. Following that, a brief translation of some of these generic principles into a specific jurisdictional context (Australia) is undertaken to illustrate the potential.

## THE PRINCIPLES AND ELEMENTS

These emergent principles and elements are grouped under the two classes of 'objects of learning' identified in Part I as targets of this investigation: problem reframing and organizing government. These empirically derived themes are key to understanding both the potential of institutional change consistent with the sustainability idea and the nature of reforms reviewed in this research. They are not forms or models of institutional change in themselves but rather conceptual and practical principles crucial to progress in institutional change for sustainability.

Grouped under problem reframing are four elements operating on the formation of an explicit conception of the sustainability problem:

- the institutional accommodation of a sustainability discourse
- normative change
- legal change
- international law and policy as drivers.

Under organizing government three characteristics emerged as critical to the organizational logic of sustainability:

- integration of policy and practice
- subsidiarity
- reiteration.

The nature of the sustainability nexus is such that it is not possible to entirely separate such principles into discrete categories. They are strongly interrelated, and the characterization presented is merely one way in which the cake might be cut in a consideration of complex, interdependent institutional systems focused on the sustainability problem. They provide different 'lenses' through which the nature of institutional change can be better understood and debated, and the intention here is not to prescribe institutional change. However, we argue that reforms undertaken without due consideration of these issues will be less likely to persist or succeed. Indeed, it is apparent that a lack of appreciation of the nature of the sustainability task and of institutional change – as expressed here through these themes – is a large part of the problem of insufficient and inadequate institutional responses. Thus the section ends with a discussion of what these themes might mean for a reconsideration of the Australian institutional and policy response to sustainable development, as an example application.

## PROBLEM REFRAMING

### The Institutional Accommodation of a Sustainability Discourse

The conceptual nexus of sustainable development has resulted from the convergence of three spheres of concern, each with its own values, problem definition, issue emphasis and language – that is, its own discourse. These concerns are for ecological integrity, economic efficiency and social justice (or equity). The realisation within each of these separate discourses that the fate of their central concerns was tied to human use of the environment drew them inexorably into the sustainable development nexus. Here they face the fact of their inextricable interdependence.

The first base of institutional change for sustainable development must therefore be the provision of a discursive space premised on this realization. The case studies evidence the fact that reconciliation of the three convergent concerns is not simple at either the conceptual or practical levels. There is no agreed vision of a sustainable future and this is unlikely to occur. This makes it vital to provide for ongoing discursive exploration of the conceptual terrain and development of agreement on principles, where possible, for moving forward down the long road of the sustainability transition. Today such exploration is undertaken in a range of locations throughout civil society (universities, NGOs, business and political think tanks) and, fragmentarily, within government policy departments. However, it appears that providing state-sanctioned forums for discussion and consensus formation is a precursor to effective formal institutional change.

The National Councils for Sustainable Development (NCSDs, Chapter 5) are the most obvious mechanism for provision of such a discursive space within the case studies here. An NCSD or equivalent provides high-level ongoing discussion of sustainability, input into government processes and a site for the seeding of related research effort, change in the private sector and broader societal debate. Councils as they exist in different countries fulfil a range of purposes, but engendering a discourse amongst key interests is a recurring one and the one most often explicitly stated. The effectiveness of the councils in fulfilling that role – let alone the substantive impact of the discourse – cannot yet be judged given the youth of NCSDs. A critical factor for success would be the eventual flow outwards from the council of discussion into other relevant parts of the institutional system and into the broader community. To do that these mechanisms must of course be well connected within the prevailing institutional system in a specific jurisdiction. Wide variations in function and form of NCSDs, and potentially of other mechanisms to serve the same purpose, indicate flexibility within the broad ideal to allow such fit. It is clear, though, that a reasonably central location and source of political support in government will enhance both the ability of an NCSD to promote the sustainability discourse and the likelihood of longevity. The 'second generation' NCSDs noted in the case study (UK, Belgium, Canada) serve to illustrate the possibility of more deeply embedding such mechanisms following success, or at least evidenced potential, of a less permanent version.

The EU case study highlighted several localities within the institutional system for such discursive reconciliation to take place. The reiterative process for the development of the Environmental Action Programmes has provided a stable ongoing space for the discussion to evolve. The case study identified many of the now commonly accepted principles of sustainable development in EAPs from the 1970s, indicating that this process provided an early host for the development of fundamentals later expressed in the Brundtland Report and at UNCED. Other sites included the Green Forum and Policy Coordination Groups, processes for development of the Sustainable Development Strategy, and so on.

The case study on New Zealand's Resource Management Act (RMA) touched on the resource management law reform (RMLR) process set up to integrate natural resource management legislation and administration across the whole country. This process was well resourced and widely consultative, and produced in a short time a sophisticated debate over both the conceptual and practical aspects of sustainable development. As we argue in the analysis of the RMA outcomes, the ongoing discursive space provided for at the national level in the institutional framework – the process specified for national policy statements – has been largely neglected, with the debate over values being left, inappropriately and unsatisfactorily, to the Environment Court. There are other spaces created in the framework for ongoing debate at the regional and local levels, but here the discussion is generally uninformed because of the failure to utilize the higher level opportunities to articulate sustainability values. The result of the neglect of this element of the sustainability puzzle is a widespread discontent with the framework. There is a tendency to blame the drafting of the Act as ambiguous and vague, on the one hand, and lack of initiative by local government on the other. It seems from our study more likely that the discontent can be traced to the lack of elaboration of agreed national values in policy statements and the empty core of the system where the discourse over values should be taking place.

Strategic environmental assessment (SEA, Chapter 6), to the limited extent that it exists in practice as an identifiable process, could provide a discursive space for sustainability, but the focus is generally on the implications of policy for the biophysical environment. However, the integrating function of the SEA intervention is to provoke either pre-emptive or subsequent consideration of how such concerns can be accommodated into high-level policy frameworks, and to do this some of the conceptual and values issues at the core of sustainability must be confronted.

The case study on the application of property rights instruments (PRIs, Chapter 7) indicated that, although this can address sustainability concerns, it is the general lack of a discussion in these terms and the then necessary confrontation of the equity concern that has contributed to social and institutional resistance to their application. The portrayal of PRIs as policy instruments with universal application and predetermined natural characteristics tends to set them apart from the normative discussion. This fallacy of misplaced correctness[5] alienates what might be an essential component of institutional systems for sustainable development from being seen in that light. Further, by not being included in the sustainability discourse, where expectations over value preferences can be aligned, their application to resource management and consequent transformative impacts can be, or at least can be perceived as being, hostile to sustainability principles.

**Normative Change**

Normative change is change in group-held values. Institutions and the configuration of institutional systems of governance embody values that, for the rules to be viable, must be resonant with those held by a sufficiently large group of the populace subject to the imposed constraints. In other words any institutional change must seek some congruence with publicly held values. This interdependence of normative and institutional change is a crucial, higher-order principle emerging from this study. In the case of institutional change for sustainability, as in other complex policy areas, the development of such congruence proceeds in an iterative manner, perhaps led from the top through the commitment of particular political figures or perhaps driven from the bottom through constituencies. Either way some degree of public debate is vital, as is political courage – or at least a proactive sensitivity to changing community values – and a suitable timeframe.

The necessary adjustment of values to secure sustainable development is generally of a high order, and hence so is the necessary degree of these factors. For example, the time-frame required to achieve general alignment of social values with sustainability could be expected to span the entire transition – perhaps six to ten decades is not an unreasonable expectation. For many the value change may only come after a generation or two of living with an institutional framework that embodies sustainability principles. Others will embrace change more readily, adjusting their lifestyles, behaviour and consumption ahead of the formal rule set. The key point is that successful institutional systems do not work through rigid and continuous enforcement of rules and application of sanctions, at least in anything other than a police state. They are effective because there exists a general consensus on the values represented in the rules – that the rules are fair and reasonable according to these values. Hence sustainability can only be viable when socially held values become aligned with those implicit in a sustainability ethic.

A great deal of the difficulty with proceeding through the sustainability transition lies in the agreement, articulation and adoption of the values set. This is because sustainability, however defined, will require the yielding of some currently dearly held values. The ideology of progress developed to its height since the Enlightenment is being challenged at its core by sustainability. What the sustainable world will be like we can only guess. How we will get there, and learn to be content with it, are equally mysterious. However, both normative change and institutional change for sustainability have commenced, and must move forward in iterative, mutually reinforcing steps. Strategies to promote the sustainability transition therefore must be cognizant of the need for normative change, and must create and support structures and processes to generate both information about sustainability concerns and an evolving consensus on values to support institutional change.

In the case study of EU environment policy in Chapter 3 we traced the development of the formal expression of sustainability principles, institutional arrangements encouraging development of the discourse and policy integration, the eventual application of binding legal rules, and the explicit inclusion of sustainability commitments in constitutional documents. This unfolded over three decades in a process that began with a relatively strong set of sustainability values and gradually built political and institutional commitment to them, while applying fairly 'soft' rules in an attempt to change behaviour. Although change in environmental and sustainability values in general society tends to be somewhat 'ghettoized,' the willingness of European leaders to endorse the sustainability strategy is taken to reflect, to a degree, such normative change, in combination with an enthusiasm for leadership on these issues.

The New Zealand RMA case was undoubtedly an attempt to push normative change through a major binding change to the governance structure and procedures for natural resource management. The Act says, thou shalt observe the embodied values in all that thou doest under this Act. This is seemingly a top-down approach to normative change but, first, the development of the RMA was subject to an open consultative process and, second, it provides for the development of a range of subordinate instruments that embody, articulate and refine values through similarly open processes at increasingly local levels. It was evident that in the period prior to the RMLR process that a relatively small group of New Zealand intellectuals had developed a rather sophisticated set of value positions that support sustainability, in part through the World Conservation Strategy mandated processes. This local intellectual leadership, and the articulation of the sustainable development thesis in the Brundtland Report at the time of the RMLR process, contributed greatly to the adoption of a high degree of normative content and implied normative change for society in the Act. The failure of central government to operationalize the national policy statement (NPS) process to extend the values debate was a serious mistake. The strategy of the Act was to embed sustainability principles at a level of generality that made agreement possible within the constraints of time and politics afforded by the electoral system. The NPS and other subordinate instruments and their associated public processes were intended to involve the wider community in a series of debates and consensual agreements (if possible) on values and policies to achieve them. The lack of articulation of these contextualized, yet still high-level, sustainability values has left the implementers of the policy and planning system to reinvent the wheel many times over and left the public confused and disappointed in the whole regime.

Mechanisms such as National Councils for Sustainable Development (Chapter 5) have a clear role to play in connecting institutional and normative change through deliberation and communication. Key interest and sectoral groups have the opportunity for sustained interaction around the sustainability idea, probably leading to normative change within individuals and perhaps, through them, within groups. Beyond that, they can serve to sensitize both parts of government and the broader policy and general communities to the new and potentially disturbing practical implications of the values associated with sustainability.

In a more prescriptive manner strategic environmental assessment (Chapter 6) as a procedural requirement embeds regard to environment – if not to sustainability – into a much wider range of policy-making contexts. This has the potential to act as a 'worm in the brain' of officials and other members of policy communities in policy sectors and agencies which have not traditionally had to think closely or routinely about the environmental or sustainability implications of activities and decisions within their domain. In the process of doing so, whether reluctantly or not, skills development will occur, but more importantly an educative process is established that may contribute to normative change. Such a process is quite common. The precursor to SEA, project scale EIA, is now considered a very normal procedure, and the values embedded in it – environmental protection within a development project – have become much more commonly held, although still not universally so, over a span of several decades. While the mechanism of EIA was of course not the sole cause of this, the practice of EIA as repeated procedure was significant, including the creation of an implicit educative process affecting previously disinterested people within industry, bureaucracies and local communities.

The use of property rights instruments (PRIs) in resource management, as explored in Chapter 7, changes the basis of access to and allocation of resources, and in so doing imposes a different set of value priorities to those prevailing under typical prior institutional arrangements. This value-set privileges economic and ecological considerations over social, and can have a range of impacts on the economy of resource use, ecological integrity and social cohesion. The state of all these factors at the time that institutional change is proposed will to some extent determine the reaction of stakeholders. However, length of cultural tradition under the existing allocation schema is also significant. There is a general correlation in the application of PRIs to fisheries management in this regard, with the greatest resistance to change coming from the oldest artisanal fishing cultures and the least from recent immigrant cultures in countries such as Australia and New Zealand.

The explanation for this lies in the implied normative change for these individualized rights to operate. The new incentive structures created that deliver the intended economic and resource conservation results are generally focused on individuals, but these disrupt trust and reciprocity relationships important to social cohesion in resource dependent communities. Such transformation of social values and relations may be viewed as a realistic trade-off in a globalized and full world, where resources are increasingly scarce and under threat of overexploitation. However, as social resistance to PRIs is widespread and can become highly politicized, the insight that this is due in large part to a mismatch of values between the instrument and stakeholder culture is worth noting in consideration of policy prescriptions. PRI regimes can be modified to make concessions to social values by trading-off potential efficiency gains without compromising ecological objectives. At the same time, consultative and educative processes may facilitate enough normative change for the adoption of PRIs with a greater understanding and willingness by stakeholders.

All the case studies serve to emphasize the importance of understanding continued policy-oriented learning as both a part and an outcome of the interdependence of normative and institutional change. This applies whether the learning is, in the terminology of our conceptual framework, instrumental, governmental, social or political, and indeed illustrates the connectivity between different forms of learning. For example, value change within policy communities may be driven by increased familiarity with the sustainability problem resulting from requirements such as to undertake SEA, to interact with an NCSD or to implement the requirements of the RMA. That familiarity and value change arising from instrumental learning may in turn contribute to incremental shifts within parts of the institutional system, involving governmental and social learning.

## Legal Change

It is through the law, constitutional documents, legislative statute and the common law, that more profound change to the formal institutional system occurs.[6] The national institutional systems of a modern state are based in this law as the codification of rules establishing order in society. Common law doctrines become established through accumulated precedent decisions involving some basic propositions of principle accepted by the Courts. Hence, for example, the Precautionary Principle (PP) has begun to recur in some legal jurisdictions in dealing with uncertainty over potential serious or irreversible environmental consequences of particular activities and may over time become a more widely recognized doctrine. However, statute law is by far the most direct and commonly used route for dealing with issues of the general public good such as sustainability, but examples of direct statutory expression of sustainability principles are still rare. In the case of the PP, it has been through (rather vague) statutory expression that this principle has entered legal discourse in the courts.

Various roles of law are evident across the case studies. In the European Union there has been a long history of slowly building the legal underpinnings of environmental policy in the wake of negotiated policy advances. Attempts to regulate to control the impacts of activities on the environment were weak at first due to the need to justify this in terms of the constitutionally defined competences of the European Community. This involved the identification of distortions in markets due to differentiated environmental laws across the member states. Combined with establishment of the right for states with more strict national environmental regulation to retain this level of protection, the system has worked to improve the environmental performance of the other states. Since the constitutional basis for environmental policy was established directly in the 1987 Single European Act, and upgraded again in the Maastricht Treaty in 1992 utilizing sustainability language, the regulations and directives promulgated by the EU have had some real force. Maastricht went further, enshrining a requirement for a high level of protection for the environment, mandating the Precautionary Principle as a fundamental tenet of policy and extending the existing requirement for policy integration. The complex array of lower-level EU environmental regulations and directives and the implementation of them represent a strongly regulatory approach, although market-based instruments are encouraged in later EAPs. If sustainability represents a bigger, more complex policy task, it follows that building and maintaining a more sophisticated policy mix is a more suitable strategy than simply relying on one or another policy instrument or style.

The use of property rights instruments in common pool natural resource management, such as for water allocation, fisheries management or pollution control, is often authorized by legislation. This is required in part due to long-standing common law doctrines that support free and unrestricted public access and use of these resources, a situation that, under scarcity, often results in both overuse and economic waste. Legislation allows the Government to control the initial characterization of the right, particularly as representing a proportional share of available resources rather than a fixed quantum, and potentially allows the disestablishment of the right by revocation of legislation. This latter power has yet to be tested in countries with constitutional clauses mandating compensation for 'takings', and this issue contributes volumes to debates on the use of property rights instruments around the world. Such instruments can offer a great deal in implementing a sustainability strategy, but like the general problem of sustainability policy in microcosm their use to change allocation patterns necessarily confronts equity norms. Where the normative debate has not occurred or, as is often the case with property rights, has been polarized and misdirected, the introduction of such instruments by legislation may cause unnecessary social dislocation, reduce citizens' commitment to the institutional system and invite legal challenge.

Provisions for both SEA and NCSDs in various countries exist variably in law and non-binding policy. Legal requirements for SEA seek to force policy integration to happen, whereas legal provision for an NCSD creates a process rather than a policy outcome. However, statutory provision for SEA has rarely been other than discretionary and that has been a key factor in lack of implementation. This emphasizes that the strength and tightness of statutory expression is as crucial as the mere existence of a legislative provision. There is arguably a greater likelihood of longevity and persistence for an initiative such as an NCSD when enabled by legislation, although this is not absolute and nor should it be. And again, the clarity of the mandate and detail of organizational design in legislation is as crucial as the provision for something like an NCSD. Importantly the process of legislative drafting, at least in a parliamentary system with adequate and transparent legislative review mechanisms, is likely to be subject to a greater degree and variety of scrutiny and debate than a more straightforward policy decision by government. In the case of sustainability, that wider scrutiny and debate should be viewed as necessary and valuable rather than a tiresome or cumbersome obligation.

The RMA as a piece of integrated legislation operates at both general and specific levels, combining a traditional planning regulatory approach with the overarching expression of sustainability in the style of the 'new public law'. At finer resolution in the institutional system the force of law is essential to bind decisions, whereas at the highest level of the hierarchy the most interesting lesson from s5 of the RMA has been to enable an ongoing discourse around what sustainability means. At the same time, this section does a rather intricate job of providing a values framework in legislation, particularly through the 'environmental bottom line' – that is, giving priority to ecological integrity over both economic efficiency and social equity. In setting sustainable management of natural and physical resources as the single purpose of the Act, and making all action taken under authority of the Act subordinate to this purpose, the RMA sets up a dynamic that seeks to define the detail of the implicit values set. In between there is a mix of regulatory intent and creation of process. At all levels the Environment Court has been essential as legal arbitrator but also as a mechanism to maintain and direct debate in the policy community. The resulting discourse has been at once inevitable and useful given the pervasiveness of the Act and the central yet contestable location of the sustainability idea in it. The desirability of other sources of values debate and definition, especially NPS, does not detract from the necessary role of a body such as the Court.

To many people recourse to the courts to argue over the meaning and application of sustainability principles is unfortunate. However, the RMA case suggests that contest is inevitable given the rudimentary state of current understanding and the multiple rationalities that must interact. The most clearly stated sustainability principle – the precautionary principle (PP) – has not attracted consensus as to meaning or implementation yet, despite a significant literature and an emerging body of jurisprudence.[7] The law and courts are one essential part of what should be an explicitly multiple strategy for learning the meaning of sustainability. Other elements include enabling and maintaining inclusive policy debate, and technical development of policy support techniques – for example, risk management frameworks in the case of the PP, or multi-criteria analyses for policy integration and public participation.

**International Law and Policy as Drivers**

Sustainability as a problem and sustainable development as a purposeful manifestation of that have arisen and been most strongly expressed at the international scale. Hence policy and institutional change within any one country is linked to international discussions, law and policy processes. National-level efforts are influenced by international processes in a number of ways (see below), and international policy and legal development is in turn influenced by individual countries or groups of countries (most often those identifiable as either powerful or inspirational leaders, or influential laggards). While this may appear obvious, the role of international law and policy as drivers of domestic normative, institutional and policy change may be less well appreciated at finer resolutions and potential positive opportunities not capitalized on.

All the case studies evidence different but significant relationships with the international level. EU environmental policy is an international process in its own right as well as having been a formative influence on emerging sustainable development policy globally. The RMA represents one of the earliest (that is, pre-Rio) responses to the unfolding idea of sustainability. NCSDs are more recent and explicit responses to developments at the international level, being often portrayed as national-scale extensions of the UN Commission on Sustainable Development. This linkage is deepened by the emerging focus of some NCSDs on achieving synergies through coordinated implementation of international environmental treaties, and the endorsement of the NCSD model at the 2002 World Summit on Sustainable Development. The future prospects for SEA are in great part tied to implementation of the EU SEA directive and the proposed SEA protocol to the Espoo Convention. Debate over and implementation of property rights instruments represent a global as well as national phenomenon, where the sustainability idea must be considered closely against neo-liberal imperatives of efficiency and competition.

Beyond the general reminder that institutional and policy change for sustainability at the national level is connected to international processes, we can identify four more specific aspects to this relationship. First, international processes – summits, conferences of parties, new treaties, protocols to existing treaties, and so on – operate to establish at least minimum (and often vague) standards of procedures and policy development. An example is the requirement from Rio in 1992 for national sustainable development strategies, an instruction fulfilled by many countries. Second, reporting and ongoing negotiation processes under international instruments serve to provide opportunities for reconsideration of, or debate about, the adequacy of domestic policy settings that are visible to stakeholders. Third, the international arena guarantees that a continued discussion of the meaning of sustainability and possible responses is maintained even if such discussion is lacking or inadequate in a particular country, and is to some degree accessible to interested parties. Fourth, international discussions and processes make available to individual countries and groups within them a wider variety of ideas about and models for policy and institutional responses, and thus much expanded sources of policy-oriented learning.

# (RE)ORGANIZING GOVERNMENT

## Integration in Policy and Practice

Integration is a fundamental, essential and pervasive element of the sustainability idea. As canvassed above 'sustainability' arises from the convergence of the concerns for ecological integrity, economic efficiency and social justice (or equity) in relation to human use of the natural environment, and the acknowledgment of their obligatory interdependence. Sustainability thus presents a series and hierarchy of challenges to integrate. The initial challenge is to conceptually integrate the above concerns into the sustainability idea – to understand the interpenetration of ecology, economy and society to form an integrated interdependent system such that action in one domain affects the whole. Flowing from this conceptual integration is the task of articulation of general principles to guide action; from that the development of strategies and policies by sector or issue; and then plans for action consistent with the policy framework. Integration at each level, whether carried out inside or outside government structures, involves the agreement of a coherent set of values and priorities covering all relevant social, economic and ecological concerns and therefore the reconciliation of differing views, priorities and interests. All interests cannot be maximized simultaneously, hence trade-offs are required and value judgements must be applied. Recognizing potential for temporal conflicts of interest as an essential consideration (intergenerational equity), integration can be seen to be the core operational aspect of the sustainability transition.

However, the 'environmental–social–economic' construction of the challenge should be accepted as only a simplistic shorthand for something more complicated, and the case studies evidence the multiple dimensions of policy integration – across those broad policy arenas but also within them (such as across resources management sectors and environmental issues) and across administrative/political and spatial/geographical scales. What clearly comes out of considering even the small set of proposed or actual options for promoting integration within institutional systems in the case studies examined in this book is that the challenge is a multi-faceted and complex one. Given the recent emergence of the sustainability problem, the relatively low status of environment in institutional systems and the traditionally compartmentalized (or disintegrated) structures of government and policy making, inherent difficulty and institutional resistance should be both expected and confronted.

As a first cut, we can separate two aspects: first, policy processes and organizational structures to encourage or allow better integration in policy making and, second, techniques and methods applicable in an operational setting. This study is more concerned with the former. But that split may serve to hide the close relationship between process and technique, an especially blurred differentiation under conditions of complexity and uncertainty (as with sustainability) where processes should be also viewed as operational pathways to enable iterative improvement in understanding and capacity (learning). Suitable processes are required to allow application of newer integrative techniques, and the experimental application of these techniques can feed back into the process and surrounding discourse.

Strategic environmental assessment (SEA) represents an integration strategy that inserts environmental considerations into existing processes for policy formulation in non-environmental sectors (loosely, social and, in the view of many, especially economic). As the oldest clearly proposed integration strategy the experience with poorly implemented SEA warns of the difficulties with implementing even a reasonably well understood integration process with available techniques to support it (Chapter 6). Factors include resistance elsewhere in the institutional system, lack of sufficiently wide-spread understanding of SEA, discretionary rather than mandatory provisions in statute and policy and the vexed question of the appropriate location and head of power for SEA within government (or at arms length from it). Against that, it is encouraging that the fate of SEA has been revived somewhat of late, with interest and implementation rising since the articulation of the sustainability idea per WCED–UNCED. That period has also focused debate over the strategy of using SEA to force environmental factors into other policy considerations against the at present less well understood but more clearly sustainability-oriented methods of sustainability assessment and integrated assessment (SA, IA). Both strategies are likely to be necessary in different circumstances and locations within the institutional system, and at present neither are well utilised or even used at all.

The long history of integrating environmental policy in the European Union (Chapter 3) offers important insights. Initially the EU relied primarily on a bottom-up approach to integration, seeking to educate and influence the process of cultural change within both regulators and their client groups in business and the community. Following the establishment of a sound legal basis for action and some normative change reflected in the values of members of the European Parliament (EP), the Directorate General (DG) Environment was able to forge a political alliance with the EP Environment Committee to force integration of environmental considerations in development planning. This imposed, under threat of blocked supply, SEA/EIA functions on the application of some $30 billion of the annual EU budget. It is important to note that within one budget cycle the powerful DG controlling these resources, and previously resistant to change, had restructured internally to accommodate the new emphasis, made commitments to environmental considerations in mission and policy documents, and generally begun what appears to be a sincere culture change. Having been forced to make some changes, it seems the organization then embraced the logic of environmental concern and reconfigured to minimize overall costs of internalization. This may be an example of pre-adapted values within the DG (normative change) being held in check by the cost of administrative change. When such change is instructed from above it is implemented efficiently with little resistance.

Other attempts to inject environmental considerations into sectoral policy have not been so effective. The use of so-called Integration Correspondents designated by each sectoral DG to act as a contact point for the Environment DG merely created an organized capacity to defend business as usual. Reports regularly highlighted 'no regrets' policies and actions but failed to reveal the basis upon which decisions were made.

New Zealand's Resource Management Act 1991 (RMA) represents an attempt to embed policy integration for sustainability across all aspects of natural resource management and land use, across spatial and administrative scales of government and across government and civil society. The framework was made possible through the concurrent reform of resource management legislation and the structure of local government. In the system, integration is driven by a singular purpose embedded in the institutional framework that expresses the logic of sustainable development. It is constructed to include social and economic imperatives but makes protection of the environment the fundamental overriding value priority. This provides valuable, although still unrefined, guidance to integrative policy making at other levels. Our interpretation would go further and say that the inclusive definition of 'environment' in the RMA generally gives social and cultural values precedence over economic value.

However, public processes to consider the values trade-off exist at each level of decision making, and these are extensively utilized. For example, a consent process for the attachment of a mobile phone transmitter to the steeple of a church adjacent to a preschool playground recently caused the Wellington City Council to consider objections on grounds of both cultural offence and potential health hazard to children. Objectors and the general public then have access to evidence, for example data from monitoring of radiation levels, witness the balance of arguments accepted in the decision, and can check this against the values and rules articulated in the planning and policy hierarchy right back to the purpose of the Act.

Whether implicitly or explicitly many National Councils for Sustainable Development (NCSD) and equivalent bodies seek policy integration through linking different parts of the institutional system (Chapter 5). This is generally a subsidiary aim, secondary to the primary goal of creating government–civil society partnerships. However, the existence of an inclusive dialogue space for the various policy communities relevant to sustainability (environment, health, transport, community development, economic development, and so on) is certainly a significant advance on not having such a mechanism. While there is little empirical evidence as to the effectiveness of NCSDs in promoting policy integration thus far, proponents and participants claim some impact. It may be that the primary integrative impact is at the conceptual level for the membership, but also for government and civil society through influence of NCSD statements and reports that articulate integrated concepts and values. The NCSD experience thus far has also helped to identify some by now familiar issues critical to policy integration – strength of political support, clarity of mandate, sufficiency of resources and identification of appropriate institutional locations.

Property rights instruments (PRIs, Chapter 7) expose different aspects of the integration challenge. A reframing of the problem is implicit in PRIs, where efficiency and ecological imperatives gain primacy over the distributional equity goal that dominated previously (and just as implicitly). This indicates the delicacy and importance of balance within the integration task, and the need to explicitly recognise competing value sets. PRIs as an implementation instrument evidence the ease with which the balance of integration can change even where that is not the intent, such as through unforeseen (yet at times arguably predictable) social equity and local economic impacts. This highlights the fact that policy integration is not simply a challenge to be implemented but one that must be catered for in the design of a policy regime, in the creation of organizational capacity and processes of implementation, and in maintenance of the policy regime through monitoring and evaluation. Not least, the case of PRIs strongly suggests that policy integration demands the presence and integration of different skills – human resources – within relevant parts of the system.

Policy integration is central to sustainability but clearly difficult and likely to be resisted as a threat to existing priorities and powers. However, the partial successes evidenced in the cases explored here and the existence of multiple operational if imperfect strategies suggest that it is possible to make a strong start given sufficiently widespread will to do so. Creation of that will require much broader and focused discussion of both the ends and the means than has taken place thus far.

## Subsidiarity

The principle of subsidiarity encapsulates the view that, in a hierarchical democratic governance system (and particularly in large, diverse systems), a decision should be taken at the level at which it can be most effective. This is important for political reasons – e.g. representation of affected parties in decision making, constituency buy-in, political accountability; for administrative reasons – e.g. economies of scale in decision making, reducing unnecessary workload, consideration of issue detail at higher levels; and for substantive reasons – e.g. information availability, significance of the problem, and the values at stake. However, in the structuring and organization of governance and the allocation of competences (responsibilities for decision making and implementation) power and control of resources and influence are being contested. Hence subsidiarity is an important but potentially controversial issue in the reorganization of government.

In structural change for sustainable development this issue is doubly important due to the factor of pervasive uncertainty operative in interactions with environmental systems. Information distance in feedback loops between decision makers and their impacts on the environment, economy and society should be minimized to reduce response times in the event of surprise. This dictates that decisions should be made at the lowest level (closest to the ground) consistent with the scope of the issue. However, as most issues have multiple dimensions that operate at different scales or scope (e.g. management of surface water within one property, a sub-catchment or a larger river basin) there will always be tensions over the appropriate level for the allocation of policy and management competence and the need for some sharing of responsibility through oversight of decision making at higher levels.

The case study of EU environment policy did not pursue the issue of subsidiarity to any great lengths but noted the political tensions generated over the issue in the negotiation of the Maastricht Treaty in particular. The situation is clouded somewhat by the nature of the EU as a confederation of sovereign states and the political utility of being seen to be a defender of sovereignty on the domestic stage, as well as the actual battle for control of particular policy spheres – despite the merits of revised allocations. However, the adoption of subsidiarity as an agreed principle of governance for the EU forces debate to focus on longer-term policy effectiveness and appropriateness as opposed to convenience or short-term political considerations, just as the acceptance of sustainability as a core policy imperative does. This re-emphasizes the importance of promoting debate and agreement on, and adoption of, principles (and possibly values) for sustainability into the formal institutional system.

An important feature of the EU system related to subsidiarity is the existence of shared central capacity. This is expressed throughout the EU system of governance but has been significant to the institutionalization of sustainability, particularly through the Directorate General for Environment (DG XI) and its sub-directorate predecessor, and the establishment of the European Environment Agency. Together with the EAP preparation and adoption cycle, which has averaged six years, such central capacity provides some degree of supra-electoral continuity in environmental and sustainability policy.

The other key expression of subsidiarity picked up in the case studies was in the RMA. The system of environmental governance set out in the Act and the coordinated local government legislation allocates competences throughout the system. It specifies roles for Ministers of the Crown, national-level processes for development and expression of consensus on values, policy and environmental standards, and responsibilities of regional and territorial authorities for the promulgation of policies and plans to control the effects of activity on the environment. The schema is such that activities that have purely local effects are regulated locally but matters deemed to be of national importance are dealt with at national level.

Although most obviously pertinent to spreading environmental sensibilities horizontally across other policy sectors, the establishment of an SEA process reflects similar issues to the RMA case of placement of rights and responsibilities vertically in hierarchical systems of policy making. The attention to tiering of SEA through policies, plans and programs (PPPs) in confederate Europe most clearly illustrates this, given that different levels in the policy system (local, provincial, national, supra-national) have differentiated responsibilities for these. Attention to this issue forces cognizance of the influence of broader policy directions, possibly unscrutinized at present, on subsidiary or related activities, in keeping with a more sophisticated understanding of complex institutional and policy systems. Negotiating rules of subsidiarity within a jurisdiction will be easier than within, say, a federal or confederate system. This is especially so when the issue is allocation of powers of scrutiny and policy assessment as well as of policy making, across traditionally disintegrated (and possibly competitive) policy sectors.

**Reiteration**

By nature the sustainability transition is a long-term project. The required shift in values and institutional arrangements to integrate across social, economic and ecological concerns may itself be an intergenerational issue, and the necessary significant structural change in the economy and resource use will take decades. Recognition of this makes the institutional provision for long-term reiterative processes a logical step. The uncertainties about the transitional path dictate periodic reassessment, adjustment and recommitment to principles, policies and actions as a prudent strategy. As values adjust under new environmental and institutional conditions, new options and trade-offs will emerge as desirable and viable. Hence any examination of institutional change for sustainable development should consider reiterative processes as fundamental building blocks for an adaptive system.

Of the case studies investigated here the EU study presented the clear benefits of iterative process. The process backbone of Europe's leading role in developing institutionalized capacity for sustainability has been the Environmental Action Plans. These have sufficient longevity to span electoral and appointment cycles in both member states and the EU polity. They have gradually built a solid and consistent basis for policy through successive iterations and have locked in commitments to protect the environment and advance the wider sustainability agenda. Part of the force of the EAPs is to remind successive generations of both politicians and bureaucrats in Brussels and in member states of what has already been agreed. The peak opportunity to do this is at the point where a new EAP is proposed for adoption. However, by this stage in the cycle those actually engaged in the process of reviewing progress under the existing plan and generating agreement among states on the new one have spent years developing a revised and strengthened agenda. The process is thus continuous, with long enough tenure of each plan and sufficient continuity between plans to provide an environment of reasonable certainty while at the same time always pursuing progressive change on a cyclical agenda.

The above principles and elements are generally applicable across most jurisdictional, and thus ecological, cultural, legal and social contexts. To indicate very briefly such a finer resolution application we finish this study with a selective consideration of one national jurisdiction: Australia.

## CHOOSING AUSTRALIAN INSTITUTIONAL PATHWAYS

It is evident that forceful yet adaptive interventions in the institutional system have not been a major part of the Australian response to sustainability.[8] Nor has it been of most countries. However, the cases examined in this study demonstrate that there are lessons available to that end. Institutional and policy resistance to the deep re-ordering of existing priorities and hierarchies inherent in any serious reading of the sustainability problem is one reason for this. While the removal of that resistance, whether in government, the private sector or the community, is not the issue here, the understanding of the nature of the institutional challenge provided above can inform dealing with such resistance or at least a better understanding of it. The following discussion proceeds on the assumption that institutional reform to promote sustainability is desired and identifies selected issues for institutional change in Australia. While it was not the intention of this study to recommend particular policy and institutional reforms, some of the case studies emphasize operational pathways whereas others serve as vehicles for informing debate at a more generic level. We will deal first with specific possibilities and then with the generalized Australian style of institutional response.

## Specific Institutional Interventions

Two of the case studies, SEA and NCSDs, represent available models to drive change in the institutional system that have been implemented elsewhere, and their suitability in the Australian context can be very briefly considered.[9] The Commonwealth and some states have provision for SEA, but these discretionary provisions have been unimplemented in the main, although analogous appraisal and assessment processes have been utilised (sectoral policy, the Resource Assessment Commission, Regional Forest Agreements, and so on). SEA remains however, the most advanced and well-understood mechanism for policy integration and one which is likely to be applied more widely in future, especially in Europe and in development aid. There seems no substantive reason not to implement SEA in Australia, whether in a coordinated manner or piecemeal, jurisdiction by jurisdiction. Careful thought as to the intent, location, targets and triggers of an SEA system would be required. Recent application of SEA to Commonwealth fisheries represents an internationally notable case and an opportunity to test the efficacy and acceptance of this policy approach.[10]

Australia has not established anything like an NCSD to further the multi-stakeholder partnership ideal inherent in sustainability at the Continental scale, although such partnerships (whether long lived or not) are evident in some specific sectors, and in developments such as in community-oriented programmes like Landcare and catchment or regional processes. Inclusive (even if corporatist) policy formulation, such as utilized in the 1990–92 ESD process, has if anything decreased since the mid-1990s. Opinions as to why this has happened, and whether it matters, would differ. Whatever the reason, the control of the overall sustainability policy agenda has been more firmly held by government. More than that, governments have tended to decompose the sustainability agenda into selected constituent issues. Opportunities for a sustained policy discourse have been less than they might otherwise have been. Whether an Australian NCSD-like body by itself would have a noticeable impact is difficult to ascertain, as details of design and function matter as much as mere existence. However, this study's general findings suggest that, to be effective, some credible commitment to sustainable development would be required at the national political level. Even without this, an NCSD-style body of sufficiently representative and weighty membership could only help to advance an Australian dialogue on sustainability, and pave the way for a change in political winds. Without credible commitment from government, resourcing of such a body might be better raised wholly independently in the interim, lest it be used as a screen for lack of official activity elsewhere in the institutional system. A key question is whether government and other stakeholders would support the establishment of an inclusive body with some influence on both the policy agenda, and especially on their own implementation of that agenda.

**Generic Themes in Australia**

This brief commentary links the themes and principles developed above to the overall trajectory and style of sustainable development policy in Australia (and to other countries with similar political and legal contexts). It is not the intention – nor is it desirable in this context – to assess in any detail Australian policy and institutional developments.

In terms of formal institutional accommodation of the sustainability discourse at a national scale, the non-continuation of the Ecologically Sustainable Development (ESD) process of the early 1990s has not been addressed by subsequent developments. Most current initiatives have been borne in the non-governmental domain, such as the strategic grouping of peak non-government organizations (environment, aid, labour, social welfare, Indigenous, consumer) in the Australian Collaboration or the independent research-oriented initiative, Australia 21. Such 'civil society' initiatives reflect a frustration with lack of forward momentum by governments evident in many parts of the world. The appearance of whole-of-government mechanisms – albeit modest ones – at state and territory level (e.g. Western Australia, Victoria, Australian Capital Territory) stands in contrast to the national scale where appropriateness of addressing sustainability via either inclusive or whole-of-government mechanisms has been actively disavowed. However, inclusive opportunities for ongoing dialogue in the formal policy and institutional system are more narrowly focused on sectors or particular regions or locations (e.g. catchments). Inclusion has been less and patchier at higher policy levels, where governments have tended to retain control of the policy agenda. Indeed, within Australian systems of government, a concentration of power in the executive at the expense of statutory authorities, the public service or parliament has been a feature of the past decade.

Normative change is difficult to identify or describe, and even more difficult is the linking of this to institutional change. There has doubtless been a significant shift in values towards the environment over recent decades but how much of an evolution of values around the broader and deeper notion of sustainability is unclear. Little investigation into this has occurred, and there are clear imperatives to gain a better understanding of public attitudes to sustainability over time.

Australia has included sustainability principles in a wide body of law (as 'ESD principles'). However, this has by and large been in a poorly defined and discretionary fashion, and such statutory expression has had little effect on public decision making.[11] Other dimensions of legal change have been less attended. Three purposes of incorporation of ESD principles into legislation can be considered. First is their expression in a manner which instructs decision makers more firmly and which even sets out techniques to operationalize it. An example is the precautionary principle being a mandatory rather than discretionary factor in decision making, and the Australia/New Zealand Risk Management Standard (AS/NZS 4360 1999) as a recommended framework for implementation. But most ESD principles are difficult to state in such a way, and the use of statute law would rather be to require a procedure addressing the principle (e.g. SEA for policy integration or provisions for public participation). That indicates the second purpose, to establish processes in the policy system. The third purpose of law is to embed the sustainability idea not in a definitive manner but in broad terms that are none the less central and thus unavoidable (such as with the RMA).

In terms of policy integration whole-of-government organizational mechanisms are not well advanced in Australia despite some recent developments. A large number of experiments have been tried with portfolio and agency structures, including natural resources and environment, over the past twenty years in various jurisdictions. At the time of writing the state of Victoria has established a Department of Sustainability and Environment, putatively to create a cross-government sustainability orientation. However, previous restructuring experiences (several of them in Victoria) have not been analysed and might yield insights even though they fell short of embracing the fuller sustainability agenda.

Use of integrative techniques has advanced, but unfortunately little coordination either at a given time or over time has been evident, and little connection of methods, application and development, and policy learning. The fragmentation of the ESD and resource and environmental management policy and management fields continues to constrain the potential for integration.

While contest and consideration of responsibilities and powers of different levels of government is a continuing feature of the Australian federation, more sophisticated discussion of subsidiarity has not been. What divisions of responsibilities that have been defined, such as a 1992 Intergovernmental Agreement on the Environment, are about environment rather than sustainability and have not included consideration of the emerging, non-traditional scales and forms of governance and management (district, catchment and regional) or, very often, that of local government. Focused and sustained discussion and reconsideration of responsibilities and linkages, especially with regard to policy integration across spatial and administrative scales of governance, would be fruitful.

Policy learning, capacity building and 'ratcheting-up' of standards of performance continue to be affected by discontinuity of policy efforts over time, with a concentration on policies, strategies and action plans with sunset clauses, with no explicit connection to later efforts and typically scant provision for later evaluation. Creation of a policy process or regime in sustainability is insufficient without continued maintenance and improvement, not only of the particular regime but also its relationship with other components of what must be a multiple institutional and policy strategy. This failure of reiteration is worsened by fragmentation within the policy field, and by a lack of both shared, ongoing capacity across the field and a supra-electoral dimension in the policy system.

A final consideration is the application of the themes and principles discussed here to existing policy and institutional settings in Australia as opposed to new responses to sustainability. As in any country there is a range of institutional and policy reforms already being pursued and, although not described or discussed here, they can usefully be reconsidered in light of the findings of this study. The extent to which existing analyses of the adequacy of Australia's response to sustainability confirms, extends or contrasts with the themes of this study also invites consideration.[12] In most countries there may be a body of useful analyses of past and current arrangements in resource and environmental policy and management or in relevant, cognate policy fields, but a lack of consolidation and synthesis of these or of their bearing on the newer and larger sustainability question.

## CONCLUDING COMMENT

The themes emerging from this study and the considerations of their relevance to future institutional reform are deeply interrelated. For example, policy integration depends on the organization of government and opportunities for shared policy discourse and learning, and may require statutory provision. And so on. That indicates two of the overarching themes explored here, the interdependent nature of institutional systems, and the need for policy discourse and learning, especially in the case of sustainability as a profound social goal pervaded by complexity and uncertainty.

Another overarching message from this study is that there are multiple institutional options available, and indeed that multiple strategies are most certainly required. Some options have featured here, but they are not the only ones and are not singular answers. For example, an NCSD might serve a range of valuable purposes as a partnership between government and civil society, whereas an office of sustainable development or a sustainability commissioner might serve other, just as necessary, roles within government in one jurisdiction. PRIs will only be effective in concert with other elements of the policy mix, just as SEA does not diminish the need for project-EIA or even for other higher-order policy assessment processes (integrated assessment or one-off sectoral reviews). So, promoting sustainability requires multiple policy and institutional strategies in a sophisticated mix and, moreover, ones that unsettle and disturb the existing institutional system. It is not apparent that modern societies have appreciated that, let alone attempted it.

If that seems too much, it does follow inevitably from a serious reading of the sustainability problem. Besides, a moment's reflection shows that sustainability's natural partners – other higher-order goals such as health or justice – are supported deeply in the institutional system through multiple strategies and constantly evolving interventions, often in quite a forceful fashion. When those goals first appeared as widely shared aspirations, however, they were not thus supported. For example, while it is now unthinkable that public health would not be supported by significant policy and institutional machinery as a core collective concern in a modern society, this took considerable time to come to pass. Recognition of public health as a 'commons' problem, and manifestation of that into public policy and institutional responses, literally took centuries from the emergence of the public health movement.[13] While it is doubtful that the transition of sustainability from its current and marginal status to central social goal, if indeed this takes place, will take centuries, it certainly can be expected to take decades.

As to choosing precise reforms it appears to be the case that, within bounds of suitability to the sustainability problem, the actual choice of institutional strategy, including organizational and policy detail, matters less than persistence of the commitment to that strategy, resources, reiteration of effort and maintenance of the policy regime. Consideration of the desired ends should precede the championing of means, especially one means in the form of a singular institutional strategy.

Sustainability is a new, big and complex social goal and policy task. Logically, promoting sustainability requires both doing more and doing better in a policy and institutional sense, and moreover requires significant interventions in the institutional system. Responses so far suggest a common assumption that just doing things a bit differently, through marginal change mostly within the environmental policy domain, will be sufficient. This study, and much else besides, shows that assumption to be misguided.

# NOTES

1.  World Commission on Environment and Development (1987); UN (1992).
2.  Recalling that here we recognize that, properly, sustainability is a long-term goal or system property that should be separated from sustainable development as a policy agenda and process of moving towards that goal, but to a degree use the terms interchangeably.
3.  This sketch of the policy agenda summarizes key elements of official policy such as the UN's Agenda 21 and the way in which these have been translated into policy statements such as in the EU or via Australia's National Strategy for ESD (see UN (1992); Chapter 3 this volume; Australia (1992)).
4.  See, for example, Buhrs and Aplin (1999); Yencken and Wilksinson (2000); Dovers (2001a).
5.  The mistaken belief that the results of abstract models are directly applicable to the real world. See Daly and Cobb (1994) for a discussion.
6.  The more common process of regulatory change and implementation targeted at specific policy and management issues exists beneath the level of legal change discussed here and is that level which has most commonly attracted the often unsupported claim that 'regulation doesn't work'.
7.  For example, see Harding and Fisher (1999).
8.  For reviews and descriptions of specific Australian structures and processes mentioned here, see Dovers (2002); Dovers and Wild River (2003).
9.  The RMA could be argued to present such a model, but it is one (possibly) applicable at state or territory rather than national level and as such would require a detailed comparative analysis of planning and related laws in each jurisdiction to assess it applicability for lesson drawing.
10. Marsden (2002).
11. Stein (2000); Bates (2003).
12. For example, the analyses by Ewing, Dore et al., Harding and Trainor, Curtis, Dovers and Eckersley in Dovers and Wild River (2003) deal with, in terms complementary to this study, respectively, catchment management arrangements, regional natural resource management, state of environment reporting, landcare, discrete policy processes and discursive approaches to policy formulation.
13. Boyden (1987).

# References

Abaza, H. and Hamwey, R. (2001), 'Integrated assessment as a tool for achieving sustainable trade policies', *Environmental Impact Assessment Review*, **21**, pp. 481–510.

Acheson, J.M. (1988), *The Lobster Gangs of Maine*, Hanover and London: University Press of New England.

Apthorpe, R. and Gasper, D. (eds) (1996), *Arguing Development Policy: Frames and Discourses*, London: Frank Cass & Co. Ltd.

Ashe, J. (2002), 'The Australian regional forest agreement process: a case study in strategic natural resource assessment', in S. Marsden and S. Dovers (eds), *Strategic Environmental Assessment in Australasia*, Sydney: Federation Press, pp. 156–81.

Aslin, H.J., Connor, R.D. and Fisher, M. (2001), 'Sharing in the catch or cashing in the share?', *Social Impacts of Individual Transferable Quotas and the South East Fishery*, **110**, Canberra: Bureau of Rural Sciences and Centre for Resource and Environmental Studies.

Australia, The Commonwealth (1992), *National Strategy for Ecologically Sustainable Development*, Canberra: Australian Government Publishing Service.

Bachurst, M., Day, M., Crawford, J.L., Ericksen, N.J., Berke, P., Laurian, L., Dixon, J.E. and Chapman, S. (2002), 'The quality of district plans and their implementation: towards environmental quality', paper presented at Impacts: Australia New Zealand Planning Congress, 8–12 April 2002, Wellington, NZ.

Baland, J.-M. and Platteau, J.-P. (1996), *Halting Degradation of Natural Resources: Is There a Role for Rural Communities?*, New York: FAO and Oxford University Press.

Barnes, P.M. and Barnes, I.G. (1999), *Environmental Policy in the European Union*, Cheltenham: Edward Elgar.

Bates, G. (2003), 'Legal perspectives', in S. Dovers and S. Wild River (eds), *Managing Australia's Environment*, pp. 255–301, Sydney: Federation Press.

Bell, S. (1997), 'Globalisation, neoliberalism and the transformation of the Australian state', *Australian Journal of Political Science*, **32**, pp. 345–67.

Bennett, C.J. and Howlett, M. (1992), 'The lessons of learning: reconciling theories of policy learning and policy change', *Policy Sciences*, **25**, pp. 275–94.

Bohm-Amtmann, A. (2001), 'EU environmental decision-making and subsidiarity', paper presented at Commissioner Wallstrom's Conference 'The Commission's White Paper on Governance: What's in it for the Environment?', 3–4 December 2001, Brussels.

Bollard, R.J. (1995), 'Some thoughts on the planning tribunal's role in resource management', *New Zealand Law Journal*, February 1995, pp. 38–9.

Bond, R., Curran, J., Kirkpatrick, C., Lee, N. and Francis, P. (2001), 'Integrated impact assessment for sustainable development: a case study approach', *World Development*, **29**, pp. 1011–24.

Boyd, R. and Dewees, C.M. (1992), 'Putting theory into practice: individual transferable quotas in New Zealand's fisheries, *Society and Natural Resources*, **5**, pp. 179–98.

Boyden, S.V. (1987), *Western Civilisation in Biological Perspective: Patterns in Biohistory*, Oxford: Clarendon Press.

Boyer, B. (2000), 'Institutional mechanisms for sustainable development: a look at national councils for sustainable development in Asia', *Global Environmental Change*, **10**, pp. 157–60.

Bridgman, P. and Davis, G. (2000), *The Australian Policy Handbook*, 2nd edn, Sydney: Allen and Unwin.

Brown, A.L. and Therivel, R. (2000), 'Principles to guide the development of strategic environmental assessment methodology', *Impact Assessment and Project Appraisal*, **18**, 183–9.

Buckley, R. (1998), 'Strategic environmental assessment', in A.L. Porter and J.J. Fittipaldi (eds), *Environmental Methods Review: Retooling Impact Assessment for the New Century*, pp. 77–86, Atlanta: Army Environmental Policy Institute.

Buhrs, T. and Aplin, G. (1999), 'Pathways towards sustainability: the Australian approach', *Journal of Environmental Planning and Management*, **42**, pp. 315–40.

Buhrs, T. and Bartlett, R.V. (1993), *Environmental Policy in New Zealand: The Politics of Clean and Green?*, Auckland: Oxford University Press.

Burger, J., Field, C., Norgaard, R.B., Ostrom, E. and Policansky, D. (2001), 'Common-pool resources and commons institutions', in J. Burger, E. Ostrom, R.B. Norgaard, D. Policansky and B.D. Goldstein (eds), *Protecting the Commons*, pp. 1–15, Washington, DC: Island Press.

Canadian Environmental Assessment Agency (1997), *Environmental Assessment of Policies, Programmes and Plans: a Training Manual*, Ottawa: CEAA.

Castles, F. (1989), 'The dynamics of policy change: what happened in the

English-speaking nations in the 1980s', *European Journal of Political Research*, **18**, 491–513.

CEC (1992), *Resolution of the Council on the continuation and implementation of a European Community programme of policy and action in relation to the environment and sustainable development – towards sustainability – Fifth Environmental Action Programme (5th EAP)*, COM. 92(23 final), 3 vols.

CEC (2000), *Sustainable governance – Institutional and procedural aspects of sustainability, Commission of the European Communities – European Consultative Forum on Environment and Sustainable Development*. 19. Luxembourg: Office for Official Publications of the European Communities.

CEC (2001a), *Environment 2010: Our future, Our choice – The Sixth Environment Action Programme*. COM(2001)31 final.

CEC (2001b), *A Sustainable Europe for a Better World: A European Union Strategy for Sustainable Development, Commission of the European Communities*. 17. Brussels: COM(2001)264 final.

CEC (2001c), *The European Consultative Forum on the Environment: Activity and Self-assessment Report, 1997–2001*. Brussels: European Commission.

Che, X., Shang, J. and Wang, J. (2002), 'Strategic environmental assessment and its development in China', *Environmental Impact Assessment Review*, **22**, pp. 101–09.

Coase, R.H. (1960), 'The problem of social cost', *Journal of Law and Economics*, **3**, pp. 1–44.

CoM (1973), 'Declaration of the Council on a programme of action of the European Communities on the Environment (First Environmental Action Programme)', *OJ C*, **112**, pp. 1–53.

CoM (1977), 'Resolution of the Council on the continuation of the implementation of a European Community policy and action programme on the Environment (Second EAP)', *OJ C*, **20** (139), pp. 1–46.

CoM (1983), 'Resolution of the Council on the continuation and implementation of a European Community policy and action programme on the Environment (1982–1987) (Third EAP)', *OJ C*, **46**, pp. 1–146.

CoM (1987), 'Resolution of the Council on the continuation and implementation of a European Community policy and action programme on the Environment (1987–1992) (Fourth EAP)', *OJ C*, **328**, pp. 1–44.

CoM (1997), Council Resolution of 7 October 1997 on the drafting, implementation and enforcement of Community environmental law.

Comhar – The National Partnership for Sustainable Development (2001), Report to the Earth Council: Assessment of progress on Agenda 21, Comhar: Dublin.

Connell, D. (ed.), (2002), *Unchartered Waters*, Canberra: Murray Darling Basin Commission.

Connor, R.D. (1997), 'Sustainability and the market: rights based fishing in Australasia', paper presented at Creating a Green Future: National Conference of the Australia New Zealand Society for Ecological Economics, 17–20 November 1997, Melbourne, Australia.

Connor, R.D. (2001a), 'Changes in fleet capacity and ownership of harvesting rights in New Zealand fisheries', in R. Shotton (ed.), *Case Studies on the Effects of Transferable Fishing Rights on Fleet Capacity and Concentration of Quota Ownership*, FAO Fisheries Technical Paper, No. 412, 238 pp, Rome: FAO, pp. 151–85.

Connor, R.D. (2001b), 'Initial allocation of individual transferable quota in New Zealand fisheries', in R. Shotton (ed.), *Case Studies on the Allocation of Transferable Quota Rights in Fisheries*, FAO Fisheries Technical Paper, No. 411, 373 pp, Rome: FAO, pp. 222–50.

Connor, R.D. and Alden, D. (2001), 'Indicators of the effectiveness of quota markets: The South East Trawl Fishery of Australia', *Australian Journal of Marine and Freshwater Research*, **52**, 4, 387–97.

Court J.D. and Associates and Guthrie Consulting (1994), *Assessment of Cumulative Impacts and Strategic Assessment in Environmental Impact Assessment*, Canberra: Commonwealth Environment Protection Agency.

Curran, G. and Hollander, R. (2002), 'Changing policy mindsets: ESD and NCP compared', *Australian Journal of Environmental Management*, **9**, 158–68.

d'Evie, F. and Beeler, B. (eds), (2002), 'Integrating global environmental conventions at national and local levels', NCSD report 2001, San José, Costa Rica: Earth Council.

d'Evie, F., McDonald, M., Mata, R. and Rodriguez, R. (eds), (2000), 'National experiences of integrative, multistakeholder processes for sustainable development', NCSD report 2000, San José, Costa Rica: Earth Council.

Daly, H.E. and John B. Cobb, Jr. (1994), *For the Common Good: Redirecting the Economy toward Community, the Environment, and a Sustainable Future*, Boston: Beacon Press.

Demmke, C. (2001), 'Towards effective environmental regulation: innovative approaches in implementing and enforcing European environmental law and policy', Jean Monnet Program Working Paper 5/01, Harvard Law School, web source: http://www.jeanmonnetprogram.org/papers/01/010501.html

Department of Environmental Affairs and Tourism (2000), *Guideline Document on Strategic Environmental Assessment in South Africa*, Pretoria: The Ministry.

Department of the Environment, Transport and the Regions (1999), *Proposals for a Good Practice Guide on Sustainability Appraisal of Regional Planning Guidance*, London: DETR.

Dietz, T., Dolsak, N., Ostrom, E. and Stern, P.C. (2002), 'The drama of the commons', in E. Ostrom, T. Dietz, N. Dolsak, P.C. Stern, S. Stonich and E.U. Weber (eds), *The Drama of the Commons*, 3–35 Division of Behavioural and Social Sciences and Education, Washington, DC: National Academy Press.

Dixon, J. (2002), 'All at SEA? Strategic environmental assessment in New Zealand', in S. Marsden and S. Dovers (eds), *Strategic Environmental Assessment in Australasia*, 195–210, Sydney: Federation Press.

Doering, R.L. (1993), 'Canadian round tables on the environment and the economy: their history, form and function', Working Paper 14, Ottawa: NRTEE.

Dore, J. and Woodhill, J. (eds) (1999), *Sustainable Regional Development: Final Report*, Canberra: Greening Australia.

Dovers, S. (1997), 'Sustainability: demands on policy', *Journal of Public Policy*, **16**, pp. 303–18.

Dovers, S. (1999), 'Institutionalising ESD', in K. Walker and K. Crowley (eds), *Australian Environmental Policy 2: Studies in Decline and Devolution*, Sydney: University of NSW Press.

Dovers, S. (2001a), 'Institutions for sustainability', Tela paper 7, Melbourne: Australian Conservation Foundation.

Dovers, S. (2001b), 'Informing institutions and policy', in J. Venning and J. Higgins (eds), *Towards Sustainability: Emerging Systems for Informing Sustainable Development*, pp. 196–220, Sydney: University of NSW Press.

Dovers, S. (2002a), 'The precautionary principle, prediction, proof and policy assessment', *New Solutions: A Journal of Environmental and Occupational Health Policy*, **12**, pp. 281–96.

Dovers, S. (2002b), 'Too deep a SEA? Strategic environmental assessment in the era of sustainability', in S. Marsden and S. Dovers (eds), *Strategic Environmental Assessment in Australasia*, pp. 24–46, Sydney: Federation Press.

Dovers, S. (2003), 'Discrete, consultative policy processes: lessons from the National Conservation Strategy for Australia and the National Strategy for Ecologically Sustainable Development', in S. Dovers and S. Wild River (eds), *Managing Australia's Environment*, pp. 133–53, Sydney: Federation Press.

Dovers, S. and Wild River, S. (eds) (2003), *Managing Australia's Environment*, Sydney: Federation Press.

Dryzek, J.S. (1996), 'The informal logic of institutional design', in R.E.

Goodin (ed.), *The Theory of Institutional Design*, pp. 103–25, Cambridge: Cambridge University Press.

Dryzek, J.S. (1997), *The Politics of the Earth: Environmental Discourses*, Oxford: Oxford University Press.

Duncan, A.G. (2000), 'The History of IMPEL', paper presented at IMPEL 2000 Conference on Compliance and Enforcement, Villach, Austria, 11–13 October, 2000, web source: http://europa.eu.int/comm/environment/impel/history.pdf

Ericksen, N.J., Crawford, J.L., Berke, P. and Dixon, J.E. (2001), *Resource Management, Plan Quality, and Governance: A Report to Government*, International Global Change Institute, Hamilton: University of Waikato.

Etheridge, L.S. (1981), 'Government learning: an overview', in S. Long (ed), *The Handbook of Political Behaviour*, pp. 73–161, vol. 2, New York: Plenum Press.

Feeny, D., Berkes, F., McCay, B.J. and Acheson, J.M. (1990), 'The tragedy of the Commons: twenty-two years later', *Human Ecology*, **18**, 1, pp. 1–19.

Fischer, T. (2002a), 'Strategic environmental assessment performance criteria: the same requirement for every assessment?', *Journal of Environmental Assessment Policy and Management*, **4**, 83–99.

Fischer, T. (2002b), *Strategic Environmental Assessment in Transport and Land Use Planning*, London: Earthscan.

Frawley, K. (1994), 'Evolving visions: environmental management and nature conservation in Australia', in S. Dovers (ed), *Australian Environmental History: Essays and Cases*, pp. 55–78, Melbourne: Oxford University Press.

Frieder, J. (1997), *Approaching Sustainability: Integrated Environmental Management and New Zealand's Resource Management Act,* Ian Axford New Zealand Fellowship, Wellington.

Goodin, R.E. (ed.) (1996), *The Theory of Institutional Design*, Cambridge: Cambridge University Press.

Goodland, R. (1998), 'Strategic environmental assessment', in A.L. Porter and J.J. Fittipaldi (eds), *Environmental Methods Review: Retooling Impact Assessment for the New Century*, pp. 87–94, Atlanta: Army Environmental Policy Institute.

Gordon, H.S. (1954), 'The economic theory of a common-property resource: the fishery', *Journal of Political Economy*, **62**, 2, pp. 124–42.

Gow, L. (1997), 'New Zealand's Resource Management Act: Implementing a major planning law reform', *Australian Planner*, **34**, 3, pp. 132–6.

Grundy, K.J. (1995), 'In search of a logic: S 5 of the Resource Management Act', *New Zealand Law Journal*, February, pp. 40–44.

Grundy, K.J. and Gleeson, B.J. (1996), 'Sustainable management and the market: the politics of planning reform in New Zealand', *Land Use Policy*, **13**, 3, pp. 197–211.

Hamilton, C. and Throsby, D. (1998), *The Ecologically Sustainable Development Process: Evaluating a Policy Experiment*, Canberra: Academy of Social Sciences.

Hanna, S. (1997a), 'The new frontier of American fisheries governance', *Ecological Economics*, **20**, pp. 221–33.

Hanna, S. (1997b), 'Social and economic path dependence in the construction of market-based fishery programs', in G. Pálsson and G. Pétursdóttir (eds), *Social Implications of Quota Systems in Fisheries*, pp. 133–46, Copenhagen: TemaNord: Nordic Council of Ministers.

Harding, R. and Fisher, E. (eds) (1999), *Perspectives on the Precautionary Principle*, Sydney: Federation Press.

Henningham, J. (ed.) (1995), *Institutions in Australian Society*, Melbourne: Oxford University Press.

Hildebrand, P.M. (2002), 'The European Community's Environmental Policy, 1957 to 1992: from incidental measures to an international regime?', in A. Jordan (ed.), *Environmental Policy in the European Union: Actors, Institutions & Processes*, pp. 13–36, London: Earthscan.

Howlett, M. and Ramesh, M. (1995), *Studying Public Policy: Policy Cycles and Policy Subsystems*, Oxford: Oxford University Press.

James, P. and Donaldson, S. (2001), 'Action for sustainability: Northwest England's tool for regional strategic sustainability appraisal', *Journal of Environmental Assessment Policy and Management*, **3**, 413–30.

Jordan, A. (1999), 'Subsidiarity and the environmental policy: Which level of government should do what in the European Union', CSERGE Working Paper, University of East Anglia and University College London: Centre for Social and Economic Research on the Global Environment.

Jordan, A. (2002a), 'Step change or stasis: EC environment policy after the Amsterdam Treaty', in A. Jordan (ed.), *Environmental Policy in the European Union: Actors, Institutions & Processes*, pp. 53–60, London: Earthscan.

Jordan, A. (2002b), 'The implementation of EU environment policy: a policy problem without a political solution', in A. Jordan (ed.), *Environmental Policy in the European Union: Actors, Institutions & Processes*, pp. 301–28, London: Earthscan.

Kerr, R. (2002), 'The Resource Management Act: fundamentally sound, or fundamentally flawed?', speech to Massey University Planning Programme, 19 April, Palmerston North: New Zealand Business Roundtable.

Lee, K.N. (1993), *Compass and Gyroscope: Integrating Science and Politics for the Environment*, Washington DC: Island Press.

Malcolm, J. (2002), 'Strategic environmental assessment: legislative developments in Western Australia', in S. Marsden and S. Dovers (eds), *Strategic Environmental Assessment in Australasia*, pp. 71–83, Sydney: Federation Press.

March, J.G. and Olsen, J.P. (1984), 'The New Institutionalism: organisational factors in political life', *American Political Science Review*, **78**, 3, 734–9.

Marsden, S. (2002), 'Strategic environmental assessment and fisheries management in Australia: how effective is the Commonwealth legal framework?', in S. Marsden and S. Dovers (eds), *Strategic Environmental Assessment in Australasia*, pp. 47–70, Sydney: Federation Press.

Marsden, S. and Dovers, S. (eds) (2002), *Strategic Environmental Assessment in Australasia*, Sydney: Federation Press.

Maurer, C. (1998), 'The US President's Council on Sustainable Development: a case study', unpublished report, Washington DC: World Resources Institute.

Maurer, C. (1999), 'Rio+8: assessment of National Councils for Sustainable Development', *Environmental Governance notes*, Washington DC: World Resources Institute.

May, P.J. (1992), 'Policy learning and policy failure', *Journal of Public Policy*, **12**, 4, pp. 331–54.

McNeil, J. (1998), 'The Resource Management Act 1992: an overview of its impact on business management. Environmental perspectives', *Araia atu ki te Tumataohikura*, **21**, pp. 1–3.

McShane, O. (1998), 'Land use control under the Resource Management Act: a "think piece" commissioned by the Minister for the Environment', in MfE (ed.), *Land Use Control under the Resource Management Act*, Wellington, NZ: Ministry for the Environment.

Memon, P.A. and Perkins, H.C. (2000), 'Environmental planning and management: the broad context', in P.A. Memon and H.C. Perkins (eds), *Environmental Planning and Management in New Zealand*, Palmerston North, NZ: Dunmore Press, pp. 11–23.

Meyer, J.W. and Rowan, B. (1977), 'Institutionalized organizations: formal structure as myth and ceremony', *American Journal of Sociology*, **83**, 2, pp. 340–63.

MfE (Ministry for the Environment) (1999), *Your Guide to the Resource Management Act*, Wellington: Ministry for the Environment.

MfE (Ministry for the Environment) (2001), *Resource Management Act: Annual Survey of Local Authorities 1999/2000*, Wellington: Ministry for the Environment.

Ministry of the Environment (2000), *Guidelines on the Environmental Impact Assessment of Legislative Proposals*, Helsinki: The Ministry.

National Research Council (1999), *Sharing the Fish: Towards a National*

*Policy on Individual Fishing Quotas*, Washington DC: National Academy Press.

National Round Table on the Environment and the Economy (2002), *Toward a Canadian Agenda for Ecological Fiscal Reform: First Steps*, Ottawa: NRTEE.

National Round Table on the Environment and the Economy (2001), NRTEE annual report 2000–2001, Ottawa: NRTEE.

Nilsson, M. and Dalkmann, H. (2001), 'Decision making and strategic environmental assessment', *Journal of Environmental Assessment Policy and Management*, **3**, pp. 305–27.

Nitz, T. and Brown, A.L. (2001), 'SEA must learn how policy works', *Journal of Environmental Assessment Policy and Management*, **3**, pp. 329–42.

Nixon, R. (1998), 'The extent to which regulatory control of land use and subdivision is justified under the Resource Management Act: comments on a paper by Owen Mcshane', in MfE (ed.), *Land Use Control under the Resource Management Act*, Wellington, NZ: Ministry for the Environment.

Noble, B.F. (2000), 'Strategic environmental assessment. What is it? & What makes it strategic?', *Journal of Environmental Assessment Policy and Management*, **2**, pp. 203–24.

Noble, B.F. (2002), 'The Canadian experience with SEA and sustainability', *Environmental Impact Assessment Review*, **22**, pp. 3–16.

Nooteboom, S. and Wieringa, K. (1999), 'Comparing strategic environmental assessment and integrated environmental assessment', *Journal of Environmental Assessment Planning and Management*, **1**, pp. 441–57.

North, D.C. (1987), 'Institutions, transaction costs and economic growth', *Economic Inquiry*, **25**, 3, pp. 419–28.

North, D.C. (1990), *Institutions, Institutional change, and Economic Performance*, Cambridge: Cambridge University Press.

North, D.C. (1993), 'Institutions and credible commitment', *Journal of Institutional and Theoretical Economics*, **149**, 1, pp. 11–23.

North, D.C. (1994), 'Economic performance through time', *The American Economic Review*, **84**, 3, pp. 359–68.

North, D.C. and Wallis, J. (1986), 'Measuring the transaction sector in the American economy, 1870–1970', in S.L. Engerman and R.E. Gallman (eds), *Long-term Factors in American Economic Growth, Income and Wealth*, pp. 95–161, Chicago: University of Chicago Press.

Olson, M. (1965), *The Logic of Collective Action. Public Goods and the Theory of Groups*, Cambridge MA: Harvard University Press.

Orchard, L. (1998), 'Managerialism, economic rationalism and public sector reform in Australia: connections, divergences, alternatives', *Australian Journal of Public Administration*, **57**, pp. 19–32.

O'Riordan, T. and Voisey, H. (1997), 'The political economy of sustainable development', in T. O'Riordan and H. Voisey (eds), *Sustainable Development in Western Europe: Coming to Terms with Agenda 21*, pp. 1–23, London, Portland OR: Frank Cass.

Ostrom, E. (1990), *Governing the Commons: The Evolution of Institutions for Collective Action*, Cambridge, MA: Cambridge University Press.

Ostrom, E. and Schlager, E. (1996), 'The formation of property rights', in S. Hanna, C. Folke and K.-G. Maler (eds), *Rights to Nature*, pp. 127–56, Washington DC: Island Press.

Palmer, K. (1999), 'Local government and resource management, *New Zealand Law Review*, pp. 487–505.

Partidario, M. (2000), 'Elements of an SEA framework: improving the added-value of SEA', *Environmental Impact Assessment Review*, **20**, pp. 647–63.

Pearce, D. and Turner, R.K. (1990), *Economics of Natural Resources and the Environment*, London: Harvester Wheatsheaf.

Perkins, H.C. and Thorns, D.C. (2001), 'A decade on: reflections on the Resource Management Act 1991 and the practice of urban planning in New Zealand', *Environment and Planning B: Planning and Design*, **28**, pp. 639–54.

Petts, J. (ed.) (1999), *Handbook of Environmental Impact Assessment*, London: Blackwell.

Pigou, A.C. (1946), *The Economics of Welfare*, London: Macmillan.

Piper, J.M. (2002), 'CEA and sustainable development: evidence from UK case studies', *Environmental Impact Assessment Review*, **22**, pp. 17–36.

Productivity Commission (1999), *Implementation of Ecologically Sustainable Development by Commonwealth Departments and Agencies*, Canberra: AGPS.

Randerson, A.P. (2001), 'Speech to celebrate the 10th anniversary of the enactment of the Resource Management Act', paper presented at Resource Management Law Association seminar, 21 August.

Ravetz, J. (2000), 'Integrated assessment for sustainability appraisal in cities and regions', *Environmental Impact Assessment Review*, **20**, pp. 31–64.

Resource Management Law Reform Core Group (1989), *Sustainability, Intrinsic Values and the Needs of Future Generations*, Wellington: Ministry for the Environment, RMLR Working Paper No. 24.

Runge, C.F. (1984), 'Institutions and the free rider: the assurance problem in collective action', *Journal of Politics*, **46**, 1, pp. 154–81.

Sabatier, P.A. (1988), 'An advocacy coalition framework of policy change and the role of policy-oriented learning therein', *Policy Sciences*, **21**, pp. 129–68.

Sadler, B. and Verheem, R. (1996), *Strategic environmental assessment: status, challenges and future directions*, Zoetermeer: Netherlands Ministry of Housing, Spatial Planning and the Environment.

Salmon, G. (1998), 'The extent to which regulatory control of land use is justified under the Resource Management Act: a commentary on the paper prepared by Owen McShane', in *Land Use Control under the Resource Management Act*, Wellington, NZ: Ministry for the Environment.

Schelling, T.C. (1960), *The Strategy of Conflict*, Oxford: Oxford University Press.

Schlager, E. and Ostrom, E. (1992), 'Property-rights regimes and natural resources: a conceptual analysis', *Land Economics*, **68**, 3, pp. 249–62.

Scott, A. (1955), 'The fishery: the objectives of sole ownership', *Journal of Political Economy*, **63**, pp. 116–24.

Scott, W.R. (1987), 'The adolescence of institutional theory', *Administrative Science Quarterly*, **32**, 493–511.

Simon, H.A. (1986), 'Rationality in psychology and economics', in R.N. Hogarth and M.W. Reder (eds), *Rational Choice: The Contrast Between Economics and Psychology*, Chicago: University of Chicago Press, pp. 25–40.

Smith, G. (1997), 'The Resource Management Act 1991: "a biophysical bottom line" vs "a more liberal regime"; a dichotomy', *Canterbury Law Review*, **6**, pp. 499–538.

Somerville, R. (2002), 'A public law response to environmental risk', *Otago Law Review*, **10**, 2, pp. 143–61.

State of Environment Advisory Committee (2001), *Australia: State of Environment 2001*, Melbourne: CSIRO Publishing.

Stein, P. (2000), 'Are decision-makers too cautious with the precautionary principle?', *Environmental and Planning Law Journal*, **17**, pp. 3–23.

Stinchcombe, K. and Gibson, R.B. (2001), 'Strategic environmental assessment as a means of pursuing sustainability: ten advantages and ten challenges', *Journal of Environmental Assessment Policy and Management*, **3**, pp. 343–72.

Taylor, M. (1995), 'Development proposals of national significance: The call-in power of the Resource Management Act', *Victoria University of Wellington Law Reporter*, **25**, 3, pp. 407–32.

Therivel, R., Wilson, E., Thompson, S., Heaney, D. and Pritchard, D. (1992), *Strategic Environmental Assessment*, London: Earthscan.

Tietenberg, T. (2002), 'The tradeable permits approach to protecting the commons: What have we learned?', in E. Ostrom, T. Dietz, N. Dolsak, P.C. Stern, S. Stonich and E.U. Weber (eds), *The Drama of the Commons*, Division of Behavioural and Social Sciences and Education, Washington, DC: National Academy Press, pp. 197–232.

United Nations (1992), *Agenda 21: The UN Programme of Action from Rio*, New York: UN.

Upton, S.D. (1991), 'Resource Management Bill Third Reading', *Hansard*, 51b (July), pp. 3018–20.
Upton, S.D. (1995), 'The Stace Hammond Grace Lecture: Purpose and principle in the Resource Management Act', *Waikato Law Review*, **3**, pp. 17–55.
van den Bergh, J.C.J.M. and de Mooij, R.A. (1999), 'An assessment of the growth debate', in J.C.J.M. van den Bergh (ed.), *Handbook of Environmental and Resource Economics*, Cheltenham: Edward Elgar.
Venning, J. and Higgins, J. (eds) (2001), *Towards Sustainability: Emerging Systems for Informing Sustainable Development*, Sydney: University of NSW Press.
Walsh, V. (2001), *Social Institutions and Background Knowledge: The Case of Tropical Pacific Marine Ecosystems*, Pittsburgh: International Studies Association.
WCED (World Commission on Environment and Development) (1987), *Our Common Future*, Oxford: Oxford University Press.
Weale, A. (2002), 'Environmental rules and rule-making in the European Union', in A. Jordan (ed.), *Environmental Policy in the European Union: Actors, Institutions & Processes*, London: Earthscan, pp. 198–213.
Wilkinson, D. (1997), 'Towards sustainability in the European Union? Steps within the European Commission towards integrating the environment into other European Union policy sectors', in T. O'Riordan and H. Voisey (eds), *Sustainable Development in Western Europe: Coming to Terms with Agenda 21*, London, Portland OR: Frank Cass, pp. 153–73.
Wilkinson, D. (2002), 'Maastricht and the environment: the implications for the EC's environment policy of the Treaty on European Union', in A. Jordan (ed.), *Environmental Policy in the European Union: Actors, Institutions & Processes*, London: Earthscan, pp. 37–52.
Williams, I.H. (2000), 'The Resource Management Act 1991: well meant but hardly done', *Otago Law Review*, **9**, 4, pp. 673–95.
Williamson, O.E. (1985), *The Economic Institutions of Capitalism*, New York: The Free Press.
Wilson, G.A., Petersen, J.-E. and Holl, A. (1999), 'EU member state responses to Agri-Environmental Regulation 2078/92/EEC – towards a conceptual framework?', *Geoforum*, **30**, pp. 185–202.
World Commission on Environment and Development (1987), *Our Common Future*, Oxford: Oxford University Press.
Yencken, D. (2002), 'Governance for sustainability', *Australian Journal of Public Administration*, **61**, 78–89.
Yencken, D. and Porter, L. (2001), *A just and sustainable Australia: a report by the Australian Collaboration*, Sydney: Australian Council of Social Service.

Yencken, D. and Wilkinson, D. (2000), *Resetting the Compass: Australia's Journey Towards Sustainability*, Melbourne: CSIRO Publishing.

Young, D. (2001), *Values as Law: the History and Efficacy of the Resource Management Act*, Wellington: Institute of Policy Studies, VUW.

Young, M.D., Gunningham, N., Elix, J., Lambert, J., Howard, B., Grabosky, P. and McCrone, E. (1996), *Reimbursing the Future*, Canberra: Department of Environment, Sport and Territories.

Zagorianakos, E. (2001), 'A case study of policy-strategic environmental assessment: the Eco-audit of the Irish National Development Plan 2000–2006', *Journal of Environmental Assessment Planning and Management*, **3**, 241–72.

# Index